Scotland's Golf Courses

SCOTLAND'S GOLF COURSES
The Complete Guide

VIC ROBBIE

MAINSTREAM
PUBLISHING

EDINBURGH AND LONDON

First published in Great Britain in 1997 by
MAINSTREAM PUBLISHING COMPANY (EDINBURGH) LTD
7 Albany Street
Edinburgh EH1 3UG

ISBN 1 85158 945 7

A catalogue record for this book is available from the British Library

Typeset in Times
Printed and bound in Great Britain by Butler and Tanner Ltd, Frome

COVER PICTURES: (FRONT) The spectacular sixth hole at Loch Lomond. At 625 yards,
it is the longest in Scottish golf; (BACK) The legendary Arnold Palmer bids farewell
to the Open Championship at St Andrews in 1995

CONTENTS

ACKNOWLEDGEMENTS

The compilation of *Scotland's Golf Courses: The Complete Guide* has taken the willing hands of many people without whose assistance it would not have been possible, and I owe them my thanks. To the club secretaries, captains, professionals and members who have provided the information about their beloved courses; and to those who have allowed me to hack around them in my research. To Bernard Gallacher, Sandy Jones of the Professional Golfers' Association, Ian Hume of the Scottish Golf Union, Michael McDonnell, golf correspondent of the *Daily Mail*, and Alister Nicol for their contributions. To Andy Hooper (*Daily Mail*), Stan Hunter and Brian Morgan for their photographs which capture perfectly the beauty of our Scottish courses. To Mainstream editor Cathy Mineards for her patience. To Alison and David Gott for technical back-up. To Jared Behmber for his expertise. Last, and certainly not least, to Christine, Gabrielle, Kirstie and Nick Robbie for their computer skills, research, hard work and support.

Vic Robbie

FOREWORD

Bernard Gallacher OBE
Three-times Ryder Cup captain

As a professional golfer, I am privileged in being able to travel around the world and play in tournaments in many exotic and exciting locations, such as Augusta and Valderrama. As Ryder Cup captain, I took the European team to the Ocean Course at Kiawah Island, The Belfry and Oak Hill at Rochester, where I experienced one of the greatest moments of my career when we defeated the United States to win the Cup. For 20 years I was Head Professional at Wentworth in Surrey, yet it still gives me a thrill to return to play in my homeland. Scotland is very much the home of golf and my golfing roots are there.

I learned to play the game as a boy at Bathgate Golf Club, near Edinburgh, and progressed through the junior ranks, representing Scotland and going on to become a Tour professional. No matter where golf takes me, however, I jump at the chance to get out my clubs and return to Scotland where there is the greatest variety of courses in the world.

That is why this book is essential reading for anyone planning to play in Scotland or just wanting to know more about the Scottish game. Apart from a history of the game in Scotland and marvellous colour photographs showing the true beauty of some of our courses, it includes a comprehensive list of Scottish clubs, giving all the information you need to plan your round, and provides a card of the course and diagrams of the signature hole of many of the top courses.

Good golfing!

PREFACE

Sandy Jones

Executive Director of the Professional Golfers' Association

As Executive Director of the PGA, may I say how honoured I am to be writing an introduction for this excellent guide. It is the result of months of tireless work, much of it no doubt taking place on the taxing but ultimately satisfying 19th hole.

The PGA can offer anyone visiting Scottish courses a vast range of benefits and information. Our members, the PGA professionals at each club, are trained to give you the best advice in every aspect of golf. On arrival at your chosen course why not visit the pro shop, where you will receive a warm welcome from the course professional and be able to view the massive range of golfing equipment and apparel? PGA professionals throughout Scotland are guaranteed to give you the right advice and the right equipment at the right price.

Why not book a lesson or two and add that little something to your Scottish golfing experience? Expert tuition will give you a whole new way of looking at the game. If you are travelling to a course on your own, our member can fix you up with a partner, possibly even himself, at a nominal fee. We really can satisfy your every golfing need and whichever courses you visit you can be safe in the knowledge that you will be treated in exactly the same way as any seasoned course member.

At the PGA we are committed to the premise that golf is a sport for everybody, and we hope that as you make your way around the courses you will be left with a good impression of our organisation and its members.

The scenery around many courses in Scotland is outstanding, but we hope that that doesn't put you off carding respectable scores as you 'bag' your courses like Munros – the only difference being that golf is rarely an uphill slog in Scotland.

Finally, let me express my congratulations to Vic Robbie for a superb book charting the courses in my homeland of Scotland. Many of those listed hold very happy memories for me and I hope that they will provide you with many hours of fantastic experiences. Scotland is a truly beautiful nation and our golf courses encapsulate perfectly that beauty.

INTRODUCTION

Imagine a fine summer's day. The turf is lush beneath your feet. A breeze emphasises the purity of the air. The fairways are ablaze with the colour of purple heather and yellow gorse, and mountains provide an impressive backdrop. All about you there is an overwhelming atmosphere of history knowing you are walking in the footsteps of the greats who made golf the game it is today.

Behind are successes and disasters in equal measure, ahead a battle between your skills as a golfer and the subtle intricacies of a course laid down many years before and made more difficult by the wind and water of the Scottish climate. It is an experience many have tried to replicate around the world. Over the years millions upon millions of pounds have been spent in this quest, most actively in Japan and America. Yet they cannot achieve that goal.

Scotland is the undoubted home of golf. No matter what standard golfers are, they have to make the pilgrimage to Scotland, where there are more than 450 spectacular and beautiful courses, otherwise they feel they haven't played the game at all. The most popular and famous, of course, are the links courses that have evolved on sandy coastal strips which, centuries ago, were beneath the sea. Here nature is the architect, the course being fashioned out of the natural terrain rather than having design imposed upon it. Then there are the magnificent inland courses which provide just as challenging a test.

Be it St Andrews, where you can almost see the ghosts of the past marching down the wide, undulating fairways; or Prestwick, the birthplace of golf's most prestigious prize, the Open Championship; or the great Open courses of Muirfield, Turnberry, Carnoustie and Royal Troon, the last of these hosting the 1997 championship; or the splendour of Royal Dornoch and Loch Lomond, or some humbler course, there is no finer country in which to play golf.

The stamp of greatness is everywhere. Almost every club has some link with the traditions of the sport. Everyone has a tale to tell of the great men who were the founding fathers of a great game. Scotland's rich history is peopled with giants like Allan Robertson, probably the first professional and certainly the first man to reduce St Andrews to fewer than 80 strokes, Old Tom Morris, the most famous name in Scottish golf, and his son, Tom, the only man to win the Open Championship four times in succession – the first time at the age of 17. Other greats include Willie Park, the first winner of the Open, and James Braid, who won the Open five times and laid down hundreds of courses. Braid's trademark was the most devilish of bunkers and his great rival, J.H. Taylor, said on seeing one of his bunkers at Prestwick, 'The man who made it should be buried here with a niblick through his heart.'

The origins of golf remain a mystery. There have been claims that the game was invented elsewhere. Play golf in Scotland and you realise that cannot be true. All civilisations have had stick-and-ball games. As early as 200 BC the Chinese were supposed to have had some such game, as were the Romans. The Dutch played a game called Kolven or Kolf, but it was more akin to ice hockey, and the Belgians and French had Chole.

The first mention of golf in Scotland was in 1457 when King James II declared that it be banned lest men be tempted not to practise their archery, which was more useful in the defence of the kingdom against the English; and in 1491 James IV's parliament ordered, 'In na place of the Realme there be used Fute-ball, Golfe, or uther sik unproffitable sportis.' But some historians claim that golf was played at St Andrews some two centuries earlier when shepherds, who grazed their flocks on the commonland along the coast, took to hitting pebbles with sticks at targets to alleviate their boredom, the name 'golf' coming from 'to gowff', a verb in the Scottish dialect meaning 'to hit'. James was eventually won over by the game and by 1513 was reportedly ordering some golf clubs to be made for him.

By 1553, the people of the Auld Grey Toon were given the rights by Archbishop John Hamilton to play golf on the links. Fourteen years later Mary, Queen of Scots perhaps set the trend for fanatical golfers by playing there only hours after the murder of her husband, Lord Darnley.

Legend has it that in 1641 Charles I escaped an injudicious defeat at Leith Links. He was trailing by six holes with eight to play when news came of the Irish rebellion. Of course, he had to take leave of his opponent immediately to attend to matters of state. Such was the growing popularity of the game that those who put a round ahead of a sermon on a Sunday morning could be fined 40 shillings for incurring their minister's displeasure.

As with all games, there came a time when the participants wanted more than just the challenge matches with hundreds of pounds at stake. They needed champions, and in 1744 The Honourable Company of Edinburgh Golfers, who then played on Leith Links and now reside at Muirfield, petitioned the Edinburgh Council to provide a Silver Club for competition. John Rattray, a surgeon and a partner of Bonny Prince Charlie in more serious issues such as the Jacobite rebellion, was the first winner. He escaped a beheading, some say, because of his prowess as a golfer. And, not far from Leith, the first ladies competition was staged in Musselburgh in 1810.

The early days of golf were an expensive affair. They played with the feathery ball, which was made of a top-hatful of feathers stuffed into a hand-stitched leather casing. At half a crown (12½ pence), it was more expensive than a club and deterred many from getting involved. Allan Robertson made a good living manufacturing the balls in the kitchen of his home at St Andrews, aided by his assistant Old Tom Morris, but when the rubber-moulded gutta-percha ball came on the market in 1848, Robertson declared, 'It's nae gowff.'

It was the gutty which started the golf boom in Scotland. More began to play and its popularity really took off with the launching of the Open Championship by the Prestwick Club in 1860, which turned the top golfers of the day into national heroes. By that time Old Tom Morris had moved to Prestwick as greenkeeper on the salary of £50 a year, and he was favourite to win. His mentor Allan Robertson had been regarded as the champion player, and he and Morris featured as partners in many foursomes matches played for stakes as high as £400. Yet they never played each other in competition.

Old Tom, an impressive figure with a full beard, was beaten in the inaugural championship by a 'foreigner from the East Coast', Willie Park, but he made his mark over the next seven years, winning it four times. Then he handed over to his son, Young Tom, who in winning his first Open recorded the first hole in one and unbelievably reduced the then 578-yard first at Prestwick to three strokes with a gutty and hickory shafts.

Young Tom made the Championship Belt his own by winning three years in succession. In 1870 there was no championship, and then a year later today's Claret Jug was put up as the trophy and he won that too. What Young Tom might have achieved is anyone's guess. His father once said, 'I could cope with Allan [Robertson] masel', but never wi' Tommy.' Tragically, Young Tom died – some say of a broken heart – on Christmas morning 1875 at the age of 24, three months after his wife had died giving birth.

Scotland's grip on the Open lasted 30 years before an English amateur, John Ball, broke the sequence. If any Scotsman took over the mantle of the Morrises, it would have been the Fife-born James Braid, who formed the great triumvirate with Harry Vardon and J.H. Taylor. He won five times between 1901 and 1910. But since those days only four Scots have won the Championship: Jock Hutchison and Tommy Armour, who were by then American citizens, George Duncan and Sandy Lyle.

Although the ultimate prize has eluded generations of Scottish golfers down the years, there have been many fine exponents of the game in John Panton, Eric Brown, Brian Barnes, Bernard Gallacher, who went on to captain the Ryder Cup team three times, Lyle and today's superstars Sam Torrance and Colin Montgomerie. They are the direct descendants of a great golfing tradition in which you can participate by playing the finest courses in the world.

OPEN CHAMPIONSHIPS IN SCOTLAND
(36 holes until 1892)

Year	Winner	Runner-up	Venue	Score
1860	W. Park	T. Morris Snr	Prestwick	174
1861	T. Morris Snr	W. Park	Prestwick	163
1862	T. Morris Snr	W. Park	Prestwick	163
1863	W. Park	T. Morris Snr	Prestwick	168
1864	T. Morris Snr	A. Strath	Prestwick	167
1865	A. Strath	W. Park	Prestwick	162
1866	W. Park	D. Park	Prestwick	169
1867	T. Morris Snr	W. Park	Prestwick	167
1868	T. Morris Jnr	R. Andrew	Prestwick	157
1869	T. Morris Jnr	T. Morris Snr	Prestwick	154
1870	T. Morris Jnr	R. Kirk, D Strath	Prestwick	149
1871	No championship			
1872	T. Morris Jnr	D. Strath	Prestwick	166
1873	T. Kidd	J. Anderson	St Andrews	179
1874	M. Park	T. Morris Jnr	Musselburgh	159
1875	W. Park	B. Martin	Prestwick	166
1876	R. Martin	D. Strath	St Andrews	176
	[Strath refused to play off]			
1877	J. Anderson	R. Pringle	Musselburgh	160
1878	J. Anderson	R. Kirk	Prestwick	157
1879	J. Anderson	J. Allan, A. Kirkaldy	St Andrews	169
1880	R. Ferguson	P. Paxton	Musselburgh	162
1881	R. Ferguson	J. Anderson	Prestwick	170
1882	R. Ferguson	W. Fernie	St Andrews	171
1883	W. Fernie	R. Ferguson	Musselburgh	159
	[Won play-off 158 to 159]			
1884	J. Simpson	D. Rolland, W. Fernie	Prestwick	160
1885	R. Martin	A. Simpson	St Andrews	171
1886	D. Brown	W. Campbell	Musselburgh	157
1887	W. Park Jnr	R. Martin	Prestwick	161
1888	J. Burns	D. Anderson, B. Sayers	St Andrews	171
1889	W. Park Jnr	A. Kirkaldy	Musselburgh	155
	[Won play-off 158 to 163]			
1890	J. Ball	W. Fernie	Prestwick	164
1891	H. Kirkaldy	A. Kirkaldy	St Andrews	166
1892	H.H. Hilton	J. Ball, H. Kirkaldy, A. Herd	Muirfield	305
1893	W. Auchterlonie	J.E. Laidlay	Prestwick	322
1895	J.H. Taylor	A. Herd	St Andrews	322

1896	H. Vardon	J.H. Taylor	Muirfield	316
	[Won play-off 157 to 159]			
1898	H. Vardon	W. Park Jnr	Prestwick	307
1900	J.H. Taylor	H. Vardon	St Andrews	309
1901	J. Braid	H. Vardon	Muirfield	309
1903	H. Vardon	T. Vardon	Prestwick	300
1905	J. Braid	R. Jones, J.H. Taylor	St Andrews	318
1906	J. Braid	J.H. Taylor	Muirfield	300
1908	J. Braid	T. Ball	Prestwick	291
1910	J. Braid	A. Herd	St Andrews	299
1912	E. Ray	H. Vardon	Muirfield	295
1914	H. Vardon	J.H. Taylor	Prestwick	306
1915–19	No championship			
1921	J. Hutchison	R.H. Wethered	St Andrews	296
	[Won play-off 150 to 159]			
1923	A.G. Havers	W. Hagen	Troon	295
1925	J. Barnes	E. Ray, A. Compston	Prestwick	300
1927	R.T. Jones Jnr	A. Boomer, F. Robson	St Andrews	285
1929	W. Hagen	J. Farrell	Muirfield	292
1931	T. Armour	J. Jurado	Carnoustie	296
1933	D. Shute	C. Wood	St Andrews	292
	[Won play-off 149 to 154]			
1935	A. Perry	A.H. Padgham	Muirfield	283
1937	T.H. Cotton	R.A. Whitcombe	Carnoustie	290
1939	R. Burton	J. Bulla	St Andrews	290
1940–45	No championship			
1946	S. Snead	A.D. Locke, J. Bulla	St Andrews	290
1948	T.H. Cotton	F. Daly	Muirfield	284
1950	A.D. Locke	R. de Vicenzo	Troon	279
1953	B. Hogan	F.R. Stranaham, A. Cerda, D.J. Rees, P.W. Thomson	Carnoustie	282
1955	P.W. Thomson	J. Fallon	St Andrews	281
1957	A.D. Locke	P.W. Thomson	St Andrews	279
1959	G. Player	F. van Donck, F. Bullock	Muirfield	284
1960	K.D.G. Nagle	A. Palmer	St Andrews	278
1962	A. Palmer	K.D.G. Nagle	Troon	276
1964	A. Lema	J. Nicklaus	St Andrews	279
1966	J. Nicklaus	D.C. Thomas, D. Sanders	Muirfield	282
1968	G. Player	J. Nicklaus, R.J. Charles	Carnoustie	289
1970	J. Nicklaus	D. Sanders	St Andrews	283
	[Won play-off 72 to 73]			
1972	L. Trevino	J. Nicklaus	Muirfield	278
1973	T. Weiskopf	N.C. Coles, J. Miller	Troon	276
1975	T. Watson	J. Newton	Carnoustie	279
	[Won play-off 71 to 72]			

13

1977	T. Watson	J. Nicklaus	Turnberry	268
1978	J. Nicklaus	S. Owen, R. Floyd, B. Crenshaw, T. Kite	St Andrews	281
1980	T. Watson	L. Trevino	Muirfield	271
1982	T. Watson	P. Oosterhuis, N. Price	Troon	284
1984	S. Ballesteros	B. Langer, T. Watson	St Andrews	276
1986	G. Norman	G.J. Brand	Turnberry	280
1987	N. Faldo	R. Davis, P. Azinger	Muirfield	279
1989	M. Calcavecchia	G. Norman, W. Grady	Troon	275
	[Won play-off over four holes]			
1990	N. Faldo	M. McNulty, P. Stewart	St Andrews	270
1992	N. Faldo	J. Cook	Muirfield	272
1994	N. Price	J. Parnevik	Turnberry	268
1995	J. Daly	C. Rocca	St Andrews	272
	[Won play-off over four holes]			

MAJOR GOLFING FIXTURES IN SCOTLAND IN 1997

March 31–April 5	Mobil Scottish Boys' Championship (Dunbar)
June 14–15	Scottish Open Amateur Stroke-play Championship (Monifieth and Panmure)
June 19–20	Claremont Scottish Mid-amateur Championship (Cawder)
June 21–22	Claremont Scottish Youths' Open Amateur Stroke-play Championship (Cawder)
July 1–2	Famous Grouse Scottish Seniors' Open Amateur Stroke-play Championship (Glasgow)
July 2–4	Bank of Scotland Scottish Boys' Open Amateur Stroke-play Championship (Downfield)
July 9–12	Loch Lomond World Invitational (Loch Lomond)
July 10	Douglas Gillespie Group Scottish Boys' Under-16 Open Stroke-play Championship (Glenbervie)
July 17–20	Open Championship (Royal Troon)
July 28–August 2	J & B Scottish Amateur Championship (Carnoustie)
August 7–10	McDonald's WPGA Championship of Europe (Gleneagles)
October 16–19	Dunhill Cup (St Andrews)

HOW TO USE THIS GUIDE

This book aims to give both the visitor to Scotland and the Scottish golfer a comprehensive guide to a great range of courses, which are listed alphabetically by area (and alphabetically by club in the index). Where possible, addresses and telephone numbers of clubs are given along with the names of secretary and professional. There are also directions and suggestions for accommodation.

To give you an idea of what to expect from the course, we detail the number of holes, yardages – in most cases from the championship or medal tees – par, standard scratch score and course record. In some cases, there is also a card of the course and a description and diagram of the club's signature hole. Clubs operate different restrictions and wherever possible these are detailed along with green fees. We also state whether clubs have a bar and catering services, and list the facilities they provide such as trolley/buggy hire, putting green, pro shop, practice ground and driving range.

While every effort has been made to compile an accurate and complete guide to Scottish courses, the publisher and author cannot be responsible for any errors, omissions or changes of details. We would welcome any information on any course that may not have been included in the guide. It is worth noting that at the time of writing, some clubs had still not decided on summer rates for 1997.

If you are planning to visit a Scottish golf course, it is worth telephoning the club in advance to ascertain availability of playing times and green fees.

DIRECTORY OF CLUBS

ABERDEEN
AUCHMILL GOLF CLUB
Address: Bonnyview Road, West Hetheryfold, Aberdeen AB2 7FQ (01224-715214; Starter: 01224-714577).
Location: On A96 Aberdeen to Inverness road.
Description: Tough municipal course. Narrow tree-lined fairways. Two new holes to be introduced in summer of 1997. Three holes are quite hilly but the rest are flat. Good views of Aberdeen. 18 holes, 5,560 yards. Par 68. Course record 67.
Visitors: Members have priority Saturdays and Wednesdays for competitions. Societies contact Aberdeen Leisure (01224-647647). **Green fees:** Summer: £6.95 per round (juniors £3.50). Winter: £4.90 per round (juniors £2.75).
Catering: Yes. Bar. **Facilities:** Putting green, practice ground.
Accommodation: The Craighaar Hotel.
Signature hole: EIGHTEENTH (455 yards, par four) – Dogleg left with out of bounds on right leading to a driving range.

CARD OF THE COURSE

Hole	Yds	Par	Hole	Yds	Par
1	311	4	10	338	4
2	149	3	11	159	3
3	353	4	12	328	4
4	213	3	13	499	5
5	186	3	14	346	4
6	179	3	15	161	3
7	340	4	16	394	4
8	485	5	17	187	3
9	477	5	18	455	4
Out	2,693	34	In	2,867	34
Total	**5,560**		**Par**	**68**	

BALNAGASK GOLF COURSE
Address: St Fitticks Road, Aberdeen AB1 3QT (01224-876407; 01224-871286).
Location: Two miles east of city centre.
Description: Undulating municipal links course without trees. Used by the Nigg Bay Club. 18 holes, 5,986 yards. Par 70 (SSS 69).
Visitors: No restrictions. Societies contact Aberdeen Leisure (01224-647647).
Green fees: Summer: £6.95 per round (juniors £3.50). Winter: £4.90 per round (juniors £2.75).
Catering: No.

Accommodation: Caledonian Thistle Hotel.
Signature hole: SIXTH (432 yards, par four) – Stroke Index 1.

CARD OF THE COURSE

Hole	Yds	Par	Hole	Yds	Par
1	368	4	10	483	5
2	447	4	11	367	4
3	406	4	12	296	4
4	360	4	13	265	4
5	133	3	14	210	3
6	432	4	15	358	4
7	310	4	16	336	4
8	316	4	17	338	4
9	345	4	18	216	3
Out	3,117	35	In	2,869	35
Total	**5,986**		**Par**	**70**	

DEESIDE GOLF CLUB

Address: Golf Road, Bieldside, Aberdeen AB15 9DL (01224-869457).
Location: Three miles from city centre on A93. Off North Deeside Road, first left beyond Bieldside Inn on Aberdeen to Culter road.
Secretary: A. Macdonald. **Professional:** Frank Coutts (01224-861041).
Description: Picturesque riverside, tree-lined courses with a stream coming into play on nine of the holes on the main course. Nine-hole course undergoing reconstruction. 18 holes, 5,971 yards. Par 71 (SSS 69). Amateur record 64. Pro record 63.
Visitors: Certain times; contact in advance. Societies on Thursdays, noon to 3.30 p.m.
Green fees: £25 per day, £30 at weekends and holidays.
Catering: Full service. Bar.
Facilities: Trolley/buggy hire, putting green, pro shop, practice ground.
Accommodation: Bieldside Inn, Cults Hotel, Waterwheel Inn.

CARD OF THE COURSE

Hole	Yds	Par	Hole	Yds	Par
1	367	4	10	169	3
2	193	3	11	338	4
3	363	4	12	476	5
4	347	4	13	165	3
5	488	5	14	406	4
6	155	3	15	349	4
7	376	4	16	491	5
8	357	4	17	275	4
9	492	5	18	164	3
Out	3,138	36	In	2,833	35
Total	**5,971**		**Par**	**71**	

HAZLEHEAD PUBLIC COURSES

Address: Groats Road, Aberdeen AB1 8BD (Starter: 01224-321830).
Location: Off Queens Road, Hazlehead Park, Aberdeen.

Description: *No. 1*: Fully mature wooded course. 18 holes, 6,204 yards. Par 71 (SSS 70).
No. 2: More parkland. 18 holes, 5,801 yards. Par 67 (SSS 68).
No. 3: Parkland. Nine holes, 5,540 yards. Par 70 (SSS 68).
Visitors: Yes. No advance bookings. **Green fees:** £7 per round.
Catering: At adjacent club.
Facilities: Trolley/buggy hire, putting green, pro shop, practice ground.
Accommodation: Stakis Treetops Hotel.

CARD OF THE NO. 1 COURSE

Hole	Yds	Par	Hole	Yds	Par
1	309	4	10	383	4
2	396	4	11	392	4
3	366	4	12	195	3
4	326	4	13	379	4
5	174	3	14	430	4
6	400	4	15	546	5
7	386	4	16	166	3
8	309	4	17	476	5
9	186	4	18	385	4
Out	2,852	35	In	3,352	36
Total	**6,204**		**Par**	**71**	

KING'S LINKS

Address: 22 Golf Road, Aberdeen AB2 1NR (01224-632269).
Location: Three-quarters of a mile north-east of city centre.
Description: Very windy municipal links course on Aberdeen sea front with no trees and plenty of bunkers and fast greens. Playable all year. The Bon Accord Club, Caledonian Club and Northern Club play over this course. 18 holes, 6,270 yards. Par 71 (SSS 71).
Visitors: Contact Starter's Box (01224-632269) to book tee times. Societies contact Aberdeen Leisure (01224-647647). **Green fees:** Summer: £6.95 per round (juniors £3.50). Winter: £4.90 per round (juniors £2.75).
Catering: No.
Accommodation: Caledonian Thistle Hotel.
Signature hole: TENTH (183 yards, par three) – Tee shot to elevated green which can vary from anything from a six-iron to a driver depending on the wind. Large bunker on left of green.

CARD OF THE COURSE

Hole	Yds	Par	Hole	Yds	Par
1	358	4	10	183	3
2	364	4	11	374	4
3	171	3	12	280	4
4	482	5	13	404	4
5	393	4	14	425	4
6	409	4	15	495	5
7	502	5	16	177	3
8	293	4	17	402	4

9	364	4	18	194	3
Out	3,336	37	In	2,934	34
Total	**6,270**		**Par**	**71**	

MURCAR GOLF CLUB

Address: Bridge of Don, Aberdeen AB23 8BD (01224-704345).
Location: Approximately five miles north-east of Aberdeen off A92 Peterhead to Fraserburgh road.
Secretary: R. Matthews. **Professional:** Gary Forbes.
Description: Typical links course with undulating fairways. 18 holes, 6,241 yards. Par 71 (SSS 71). Course record 65.
Visitors: Mondays and Tuesdays after 12.30 p.m. Wednesdays before 12 noon. Thursdays, Fridays and Saturdays after 4 p.m. Sundays after 12 noon.
Green fees: £28 per round weekdays, £38 per day. £43 weekends.
Catering: Yes, but snacks only on Tuesdays. Bar.
Facilities: Trolley hire, putting green, pro shop, practice ground.
Accommodation: Quality Hotel, The Mill of Mundorno Travel Inn.
Signature hole: SIXTH (439 yards, par four) – Dogleg to left. Most challenging, particularly if wind against. Difficult to judge second shot to green with undulating fairway.

CARD OF THE COURSE

Hole	Yds	Par	Hole	Yds	Par
1	322	4	10	395	4
2	367	4	11	338	4
3	401	4	12	152	3
4	489	5	13	383	4
5	162	3	14	476	5
6	439	4	15	351	4
7	423	4	16	160	3
8	383	4	17	359	4
9	312	4	18	329	4
Out	3,298	36	In	2,943	35
Total	**6,241**		**Par**	**71**	

NEWMACHAR GOLF CLUB

Address: Swailend AB2 0UU (01651-863002).
Location: Two miles north of Dyce, off A947. **Professional:** Glenn Taylor.
Description: *Hawkshill*: Championship-standard parkland, known as 'the thinking man's course'. Highly praised for its layout and use of several lakes, which affect five of the holes. Opened in 1991, it was designed by Dave Thomas and Peter Alliss. 18 holes, 6,623 yards. Par 72 (SSS 74). Course record 68. *Swailend*: Opened in June 1997. Not as much water, not so many trees. 18 holes, 6,388 yards. Par 72 (SSS 70).
Visitors: Restricted at weekends. Must have handicap certificate.
Green fees: *Hawkshill*: Weekdays: Before 11 a.m. £15 per round, 11–7 p.m. £25 per round, £35 per day. Weekends: £30 per round, £40 per day. *Swailend*: Weekdays: Before 11 a.m. £10 per round, 11–7 p.m. £15 per round, £25 per day. Weekends: £20 per round, £30 per day.

Catering: Bar. **Facilities:** Trolley/buggy hire, putting green, pro shop.
Accommodation: Strathburn Hotel.

PORTLETHEN GOLF CLUB

Address: Badentoy Road, Portlethen, Aberdeen AB12 4YA (01224-781090).
Location: Six miles south of Aberdeen on A90.
Secretary: B. Mole. **Professional:** Muriel Thomson (01224-782571).
Description: Rolling parkland course with water. 18 holes, 6,707 yards. Par 72
(SSS 72). Amateur record 67 (J. Murray 1995). Pro record 62 (D. Vannet 1996).
Visitors: Weekdays 9.30 a.m. to 4.30 p.m. Saturdays as available. Sundays after 1 p.m
Green fees: £14 per round weekdays, £21 per day. £21 per round weekends.
Catering: Yes. Bar.
Facilities: Trolley hire, putting green, pro shop, practice ground.
Accommodation: Travel Inn next door.
Signature hole: EIGHTEENTH (506 yards, par five) – Out of bounds left with a
burn crossing the fairway 140 yards short of the green.

CARD OF THE COURSE

Hole	Yds	Par	Hole	Yds	Par
1	384	4	10	237	3
2	498	5	11	334	4
3	418	4	12	188	3
4	485	5	13	538	5
5	135	3	14	371	4
6	382	4	15	399	4
7	431	4	16	367	4
8	178	3	17	418	4
9	438	4	18	506	5
Out	3,349	36	In	3,358	36
Total	**6,707**		**Par**	**72**	

ROYAL ABERDEEN GOLF CLUB

Address: Balgownie Links, Links Road, Bridge of Don, Aberdeen AB23 8AT
(01224-702571).
Location: Northbound on the main road from Aberdeen (A92 to Fraserburgh). Turn
right at traffic lights after crossing the Bridge of Don and fork left some 50 yards
onwards.
Professional/Director of Golf: R. MacAskill.
Description: Founded in 1780, it is the sixth oldest golf club in the world, and has
two courses.
Balgownie Links: Challenging championship course set amongst hill, sand and sea.
Many of the great names of golf – Morris, Hagen, Cotton, Lema, Jacklin and Norman
to name but a few – have played here. 18 holes, 6,372 yards. Par 70 (SSS 71).
Silverburn course: Shorter for high handicappers. 18 holes.
Visitors: During the week. **Green fees:** £40 per round on weekdays, £50 per round
at weekends. £60 for day ticket (2 rounds).
Catering: Dining-room holds a maximum of 36. Lounge and bar.
Facilities: Trolley/buggy hire, putting green, pro shop, practice ground.

Accommodation: Atholl Hotel, Udny Arms Hotel, Maryculter House Hotel, The Marcliffe.
Signature hole: EIGHTEENTH (434 yards, par four) – One of the best finishing holes in Scottish golf. The tee is modestly elevated, displaying the hole and its dangers. Bunkers, long links grasses, thick gorse. Then, for a second shot, a long iron to a plateau green. (See diagram opposite.)

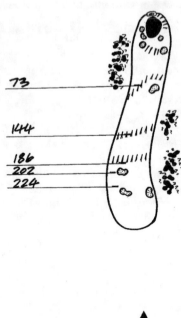

CARD OF THE BALGOWNIE LINKS COURSE

Hole	Yds	Par	Hole	Yds	Par
1	409	4	10	342	4
2	530	5	11	166	3
3	223	3	12	383	4
4	423	4	13	375	4
5	326	4	14	390	4
6	486	5	15	341	4
7	375	4	16	389	4
8	147	3	17	180	3
9	453	4	18	434	4
Out	3,372	36	In	3,000	34
Total	**6,372**		**Par**	**70**	

WESTHILL GOLF CLUB

Address: Skene, Aberdeen AB32 6RY (01224-742567).
Location: Six miles north-west of city centre off A944.
Professional: Ronnie McDonald.
Description: Inland course with a mix of undulating heathland and parkland holes. Greens usually fast. 18 holes, 5,921 yards. Par 69 (SSS 69). Course record 65.
Visitors: Contact in advance. **Green fees:** £12 per round weekdays, £16 per day. £18 per round weekends, £22 per day.
Catering: Full service. Bar.
Facilities: Trolley/buggy hire, putting green, pro shop, practice ground.
Accommodation: Westhill Hotel.

ABERDOUR

ABERDOUR GOLF CLUB

Address: Seaside Place, Aberdour KY3 0TX (01383-860080).
Location: Six miles south-east of Dunfermline.
Secretary: John Train. **Professional:** G. McCallum (01383-860256).
Description: Parkland course running along shore of River Forth with views across the Forth to Edinburgh and beyond. 18 holes, 5,460 yards. Par 67 (SSS 66). Course record 63.
Visitors: Not Saturdays. **Green fees:** £17 per round, £28 per day.
Catering: Full. Bar. **Facilities:** Trolley hire, putting green, pro shop.

Accommodation: Woodside Hotel.
Signature hole: FIRST (159 yards, par three) – Falls over 100 feet to the green which is on a promontory into the Firth of Forth.

CARD OF THE COURSE

Hole	Yds	Par	Hole	Yds	Par
1	159	3	10	530	5
2	159	3	11	340	4
3	343	4	12	163	3
4	287	4	13	251	4
5	359	4	14	318	4
6	365	4	15	171	3
7	163	3	16	449	4
8	458	4	17	354	4
9	394	4	18	197	3
Out	2,687	33	In	2,773	34
Total	**5,460**		**Par**	**67**	

ABERFELDY
ABERFELDY GOLF CLUB

Address: Taybridge Road, Aberfeldy PH15 2BA (01887-820535).
Location: Come off the A9 at Ballinwig Junction, approximately 10 miles from A9. Turn right at Blackwatch Inn. Course approximately 500 yards.
Secretary: Chris Henderson.
Description: Pleasant parkland course set on the north and south banks of the River Tay, incorporating some of the best scenery of highland Perthshire. Tricky but not too demanding test. 18 holes, 5,283 yards. Par 68 (SSS 66). Amateur record 67.
Visitors: All year round. **Green fees:** £14 per round, £22 per day, £55 weekly.
Catering: Snacks, lunch, high teas, evening meals. Bar. **Facilities:** Trolley hire.
Accommodation: Crown Hotel, Palace Hotel.
Signature hole: THIRTEENTH (309 yards, par four) – Sharp dogleg to the right. A four-iron and wedge for the cautious or a driver to carry the trees for the brave, but beware: the Tay awaits a slice.

CARD OF THE COURSE

Hole	Yds	Par	Hole	Yds	Par
1	229	3	10	174	3
2	337	4	11	305	4
3	382	4	12	309	4
4	515	5	13	309	4
5	335	4	14	163	3
6	280	4	15	289	4
7	142	3	16	363	4
8	308	4	17	367	4
9	361	4	18	115	3
Out	2,889	35	In	2,394	33
Total	**5,283**		**Par**	**68**	

ABERFOYLE
ABERFOYLE GOLF CLUB

Address: Braeval, Aberfoyle FK8 3UY (01877-382493).
Location: One mile outside Aberfoyle on main Stirling road.
Secretary: Roddy Steele.
Description: Parkland course. 18 holes, 5,218 yards. Par 66 (SSS 66).
Visitors: Restrictions at weekends. **Green fees:** £12 per round weekdays, £16 per day. £16 per round weekends, £24 per day.
Catering: Yes. Bar. **Facilities:** Trolley hire, putting green.
Accommodation: Rob Roy Motel (walking distance from course).
Signature hole: FOURTH (271 yards, par four) – Good tee shot leaves a short uphill approach to a small green cut into the hillside.

CARD OF THE COURSE

Hole	Yds	Par	Hole	Yds	Par
1	324	4	10	127	3
2	357	4	11	401	4
3	363	4	12	168	3
4	271	4	13	156	3
5	225	3	14	421	4
6	157	3	15	327	4
7	310	4	16	338	4
8	162	3	17	356	4
9	373	4	18	382	4
Out	2,542	33	In	2,676	33
Total	**5,218**		**Par**	**66**	

ABERLADY
KILSPINDIE GOLF CLUB

Address: The Clubhouse, Aberlady, East Lothian EH32 0QD (01875-870358).
Location: 24 miles east of Edinburgh on A198.
Secretary: Bob McInnes. **Professional:** Graham Sked (01875-870695).
Description: Typical Scottish links course with four holes bordering the River Forth estuary. Course has been in its present situation since 1898. Short but tight with well-bunkered holes which become increasingly difficult when the wind blows. 18 holes, 5,471 yards. Par 69 (SSS 66). Amateur record 60. Pro record 59.
Visitors: After 9.15 a.m. weekdays. After 10.30 a.m. weekends.
Green fees: £20 per round weekdays, £30 per day. £25 per round weekends, £30 per day.
Catering: Full catering facilities and bar snacks available.
Facilities: Trolley hire, putting green, pro shop, practice ground.
Accommodation: Kilspindie House Hotel.
Signature hole: EIGHTH (162 yards, par three) – From a new elevated tee, you play across Gosford Bay – after which it is named – to a far from generous green, close to a barrier of sleepers that provide protection from the tide. Guarded by bunkers to the front and left, there is little to spare at the back. On a calm day you could take a wedge but later when the wind gets up it might need a full-blooded driver.

CARD OF THE COURSE

Hole	Yds	Par	Hole	Yds	Par
1	167	3	10	155	3
2	515	5	11	295	4
3	413	4	12	269	4
4	365	4	13	185	3
5	290	4	14	339	4
6	279	4	15	436	4
7	375	4	16	412	4
8	162	3	17	276	4
9	286	4	18	252	4
Out	2,852	35	In	2,619	34
Total	**5,471**		**Par**	**69**	

LUFFNESS NEW GOLF CLUB

Address: Aberlady, East Lothian EH32 0QA (01620-843336).
Location: Between Aberlady and Gullane on A198.
Secretary: Lt.-Col. Ian Tedford.
Description: Championship links course. Final qualifying course when Open is held at Muirfield. 18 holes, 6,122 yards. Par 69 (SSS 70). Amateur record 63 (R. Winchester). Pro record 62 (C. O'Connor).
Visitors: Weekdays, except public holidays.
Green fees: £29 per round, £40 per day.
Catering: Yes (Tuesday to Friday). Bar.
Facilities: Putting green, pro shop, practice ground.
Accommodation: Old Aberlady Inn, Golf Hotel, Mallard Hotel, Marine Hotel.
Signature hole: THIRD (196 yards, par three) – Challenging. Six-iron to three-wood depending on the wind.

CARD OF THE COURSE

Hole	Yds	Par	Hole	Yds	Par
1	332	4	10	176	3
2	420	4	11	445	4
3	196	3	12	336	4
4	531	5	13	393	4
5	326	4	14	435	4
6	155	3	15	346	4
7	293	4	16	163	3
8	383	4	17	349	4
9	427	4	18	416	4
Out	3,063	35	In	3,059	34
Total	**6,122**		**Par**	**69**	

ABOYNE
ABOYNE GOLF CLUB

Address: Formaston Park, Aboyne AB34 5HP (013398-86328).
Location: East of village, north of A93.

Professional: Innes Wright.
Description: First nine is well-maintained parkland with the back nine over hilly, almost heath land. Two lochs with beautiful views. Finishes with two par threes. 18 holes, 5,975 yards. Par 69 (SSS 68). Course record 62.
Visitors: Any time. Contact in advance. **Green fees:** £16 per round weekdays, £21 per day. £20 per round weekends, £25 per day.
Catering: Full service. Bar.
Facilities: Trolley hire, putting green, pro shop, practice ground.
Accommodation: Birse Lodge Hotel.

AIRDRIE
AIRDRIE GOLF CLUB

Address: Rochsoles, Airdrie ML6 0PQ (01236-762195).
Location: One mile north on B802.
Professional: A. McCloskey.
Description: Picturesque wooded parkland course with good views. 18 holes, 6,004 yards. Par 69 (SSS 69). Course record 64.
Visitors: Must contact in advance. Guests of members only at weekends and bank holidays. **Green fees:** £15 per round, £25 per day.
Catering: Bar. **Facilities:** Trolley hire, putting green, pro shop, practice ground.
Accommodation: Westerwood Hotel Golf and Country Club.

EASTER MOFFAT GOLF CLUB

Address: Mansion House, Plains ML6 8NP (01236-842878).
Location: Two miles east on Old Edinburgh Road.
Professional: Brian Dunbar.
Description: Moorland, parkland course. 18 holes, 6,221 yards. Par 72 (SSS 70).
Visitors: Weekdays only. **Green fees:** £15 per round, £20 per day.
Catering: Bar. **Facilities:** Pro shop.
Accommodation: Westerwood Hotel Golf and Country Club.

ALEXANDRIA
VALE OF LEVEN GOLF CLUB

Address: Bonhill, Alexandria G83 9ET (01389-752351).
Location: A82 to Dumbarton then Bonhill and Alexandria.
Secretary: John Stewart (01389-757691).
Description: Tricky parkland course on hillside with several holes overlooking Loch Lomond. 18 holes, 5,162 yards. Par 67 (SSS 66). Amateur record 60 (Gordon Brown). Pro record 63 (Eric Brown).
Visitors: Any time, except Saturdays. **Green fees:** £12 per round weekdays, £18 per day. £18 per round weekends, £25 per day.
Catering: Yes, except Tuesdays. Bar.
Facilities: Trolley hire, putting green, pro shop.
Accommodation: Balloch Hotel, Lomond Park Hotel.
Signature hole: SEVENTEENTH (178 yards, par three) – Looks down on Loch Lomond from an elevated tee. Gorse to be carried. Three bunkers to left of green. (See diagram on opposite page.)

CARD OF THE COURSE

Hole	Yds	Par	Hole	Yds	Par
1	361	4	10	292	4
2	485	5	11	350	4
3	259	4	12	164	3
4	411	4	13	180	3
5	174	3	14	315	4
6	345	4	15	248	4
7	190	3	16	272	4
8	375	4	17	178	3
9	198	3	18	365	4
Out	2,798	34	In	2,364	33
Total	**5,162**		**Par**		**67**

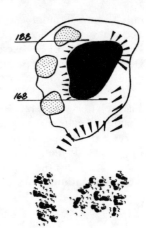

ALFORD
ALFORD GOLF CLUB

Address: Montgarrie Road, Alford AB33 8AE (01975-562178).
Location: 25 miles west of Aberdeen on A944.
Secretary: Bob Fiddes.
Description: Parkland course which is challenging without being physically demanding. Lush fairways with areas of mature and semi-mature trees. Course divided by a road, a railway and a burn. 18 holes, 5,290 yards. Par 69 (SSS 66). Course record 64.
Visitors: Contact in advance. **Green fees:** £12 per round, weekdays, £17 per day. £19 per round weekends, £24 per day. **Catering:** Full meals and snacks. Bar.
Facilities: Trolley hire, golf shop, practice ground.
Accommodation: Kildrummy Castle Hotel, Forbes Arms Hotel.

CARD OF THE COURSE

Hole	Yds	Par	Hole	Yds	Par
1	275	4	10	271	4
2	371	4	11	273	4
3	165	3	12	190	3
4	328	4	13	503	5
5	372	4	14	320	4
6	132	3	15	299	4
7	280	4	16	150	3
8	293	4	17	291	4
9	394	4	18	383	4
Out	2,610	34	In	2,680	35
Total	**5,290**		**Par**		**69**

ALLOA
ALLOA GOLF CLUB

Address: Schawpark Course, Sauchie, Alloa FK10 3AX (01259-722745).
Location: Seven miles from Stirling on A908 road from Alloa to Tillicoultry. Five

miles from Kincardine Bridge.
Secretary: P. Ramage (01259-722745).
Professional: Bill Bennett (01259-724476).
Description: Rolling parkland course with tree-lined fairways. Ideal variety of all types of holes with spectacular views. Ideal test for all discerning golfers. 18 holes, 6,229 yards. Par 70 (SSS 71). Amateur record 63. Pro record 65.
Visitors: On weekdays. **Green fees:** £17 per round weekdays, £26 per day. £21 per round weekends, £32 per day.
Catering: All types of meals available. Bar.
Facilities: Trolley hire, putting green (being constructed), pro shop, practice ground.
Accommodation: Claremont Lodge Hotel.
Signature hole: NINTH (467 yards, par four) – Panoramic views of the Ochil Hills and the Forth valley. Green guarded by two large bunkers. (See diagram opposite.)

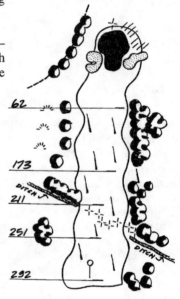

CARD OF THE COURSE

Hole	Yds	Par	Hole	Yds	Par
1	333	4	10	315	4
2	478	5	11	346	4
3	325	4	12	428	4
4	168	3	13	313	4
5	508	5	14	422	4
6	317	4	15	173	3
7	162	3	16	404	4
8	393	4	17	474	4
9	467	4	18	203	3
Out	3,151	36	In	3,078	34
Total	**6,229**		**Par**	**70**	

BRAEHEAD GOLF CLUB

Address: Cambus, by Alloa FK10 2NT (01259-725766).
Location: One mile west of Alloa on A706.
Secretary: Paul MacMichael. **Professional:** Paul Brookes (01259-722078).
Description: Undulating parkland course with a fine variety of challenging holes. Scenic views from many parts of the course. 18 holes, 6,052 yards. Par 70 (SSS 69). Amateur record 64.
Visitors: Societies by prior booking. Visitors advised to telephone in advance.
Green fees: £18 per round weekdays, £24 per day. £24 per round weekends, £32 per day.
Catering: Full range of catering throughout the season. Bar.
Facilities: Trolley/buggy hire, putting green, pro shop, practice ground.
Accommodation: Harviestoun Inn, Royal Hotel, Dunblane Hydro.
Signature hole: FOURTEENTH (210 yards, par three) – Picturesque and challenging hole. Bunkers to the left and right will catch the slightly wayward shot while out of bounds lurks to the rear.

CARD OF THE COURSE

Hole	Yds	Par	Hole	Yds	Par
1	350	4	10	467	4
2	332	4	11	139	3
3	356	4	12	518	5
4	297	4	13	400	4
5	344	4	14	210	3
6	157	3	15	376	4
7	505	5	16	270	4
8	164	3	17	467	4
9	273	4	18	427	4
Out	2,778	35	In	3,274	35
Total	**6,052**		**Par**	**70**	

ALNESS

ALNESS GOLF CLUB

Address: Ardross Road, Alness, Ross-shire IV17 0QA (01349-882389).
Location: 23 miles north of Inverness on A9. Follow signs into Alness town centre. Turn left after crossing bridge.
Secretary: Mrs Betty Taylor.
Description: Overlooking the Cromarty Firth with scenic views on all tees. Interesting and tricky course. Nine holes, 4,946 yards. Par 66 (SSS 64). Amateur record 62.
Visitors: Any time, except competition days.
Green fees: £8 per round weekdays, £10 per round weekends. Juniors £5.
Catering: Bar snacks, teas and coffees.
Facilities: Practice ground.
Accommodation: Commercial Hotel, Station Hotel, Morven House Hotel.
Signature hole: FOURTH (322 yards, par four) – Downhill with trouble on the left. Panoramic views.

CARD OF THE COURSE

Hole	Yds	Par
1	365	4
2	102	3
3	283	4
4	322	4
5	121	3
6	212	3
7	369	4
8	331	4
9	368	4
Out	2,473	33
Total	**4,946**	**Par** 66

ALVA
ALVA GOLF CLUB

Address: Beauclerc Street, Alva FK12 5LH (01259-760431).
Location: Seven miles from Stirling on A91 (Stirling to St Andrews road).
Description: Sloping fairways and fast greens. Course at foot of Ochil Hills. Nine holes, 4,846 yards. Par 66 (SSS 64). Course record 62.
Visitors: Any time, except during medal competitions and Thursday evenings (ladies' night). **Green fees:** £9 per round weekdays, £15 per day. £12 per round weekends. Weekly ticket (weekdays) £30.
Catering: Bar.
Accommodation: Harviestoun Country Inn.

ALYTH
THE ALYTH GOLF CLUB

Address: Pitcrocknie, Alyth, Perthshire PH11 8HF.
Location: Follow signs from Perth to Blairgowrie. Then to Alyth and follow signs to Glenisla.
Secretary: J. Docherty (01828-632268).
Professional: Tom Melville (01828-632411).
Description: Moorland course with tricky greens. Designed by James Braid. 18 holes, 6,205 yards. Par 70 (SSS 71).
Visitors: Most days. **Green fees:** £18 per round weekdays, £30 per day. £23 per round weekends, £35 per day.
Catering: Full range from bar snacks to dinner.
Facilities: Trolley/buggy hire, putting green, pro shop, practice ground.
Accommodation: Local hotels.
Signature hole: FIFTH (325 yards, par four) – A difficult par four with out of bounds on right. Dogleg with criss cross burn leaving a second shot to plateau green with out of bounds at rear.

CARD OF THE COURSE

Hole	Yds	Par	Hole	Yds	Par
1	398	4	10	436	4
2	417	4	11	504	5
3	155	3	12	308	4
4	368	4	13	318	4
5	325	4	14	198	3
6	388	4	15	446	4
7	130	3	16	545	5
8	255	4	17	202	3
9	456	4	18	356	4
Out	2,892	34	In	3,313	36
Total	**6,205**		**Par**	**70**	

STRATHMORE GOLF CENTRE

Address: Leroch, Alyth, Blairgowrie, Perthshire PH11 8NZ (01828-633322).
Location: South of A926 Blairgowrie to Kirriemuir road.

Managing Director: Pat Barron.
Description: *Rannaleroch Course*: Challenging but forgiving. Rolling parkland with views over the valley of Strathmore. 18 holes, 6,490 yards. Par 72 (SSS 72). Course record 69.
Leitfie Links: Ideal for beginners or older golfers. Nine holes, 3,438 yards. Par 58 (SSS 58).
Visitors: Any time.
Green fees: *Rannaleroch*: £14 weekdays, £18 weekends. *Leitfie*: £5 and £6.
Catering: Yes. Bar.
Facilities: Trolley hire, putting green, pro shop, practice ground, driving range.
Accommodation: Alyth Hotel, Drumnacree House Hotel.
Signature hole: FIFTH (470 yards, par five) – Elevated tee. Carry of 160 yards over water and rough to fairway with out of bounds on left. Fairway doglegs right around trees to a large green with water behind.

CARD OF THE RANNALEROCH COURSE

Hole	Yds	Par	Hole	Yds	Par
1	516	5	10	288	4
2	363	4	11	315	4
3	339	4	12	549	5
4	190	3	13	161	3
5	470	5	14	471	4
6	124	3	15	339	4
7	401	4	16	343	4
8	452	4	17	226	3
9	416	4	18	527	5
Out	3,271	36	In	3,219	36
Total	**6,490**		**Par**	**72**	

ANNAN
POWFOOT GOLF CLUB

Address: Powfoot DG12 5QE (01461-700276).
Location: Half a mile off B724.
Professional: Gareth Dick.
Description: Compact seaside semi-links course on the Solway shore. Great views of hills of Cumbria and on a good day the Isle of Man. 18 holes, 6,283 yards. Par 71 (SSS 70).
Visitors: May not play between 8.45 a.m. and 10 a.m., and between noon and 1.30 p.m. on weekdays, and until after 2 p.m. at weekends. Contact in advance.
Green fees: £20 per round weekdays, £27 per day. £20 Sundays after 2 p.m.
Catering: Yes. Bar.
Facilities: Trolley hire, putting green, pro shop, practice ground.
Accommodation: Golf Hotel, Powfoot.

ANSTRUTHER
ANSTRUTHER GOLF CLUB

Address: Shore Road, 'Marsfield', Anstruther KY10 3DZ (01333-310956; 312282).
Location: South-west of A917.
Description: Seaside links course, kept in good condition. Some unusual holes and excellent par threes. Nine holes, 4,532 yards. Par 62 (SSS 63).
Visitors: Contact in advance. Societies welcome, except June to August.
Green fees: £12 per round weekdays, £15 weekends.
Catering: Bar June to August. **Accommodation:** Smugglers Inn.

ARBROATH
ARBROATH ARTISAN GOLF CLUB

Address: Elliot, Arbroath, Angus DD11 2PE (01241-875837).
Location: A92 Dundee road to Arbroath heading north. Before Elliot turn right.
Secretary: Chris Frith. **Professional:** Lindsay Ewart.
Description: Links course with heavily sand-trapped greens. 18 holes, 6,185 yards. Par 70 (SSS 70).
Visitors: All week from 10 to 11 a.m., 2.30 to 3.30 p.m.
Green fees: £13 per round weekdays, £18 per round weekends.
Catering: All week 9 a.m. to 7 p.m. Bar.
Facilities: Trolley hire, putting green, pro shop, practice ground.
Accommodation: Hotel Seaforth.
Signature hole: THIRTEENTH (412 yards, par four) – railway line and out of bounds down the right. Burn crosses fairway 120 yards from green leaving a tricky second shot to smallest green on the course. (See diagram opposite.)

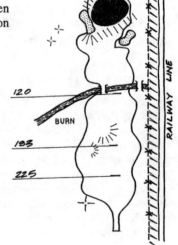

CARD OF THE COURSE

Hole	Yds	Par	Hole	Yds	Par
1	367	4	10	407	4
2	481	5	11	326	4
3	348	4	12	316	4
4	166	3	13	412	4
5	405	4	14	239	3
6	375	4	15	355	4
7	159	3	16	182	3
8	372	4	17	495	5
9	373	4	18	407	4
Out	3,046	35	In	3,139	35
Total	**6,185**		**Par**	**70**	

LETHAM GRANGE HOTEL AND GOLF COURSE

Address: Letham Grange, Colliston DD11 4RL (01241-890373).
Location: Four miles north on A933.
Description: *Old Course*: A championship course. Open parkland, wooded with water hazards. 18 holes, 6,632 yards. Par 73 (SSS 73). Course record 69.

New Course: Open parkland. 18 holes, 5,528 yards. Par 68 (SSS 68). Course record 63.

Visitors: No visitors at weekends before 9.30 a.m.; Old Course before 10 a.m. on Tuesdays; and New Course before 10 a.m. on Fridays.

Green fees: *Old Course*: £23 per round weekdays, £35 per day. £32 per round weekends, £64 per day. *New Course*: £14.50 per round weekdays, £21 per day. £17 per round weekends, £27 per day.

Catering: Full service available. Bar.

Facilities: Trolley/buggy hire, putting green, pro shop, practice ground.

Accommodation: Letham Grange Hotel.

ARISAIG
TRAIGH GOLF CLUB

Address: Arisaig, Inverness-shire PH39 4NT (01687-450645).

Location: On A830 Fort William to Mallaig road. Course three miles north of Arisaig.

Secretary: A. Simpson (01687-450221).

Description: Seaside course featuring a line of grassy hills which used to be sand dunes. Spectacular views over Traigh Sands and the Sound of Sleat to the islands of Eigg, Rhum and Skye. Nine holes, 4,810 yards. Par 68 (SSS 65). Amateur record 69.

Visitors: Any time. **Green fees:** £10 per day, £40 per week.

Catering: Soft drinks, coffee and snacks. **Facilities:** Trolley hire.

Accommodation: Arisaig House Hotel, Arisaig Hotel, Morar Hotel, Marine Hotel, West Highland Hotel.

Signature hole: NINTH (180 yards, par three) – Elevated tee down to a challenging green. Depending on the wind, it can be anything from a full driver to an easy nine-iron. Spectacular views to the islands.

ARRAN (Isle of)
BRODICK GOLF CLUB

Address: Brodick, Isle of Arran KA27 8DL (01770-302349; 01770-302513).

Location: North side of village.

Professional: Peter McCalla.

Description: Short, very flat seaside course adjoining beach. 18 holes, 4,405 yards. Par 62 (SSS 62). Course record 60.

Visitors: Any time, except competition days. Contact in advance.

Green fees: £10 per round weekdays, £15 per day. £15 per round weekends, £20 per day.

Catering: Bar. **Facilities:** Trolley hire, pro shop, practice ground.

Accommodation: Auchrannie Country House Hotel.

CORRIE GOLF CLUB

Address: Sannox, Isle of Arran KA27 8JD (01770-810223).

Location: Six miles north of Brodick ferry port on A841.

Secretary: R. Stevenson (01770-810268).

Description: A short heathland course on the coast. Very picturesque. When the winds blow, it changes character. Nine holes, 3,896 yards. Par 62 (SSS 61). Amateur record 56.
Visitors: Yes. **Green fees:** £7 per day.
Catering: Yes. Tea room open 8 a.m. to 8 p.m., April to October.
Facilities: Driving net.
Accommodation: Ingledene Hotel, Corrie Hotel, Blackrock Guest House.
Signature hole: SECOND (199 yards, par three) – Magnificent views of mountains.

CARD OF THE COURSE

Hole	Yds	Par	
1	139	3	
2	199	3	
3	251	4	
4	171	3	
5	128	3	
6	320	4	
7	306	4	
8	160	3	
9	274	4	
Out	1,948	31	
Total	**3,896**	**Par**	**62**

LAMLASH GOLF CLUB

Address: Lamlash, Isle of Arran KA27 8JU (01770-600296; Starter: 01770-600196).
Location: Three miles south of ferry terminal.
Secretary: J. Henderson.
Description: Undulating heathland. 18 holes, 4,640 yards, Par 64 (SSS 64). Course record 62 (Douglas McFarlane).
Visitors: Any time.
Green fees: 1996 rates: £12 per day weekdays; £15 per day weekends.
Catering: Yes. **Facilities:** Trolley/buggy hire, putting green, pro shop.
Accommodation: Auchrannie Country House Hotel.
Signature hole: SIXTEENTH (102 yards, par three) – Elevated tee. Green protected by two bunkers at the front. Burn at the rear.

CARD OF THE COURSE

Hole	Yds	Par	Hole	Yds	Par
1	346	4	10	276	4
2	189	3	11	271	4
3	389	4	12	233	3
4	183	3	13	191	3
5	208	3	14	215	3
6	325	4	15	275	4
7	294	4	16	102	3
8	266	4	17	226	3
9	355	4	18	296	4

| Out | 2,555 | 33 | In | 2,085 | 31 |
| Total | **4,640** | | **Par** | **64** | |

LOCHRANZA GOLF CLUB

Address: Lochranza, Isle of Arran KA27 8HL (01770-830273).
Description: Level course opened in 1991. Water hazards including a river. Nine greens and 18 tees. Nine holes, 5,506 yards. Par 70 (SSS 70). Course record 74.
Visitors: Any time. Closed November to April.
Green fees: £10 per round, £15 per day.
Catering: Bar. **Facilities:** Trolley hire, putting green, pro shop.
Accommodation: The Lagg Hotel.

MACHRIE BAY GOLF CLUB

Address: Machrie, Isle of Arran KA27 8DZ (01770-850232).
Location: Nine miles from Brodick.
Secretary: John Malesi.
Description: Seaside links course on west coast of Arran. Designed by William Fernie. Nine holes, 4,400 yards. Par 66 (SSS 62). Amateur record 59. Pro record 53 (Walter Hagen, US Ryder Cup captain).
Visitors: Any time. **Green fees:** £5 per day.
Catering: Meals, snacks, tea, coffee. No bar.
Facilities: Putting green, practice ground.
Accommodation: Kinloch Hotel.
Signature hole: FIRST (315 yards, par four) – Shore to the right, road to the left. Both out of bounds.

CARD OF THE COURSE

Hole	Yds	Par	
1	315	4	
2	175	3	
3	169	3	
4	281	4	
5	198	3	
6	281	4	
7	281	4	
8	250	4	
9	250	4	
Out	2,200	33	
Total	**4,400**	**Par**	**66**

SHISKINE GOLF CLUB

Address: Shiskine Shore Road, Blackwaterfoot, Isle of Arran KA27 8AH (01770-860226).
Location: West side of village off A841.
Description: Unique 12-hole links course with magnificent outlook to Mull of Kintyre. 12 holes, 2,990 yards. Par 41 (SSS 42).
Visitors: Contact in advance. July and August no parties.
Green fees: £8 per round, £12 for two rounds.

Catering: Yes. **Facilities:** Trolley/buggy hire, putting green, pro shop.
Accommodation: The Lagg Hotel.

WHITING BAY GOLF CLUB

Address: Whiting Bay, Isle of Arran KA27 8QT (01770-700487).
Location: North-west of village, off A841.
Secretary: Mrs I. Ianson (01770-700307).
Description: Hilly, testing course. 18 holes, 4,405 yards. Par 63 (SSS 63). Course record 59.
Visitors: 8.45 a.m. to 9.30 a.m. weekdays. Also Sundays 11.45 a.m. to 1 p.m.
Green fees: £10 per round weekdays, £13 per day. £25 weekends.
Catering: Bar. **Facilities:** Trolley/buggy hire, putting green, pro shop.
Accommodation: The Lagg Hotel.

AUCHENBLAE
AUCHENBLAE GOLF CLUB

Address: Auchenblae AB30 1BU (01561-320002).
Location: Half a mile north-east of village.
Description: Undulating parkland course. Picturesque views. Nine holes, 4,348 yards. Par 64 (SSS 60). Course record 60.
Visitors: Restricted Wednesday and Friday evenings.
Green fees: £8 per day weekdays, £10 per day weekends.
Accommodation: County Hotel.

AUCHTERARDER
AUCHTERARDER GOLF CLUB

Address: Orchil Road, Auchterarder DH3 1LS (01764-662804).
Location: A9 to south-west of town.
Secretary: W. Campbell. **Professional:** Gavin Baxter (01764-663711).
Description: Flat parkland course, part woodland. 18 holes, 5,775 yards. Par 69 (SSS 68). Course record 64.
Visitors: Weekdays and weekends. Restricted on Sundays and competition days.
Green fees: £17 per round weekdays, £25 per day. £23 per round weekends, £36 per day.
Catering: Yes. Bar.
Facilities: Trolley hire, putting green, pro shop, practice ground.
Accommodation: The Cairn Lodge Hotel

CARD OF THE COURSE

Hole	Yds	Par	Hole	Yds	Par
1	380	4	10	359	4
2	303	4	11	339	4
3	343	4	12	167	3
4	142	3	13	291	4

5	406	4	14	211	3
6	476	5	15	513	5
7	365	4	16	225	3
8	151	3	17	438	4
9	478	5	18	188	3
Out	3,044	36	In	2,731	33
Total	**5,775**		**Par**	**69**	

THE GLENEAGLES HOTEL GOLF COURSES

Address: Auchterarder PH3 1NF (01764-663543).
Location: Two miles south-west of A823.
Professional: Greg Schofield.
Description: One of the foremost golfing centres in the country surrounded by the Grampian mountains, the Trossachs and the Ochil Hills. Undulating moorland courses set alongside this five-star hotel. Spectacular views.
King's Course: Championship course designed by James Braid. 18 holes, 6,471 yards. Par 70 (SSS 73).
Queen's Course: Championship course designed by James Braid. 18 holes, 5,965 yards. Par 68 (SSS 70).
Monarch's Course: Jack Nicklaus-designed, American-style championship course. 18 holes, 6,551 yards. Par 72 (SSS 73).
Wee Course: Nine holes, 2,962 yards. Par 54.
Golf Academy: Long and short game.
Visitors: Members and hotel residents only.
Green fees: *King's*, *Queen's* and *Monarch's*: £65 per round. *Wee*: £15 per round.
Catering: Full service available. Bar. **Facilities:** Trolley/buggy hire, putting green, pro shop, practice ground, driving range.
Accommodation: Gleneagles Hotel.

CARD OF THE KING'S COURSE

Hole	Yds	Par	Hole	Yds	Par
1	362	4	10	447	4
2	405	4	11	230	3
3	374	4	12	395	4
4	466	4	13	448	4
5	161	3	14	260	4
6	476	5	15	459	4
7	439	4	16	135	3
8	158	3	17	377	4
9	354	4	18	525	5
Out	3,195	35	In	3,276	35
Total	**6,471**		**Par**	**70**	

AYR
BELLEISLE GOLF CLUB

Address: Belleisle Park, Ayr KA7 4DU (01292-441258).
Location: Two miles south on A719.

Professional: David Gemmell (01292-441314).

Description: *Belleisle Course*: Heathland/parkland course with trees and a burn influencing shots. A good short game is needed here with large undulating greens, several on plateaus, protected by bunkers. Beautiful sea views. Designed by James Braid. 18 holes, 6,477 yards. Par 71 (SSS 72).

Seafield Course: A tight, hazardous course with some dangerous bunkers. Wooded and rolling, it has only three holes that exceed 400 yards. 18 holes, 5,498 yards. Par 68 (SSS 66).

Visitors: Any time after 9.36 a.m. Contact in advance.

Green fees: *Belleisle*: £17 per round, £24 per day. *Seafield*: £11 per round, £18 per day. Day ticket: £24 (rounds on both courses).

Catering: Yes. Bar. **Facilities:** Trolley/buggy hire, putting green, pro shop.

Accommodation: Quality Friendly Hotel, Jarvis Caledonian Hotel.

CARD OF THE BELLEISLE COURSE

Hole	Yds	Par	Hole	Yds	Par
1	470	5	10	185	3
2	470	5	11	429	4
3	176	3	12	425	4
4	420	4	13	430	4
5	401	4	14	196	3
6	432	4	15	480	5
7	153	3	16	403	4
8	334	4	17	194	3
9	347	4	18	532	5
Out	3,203	36	In	3,274	35
Total	**6,477**	**Par**	**71**		

DALMILLING GOLF CLUB

Address: Westwood Avenue, Ayr KA8 0QY (01292-263893).

Location: One and a half miles east of town off A719.

Professional: Philip Cheyney.

Description: Meadowland course with easy walking. Forgiving 18 holes, 5,724 yards. Par 68 (SSS 68).

Visitors: Any time. Contact in advance.

Green fees: £11 per round, £18 per day.

Catering: Bar. **Facilities:** Trolley/buggy hire, pro shop.

Accommodation: Carlton Toby Hotel.

CARD OF THE COURSE

Hole	Yds	Par	Hole	Yds	Par
1	461	4	10	350	4
2	360	4	11	407	4
3	309	4	12	418	4
4	162	3	13	165	3
5	360	4	14	500	5
6	122	3	15	174	3
7	356	4	16	296	4

8	137	3	17	458	4
9	284	4	18	405	4
Out	2,551	33	In	3,173	35
Total	**5,724**		**Par**	**68**	

BALLATER
BALLATER GOLF CLUB ✓

Address: Victoria Road, Ballater, Aberdeen AB35 5QX (013397-55567).
Location: 40 miles west of Aberdeen on A93.
Secretary: A.E. Barclay. **Professional:** F. Smith (013397-55658).
Description: Ballater was founded in 1892 and the course was expanded from nine to 18 holes in 1905. It is a slightly undulating, medium-length course situated in one of the most beautiful parts of upper Deeside. Several holes lie close to the River Dee. Ballater and the course lies within a circle of hills with glorious views. 18 holes, 6,094 yards. Par 70 (SSS 69).
Visitors: No restrictions (except during medal competitions).
Green fees: £17 per round weekdays, £26 per day. £20 per round weekends, £30 per day.
Catering: Full service April to October. Bar.
Facilities: Trolley/buggy hire, putting green, pro shop, practice ground.
Accommodation: Stakis Royal Deeside Hotel, Glen Lui Hotel, Darroch Learg Hotel, Alexandra Hotel, Coyles Hotel plus many others.
Signature hole: FIFTH (186 yards, par three) – Arguably the best hole on the course. It demands the perfect tee shot. Miss the green and you are in a lot of trouble.

CARD OF THE COURSE

Hole	Yds	Par	Hole	Yds	Par
1	464	5	10	381	4
2	422	4	11	477	5
3	223	3	12	403	4
4	419	4	13	161	3
5	186	3	14	319	4
6	368	4	15	368	4
7	509	5	16	346	4
8	333	4	17	160	3
9	220	3	18	335	4
Out	3,144	35	In	2,950	35
Total	**6,094**		**Par**	**70**	

BALLOCH
CAMERON HOUSE HOTEL AND COUNTRY ESTATE

Address: Loch Lomond G83 8QZ (01389-757211).
Description: The Wee Demon Course is challenging with water hazards. Nine holes, 4,532 yards. Par 64.
Visitors: Residents only. **Green fees:** £15 per day.

Catering: Full service. Bar. **Facilities:** Trolley hire, practice nets.
Accommodation: Cameron House Hotel.

BANCHORY
BANCHORY GOLF CLUB

Address: Kinneskie Road, Banchory AB31 5TA (01330-822365).
Location: 18 miles west of Aberdeen off A93. 200 yards from town centre.
Secretary: W. Donaldson. **Professional:** Charles Dernie.
Description: Short, easy-walking, parkland course with views of River Dee and tree-clad hills. 18 holes, 5,775 yards. Par 69 (SSS 68). Amateur record 60 (D. Reith). Pro record 61 (A. Thomson, D. Matthew).
Visitors: Weekdays, except Thursdays. **Green fees:** £17 per round weekdays, £23 per day. £21 per round weekends, £26 per day.
Catering: Yes. Bar.
Facilities: Trolley hire, putting green, pro shop, practice ground.
Accommodation: Burnett Arms Hotel, Torna-coille Hotel.
Signature hole: SIXTEENTH (88 yards, par three) – A short iron to an elevated green with the distinctive dovecote a main feature.

CARD OF THE COURSE

Hole	Yds	Par	Hole	Yds	Par
1	315	4	10	514	5
2	224	3	11	353	4
3	125	3	12	183	3
4	444	4	13	420	4
5	354	4	14	302	4
6	485	5	15	521	5
7	188	3	16	88	3
8	326	4	17	430	4
9	149	3	18	354	4
Out	2,610	33	In	3,165	36
Total	**5,775**		**Par**	**69**	

BANFF
DUFF HOUSE ROYAL GOLF CLUB

Address: The Barnyards, Banff AB4 3SX (01261-812062).
Location: On Moray Firth coast, in centre of Banff. On A98 Aberdeen to Inverness road.
Secretary: Mrs J. Maison. **Professional:** Bob Strachan.
Description: Flat parkland course. Large two-tier greens. Lush tree-lined fairways. Bunkers well positioned on fairways and around greens. 18 holes, 6,161 yards. Par 68 (SSS 69).
Visitors: Welcome but restrictions during monthly medal competitions.
Green fees: £16 per round weekdays, £20 per day. £23 per round weekends, £28 per day.
Catering: Full catering available during season. Bar.

Facilities: Trolley/buggy hire, putting green, pro shop, practice ground.
Accommodation: Banff Springs Hotel.
Signature hole: TWELFTH (498 yards, par five) – Testing hole. Dogleg. Two-tier green. (See diagram opposite.)

CARD OF THE COURSE

Hole	Yds	Par	Hole	Yds	Par
1	314	4	10	403	4
2	366	4	11	214	3
3	392	4	12	498	5
4	367	4	13	175	3
5	330	4	14	434	4
6	139	3	15	468	4
7	460	4	16	242	3
8	381	4	17	462	4
9	172	3	18	344	4
Out	2,921	34	In	3,240	34
Total	**6,161**		**Par**	**68**	

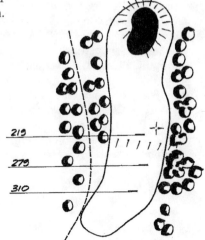

BARRHEAD

FERENEZE GOLF CLUB

Address: Fereneze Avenue, Barrhead, Glasgow G78 1HJ (0141-881-1519).
Location: Eight miles south of Glasgow city centre, off B774.
Secretary: A. Johnston. **Professional:** Darren Robinson.
Description: Hilly moorland course on Fereneze Braes. 18 holes, 5,962 yards. Par 71 (SSS 70). Course record 66.
Visitors: Yes, on written request. **Green fees:** £20 per round.
Catering: Yes. Bar.
Facilities: Trolley hire, putting green, pro shop, practice ground.
Accommodation: Dalmeny Park Country House.

CARD OF THE COURSE

Hole	Yds	Par	Hole	Yds	Par
1	280	4	10	379	4
2	145	3	11	330	4
3	518	5	12	355	4
4	168	3	13	372	4
5	315	4	14	182	3
6	500	5	15	474	4
7	150	3	16	299	4
8	500	5	17	309	4
9	312	4	18	374	4
Out	2,888	36	In	3,074	35
Total	**5,962**		**Par**	**71**	

BATHGATE
BATHGATE GOLF CLUB

Address: Edinburgh Road, Bathgate EH48 1BA.
Location: Five minutes' walk from town and train station.
Secretary: W. Osborne (01506-630505).
Professional: Sandy Strachan (01506-630553).
Description: Pleasant, easy-walking course which has produced two Ryder Cup captains. 18 holes, 6,250 yards. Par 71 (SSS 70). Course record 58 (Sam Torrance).
Visitors: Welcome any time. Societies on weekdays.
Green fees: £20 per day weekdays, £30 per day weekends.
Catering: Full catering and bar service all week.
Facilities: Trolley/buggy hire, putting green, pro shop, practice ground.
Accommodation: Dreadnought Hotel, Fairway Hotel, Kaim Park Hotel.

CARD OF THE COURSE

Hole	Yds	Par	Hole	Yds	Par
1	476	5	10	398	4
2	451	4	11	175	3
3	329	4	12	505	5
4	216	3	13	215	3
5	480	5	14	429	4
6	324	4	15	504	5
7	373	4	16	337	4
8	145	3	17	142	3
9	346	4	18	405	4
Out	3,140	36	In	3,110	35
Total	**6,250**		**Par**	**71**	

BALBARDIE PARK GOLF CLUB

Address: Balbardie Park, Bathgate, West Lothian EH48 4LE (01506-634561).
Location: North side of Bathgate off Torphichen Road.
Description: Challenging par-three course with good greens. Nine holes, 2,474 yards.
Visitors: Any time. **Green fees:** £1.40 Monday to Saturday, £1.95 Sundays.
Catering: Snacks only.
Facilities: Practice green.

BEITH
BEITH GOLF CLUB

Address: Threepwood Road, Beith KA15 2JR (01505-503166).
Location: One and a half miles north-east of A737.
Description: Inland, hilly course with panoramic views. 18 holes, 5,616 yards. Par 68 (SSS 68).
Visitors: Contact in advance. **Green fees:** £12 per round weekdays, £18 weekends.
Catering: Yes.
Accommodation: Bowfield Hotel and Country Club.

BELLSHILL

BELLSHILL GOLF CLUB

Address: Orbiston, Bellshill, Lanarkshire ML4 2RZ (01698-745124).
Location: Exit 5 (A725) off M74 north or the A725 exit off the A8 east–west trunk road.
Administrator: Mrs L. Kennedy.
Description: Inland parkland course. Although most holes appear straightforward, there are enough out of bounds, fairway bunkers and small tree plantations to catch the unwary, especially in the prevailing westerly breeze. Most greens are well protected by bunkers and the sculptured fairways make accuracy a benefit. 18 holes, 6,315 yards. Par 70 (SSS 69). Course record 67.
Visitors: Contact administrator on arrival. Societies must book in advance in writing. **Green fees:** £25 weekdays, £30 weekends. (All-inclusive package includes morning coffee, midday snack and high tea.)
Catering: Yes. Bar. **Facilities:** Putting green.
Accommodation: Bothwell Bridge Hotel, Moorings House Hotel, Silvertrees Hotel.
Signature hole: NINTH (483 yards, par five) – Out of bounds to the left. A dogleg left to a generous green guarded by two large chestnut trees and a large fairway bunker. A good drive to right of centre opens up the green for big hitters. A birdie here is hard-earned.

CARD OF THE COURSE

Hole	Yds	Par	Hole	Yds	Par
1	473	4	10	399	4
2	397	4	11	414	4
3	452	4	12	367	4
4	409	4	13	310	4
5	231	3	14	381	4
6	294	4	15	333	4
7	305	4	16	384	4
8	165	3	17	154	3
9	483	5	18	364	4
Out	3,209	35	In	3,106	35
Total	**6,315**		**Par**	**70**	

BIGGAR

BIGGAR GOLF CLUB

Address: The Park, Broughton Road, Biggar ML12 6HA.
Location: Half a mile from police station. Signposted off A702.
Description: Flattish, scenic parkland course in rolling border countryside. 18 holes, 5,537 yards. Par 68 (SSS 67). Amateur record 61 (G. Kerr). Pro record 63 (Paul Lawrie).
Visitors: Any time. Prior booking on 01899-220319.
Green fees: £8.50 per round weekdays, £14.50 weekends.
Catering: Full licence and catering. Pre-book on 01899-220618.
Facilities: Trolley hire, putting green.
Accommodation: Shieldhill Hotel.

Signature hole: NINTH (200 yards, par three) – Water hazard on left and out of bounds on right.

CARD OF THE COURSE

Hole	Yds	Par	Hole	Yds	Par
1	254	4	10	130	3
2	407	4	11	408	4
3	294	4	12	425	4
4	412	4	13	201	3
5	159	3	14	353	4
6	317	4	15	368	4
7	161	3	16	482	5
8	504	5	17	252	4
9	200	3	18	210	3
Out	2,708	34	In	2,829	34
Total	**5,537**		**Par**		**68**

BISHOPTON
ERSKINE GOLF CLUB

Address: Golf Road, Bishopton, Renfrewshire PA7 5PH (01505-862302).
Location: Three-quarters of a mile north-east off B815.
Professional: Peter Thomson.
Description: Tight parkland course. 18 holes, 6,287 yards. Par 71 (SSS 70).
Visitors: Must be accompanied by member and have handicap certificate.
Green fees: On application.
Catering: Bar. **Facilities:** Pro shop.
Accommodation: Forte Posthouse.

BLAIR ATHOLL
BLAIR ATHOLL GOLF CLUB

Address: Blair Atholl, Perthshire PH18 5TG (01796-481407).
Location: Leave A9 north of Pitlochry at sign for Blair Atholl. Enter village and turn left at Tilt Hotel.
Secretary: J. McGregor.
Description: Inland flat parkland. Easy walking. River runs by three holes. Nine holes, 6,246 yards. Par 69 (SSS 69). Course record 64.
Visitors: Any time.
Green fees: £12 per day weekdays, £15 per day weekends.
Catering: Yes. Bar. **Facilities:** Trolley/buggy hire, practice ground.
Accommodation: Atholl Arms Hotel, Tilt Hotel.

BLAIRGOWRIE
BLAIRGOWRIE GOLF CLUB

Address: Rosemount PH10 6LG (01250-872622).
Location: Two miles south of A93.

Professional: Gordon Kinnoch.
Description: Two wooded heathland courses with pines, silver birch, gorse, broom and heather. Also a nine-hole course.
Rosemount Course: 18 holes, 6,588 yards. Par 72 (SSS 72).
Lansdowne Course: 18 holes, 6,895 yards. Par 72 (SSS 73).
Wee Course: Nine holes, 4,654 yards. Par 64 (SSS 63).
Visitors: Contact in advance. Must have handicap certificate. Restricted Wednesdays, Fridays and weekends.
Green fees: £35 per round weekdays, £48 per day. £40 per round weekends.
Catering: Full service. Bar.
Facilities: Putting green, pro shop, practice ground.
Accommodation: Kinloch House Hotel.

BOAT OF GARTEN
BOAT OF GARTEN GOLF CLUB

Address: Boat of Garten PH24 3BQ (01479-831282).
Location: 30 miles south of Inverness just off the A9.
Secretary: Paddy Smyth.
Description: Heathland course with birch-lined fairways and spectacular views of Cairngorm mountains with snow-capped peaks. 18 holes, 5,866 yards. Par 69 (SSS 69). Amateur record 67. Pro record 64.
Visitors: On application. **Green fees:** £20 weekdays, £25 weekends.
Catering: All-day package from £8. Bar.
Facilities: Trolley/buggy hire, putting green, pro shop.
Accommodation: The Boat Hotel, The Craigard Hotel.
Signature hole: TWELFTH (349 yards, par four) – Tricky but not too difficult. From an elevated tee you drive down an avenue of silver birches. The two-tiered green is guarded by bunkers and an overhit approach shot will find deep rough.

CARD OF THE COURSE

Hole	Yds	Par	Hole	Yds	Par
1	188	3	10	271	4
2	360	4	11	379	4
3	163	3	12	349	4
4	514	5	13	432	4
5	333	4	14	323	4
6	403	4	15	307	4
7	386	4	16	168	3
8	355	4	17	344	4
9	154	3	18	437	4
Out	2,856	34	In	3,010	35
Total	**5,866**		**Par**	**69**	

BONAR BRIDGE
BONAR BRIDGE-ARDGAY GOLF CLUB

Address: Migdale Road, Bonar Bridge IV24 3EB.

Location: From south, immediately after crossing the bridge, go straight on up hill for quarter of a mile. Course on right.
Joint Secretaries: F. Mussard (01863-766375), A. Turner (01549-421248).
Description: A heath and moorland course. Narrow tree-lined fairways favour the accurate rather than the long hitter. Rough is not fierce and course is suitable for high handicap players and the visitor in search of family golf. Nine holes, 4,626 yards. Par 66 (SSS 63). Amateur record 63.
Visitors: Any time. Societies weekdays. **Green fees:** £10 per day.
Catering: Limited (soup and sandwiches) May to September. No licence.
Accommodation: Local hotels and guest houses.

CARD OF THE COURSE

Hole	Yds	Par	
1	339	4	
2	297	4	
3	278	4	
4	190	3	
5	302	4	
6	174	3	
7	285	4	
8	137	3	
9	311	4	
Out	2,313	33	
Total	**4,626**	**Par**	**66**

BONNYBRIDGE
BONNYBRIDGE GOLF CLUB

Address: Larbert Road, Bonnybridge FK4 1NY (01324-812822).
Location: One mile north-east, off A883.
Description: Inland course. Testing heathland but plays similar to links. Guarded greens. Easy walking. Nine holes, 6,060 yards. Par 72 (SSS 69).
Visitors: Must be accompanied by member. Contact in advance.
Green fees: On application.
Facilities: Pro shop.
Accommodation: Inchyra Grange Hotel.

BONNYRIGG
BROOMIEKNOWE GOLF CLUB LTD

Address: 36 Golf Course Road, Bonnyrigg EH19 2HZ (0131-663-9317).
Location: One and a half miles west of roundabout on A7/A6094.
Secretary: John White. **Professional:** Mark Patchett (0131-660-2035).
Description: Interesting mature parkland course. Elevated with good views. 18 holes, 6,150 yards. Par 70 (SSS 69). Course record 65.
Visitors: Midweek after 9.30 a.m. Not weekends.
Green fees: £17 per round weekdays, £25 per day. £20 per round weekends.
Catering: Bar snacks, lunches and high teas Tuesday to Sunday.

Facilities: Trolley hire, putting green, pro shop, practice ground. Independent driving range next to course.
Accommodation: Eskbank Hotel.

CARD OF THE COURSE

Hole	Yds	Par	Hole	Yds	Par
1	316	4	10	402	4
2	347	4	11	183	3
3	369	4	12	441	4
4	321	4	13	430	4
5	167	3	14	408	4
6	401	4	15	153	3
7	468	4	16	297	4
8	470	5	17	309	4
9	350	4	18	318	4
Out	3,209	36	In	2,941	34
Total	**6,150**		**Par**	**70**	

BOTHWELL
BOTHWELL CASTLE GOLF CLUB

Address: Blantyre Road, Bothwell G71 8BR (01698-853177).
Location: North-west of village, off B7071.
Professional: Gordon Niven.
Description: Inland flat parkland course. 18 holes, 6,243 yards. Par 71 (SSS 70). Amateur record 63. Pro record 61.
Visitors: Tuesdays only. Tee off 9.30 a.m. and/or 2 p.m.
Green fees: £20 per round, £28 per day.
Catering: Full service. Bar.
Facilities: Trolley/buggy hire, putting green, pro shop, practice ground.
Accommodation: Silvertrees Hotel, Bothwell Bridge Hotel, Redstones Hotel.
Signature hole: SIXTH (159 yards, par three).

CARD OF THE COURSE

Hole	Yds	Par	Hole	Yds	Par
1	341	4	10	327	4
2	333	4	11	384	4
3	397	4	12	184	3
4	398	4	13	327	4
5	423	4	14	402	4
6	159	3	15	185	3
7	482	5	16	512	5
8	314	4	17	463	5
9	179	3	18	433	4
Out	3,026	35	In	3,217	36
Total	**6,243**		**Par**	**71**	

BRAEMAR
BRAEMAR GOLF CLUB

Address: Cluniebank Road, Braemar, Aberdeenshire AB35 5XX (013397-41618).
Location: Half a mile from village centre.
Secretary: John Pennet (01224-704471).
Description: Parkland course situated in the bottom of Glen Clunie with the River Clunie running through the centre. Highest 18-hole course in Scotland but easy walking. 18 holes, 4,935 yards. Par 65 (SSS 64). Amateur record 61. Pro record 64.
Visitors: Any time by phoning club day before play. Societies by phoning secretary.
Green fees: £11 per round weekdays, £16 per day. £15 per round weekends, £20 per day. £60 per week.
Catering: Full catering available. Bar.
Facilities: Trolley hire.
Accommodation: Invercauld Arms, Fife Arms Hotel, Braemar Lodge, Moorfield House Hotel.
Signature hole: SECOND (369 yards, par four) – Because green is 40 feet above the fairway, it plays a lot longer. River Clunie cuts in and out the whole length of the right side of the fairway, and the rough does the same on the left. A ditch runs across the fairway at about 250 yards. Fives, sixes, sevens or more are common. (See diagram opposite.)

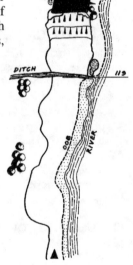

CARD OF THE COURSE

Hole	Yds	Par	Hole	Yds	Par
1	375	4	10	409	4
2	369	4	11	277	4
3	185	3	12	334	4
4	403	4	13	173	3
5	231	3	14	310	4
6	103	3	15	421	4
7	207	3	16	261	4
8	253	4	17	245	3
9	257	4	18	122	3
Out	2,383	32	In	2,552	33
Total	**4,935**		**Par**	**65**	

BRECHIN
BRECHIN GOLF CLUB

Address: Trinity, by Brechin, Angus DD9 7PD (01356-622383; Pro: 01356-625270).
Location: From Brechin take the Aberdeen road. Club is half a mile outside town on left. From the north entry to Brechin from A90, club is a mile from the motorway on the right.
Description: Rolling parkland with delightful views of the Grampian mountains. 18 holes, 6,190 yards. Par 72 (SSS 69). Amateur record 66.
Visitors: Any time midweek. Weekends 10 a.m. to 12 noon, 2.30 p.m. to 4 p.m.

Green fees: £14 per round weekdays, £19 per day. £18 per round weekends, £27 per day.
Catering: Yes. Bar. **Facilities:** Driving range.
Accommodation: Northern Hotel.
Signature hole: THIRTEENTH (213 yards, par three) – Stroke Index 2. Very tricky. Out of bounds on left and a fairway which slopes left to right.

BRIDGE OF ALLAN
BRIDGE OF ALLAN GOLF CLUB

Address: Sunnylaw, Bridge of Allan, Stirling FK9 4LY (01786-832332).
Location: One and a half miles from Dunblane roundabout on M9. Follow signs for Bridge of Allan.
Secretary: Jim Black (01786-813676).
Description: Very picturesque and hilly course in good condition. Overlooks Stirling Castle and the Wallace Monument. Nine holes, 5,120 yards. Par 66 (SSS 65). Course record 62 (men), 66 (ladies).
Visitors: Mondays, Wednesdays, Thursdays and Fridays.
Green fees: £8 per round weekdays, £10 weekends.
Catering: Seven days a week. Weekends only in winter. Bar.
Facilities: Trolley hire, putting green, small practice ground.
Accommodation: Royal Hotel.
Signature hole: FIRST (223 yards, par three) – Said by many to be the most difficult par three anywhere. Six-foot-high dyke 175 yards from tee.

CARD OF THE COURSE

Hole	Yds	Par	
1	223	3	
2	277	4	
3	362	4	
4	314	4	
5	208	3	
6	330	4	
7	289	4	
8	390	4	
9	167	3	
Out	2,560	33	
Total	**5,120**	**Par**	66

BRIDGE OF WEIR
THE OLD COURSE RANFURLY GOLF CLUB LTD

Address: Ranfurly Place, Bridge of Weir, Renfrewshire (01505-613214).
Location: 10 miles south-west of Glasgow.
Description: Interesting inland course with some very challenging holes, particularly the par-three 16th and 18th. 18 holes, 6,089 yards. Par 70 (SSS 70).
Visitors: Welcome but must apply to secretary.
Green fees: £15 per round, £30 per day.

49

Catering: Yes. Bar. **Facilities:** Putting green.
Accommodation: Gryffe Arms Hotel.

CARD OF THE COURSE

Hole	Yds	Par	Hole	Yds	Par
1	454	4	10	382	4
2	355	4	11	482	5
3	364	4	12	415	4
4	506	5	13	121	3
5	166	3	14	389	4
6	502	5	15	321	4
7	224	3	16	201	3
8	301	4	17	338	4
9	426	4	18	142	3
Out	3,298	36	In	2,791	34
Total	**6,089**		**Par**	**70**	

THE RANFURLY CASTLE GOLF CLUB LTD

Address: The Clubhouse, Golf Road, Bridge of Weir PA11 3HN (01505-612609).
Location: From Glasgow Airport (five miles), follow Irvine road and Bridge of Weir signs. Turn left immediately on entering village.
Secretary: Jack Walker. **Professional:** Tom Eckford (01505-614795).
Description: Magnificent inland moorland course, hilly and open. 18 holes, 6,284 yards. Par 70 (SSS 71). Amateur record 65 (W. Brown). Pro record 65 (A. Lockie).
Visitors: Casual visitors (golf club members) any weekday. Societies Tuesdays only. **Green fees:** £25 per round, £35 per day.
Catering: Full catering available. Bar.
Facilities: Trolley hire, putting green, pro shop, practice ground.
Accommodation: Gryffe Arms Hotel.

CARD OF THE COURSE

Hole	Yds	Par	Hole	Yds	Par
1	319	4	10	294	4
2	396	4	11	441	4
3	490	5	12	381	4
4	269	4	13	370	4
5	139	3	14	185	3
6	403	4	15	389	4
7	184	3	16	347	4
8	461	4	17	411	4
9	383	4	18	422	4
Out	3,044	35	In	3,240	35
Total	**6,284**		**Par**	**70**	

BRORA

BRORA GOLF CLUB

Address: Golf Road, Brora, Sutherland KW9 6QS (01408-621417).

Location: Five miles north of Golspie on A9. 51 miles from Inverness. Turn right in centre of village to seaside car park.
Secretary: James Fraser.
Description: James Braid-designed links course. Maintained in traditional fashion. Noted for fast, true greens. 18 holes, 6,110 yards. Par 69 (SSS 69). Amateur record 61 (J. Miller).
Visitors: All year round except competition days.
Green fees: £18 per round, £24 per day.
Catering: May to October. Bar.
Facilities: Trolley hire, putting green, pro shop, practice ground.
Accommodation: Several close to course, including Royal Marine.
Signature hole: TWELFTH (362 yards, par four) – Rolling fairway. The perfect drive is down the right but beware out of bounds. If you choose the left then the second shot has to contend with bunkers. (See diagram opposite.)

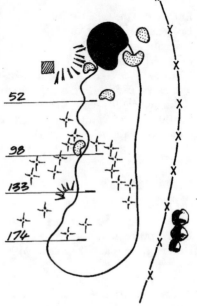

CARD OF THE COURSE

Hole	Yds	Par	Hole	Yds	Par
1	297	4	10	435	4
2	344	4	11	412	4
3	447	4	12	362	4
4	325	4	13	125	3
5	428	4	14	334	4
6	174	3	15	430	4
7	350	4	16	345	4
8	501	5	17	438	4
9	162	3	18	201	3
Out	3,028	35	In	3,082	34
Total	**6,110**		**Par**	**69**	

BUCKIE
BUCKPOOL GOLF CLUB

Address: Barrhill Road, Buckpool AB56 1DU (01542-832933).
Location: Off A98.
Description: Seaside course overlooking Moray Firth. Whin and broom line fairways. Can be windy but easy walking. 18 holes, 6,257 yards. Par 70 (SSS 70). Course record 64.
Visitors: Apply in advance. **Green fees:** £8 per round weekdays, £12 per day. £10 per round weekends, £18 per day.
Catering: Yes. Bar. **Facilities:** Trolley hire, Putting green.
Accommodation: Marine Hotel.

STRATHLENE GOLF CLUB

Address: Strathlene Road, Buckie AB56 1DJ (01542-831798).
Location: Three miles east on A942.
Description: Seaside links course. Good views. Windy with raised greens which

can cause problems. 18 holes, 5,980 yards. Par 69 (SSS 69). Course record 65.
Visitors: Book at weekends. Societies telephone for Mondays to Fridays and write for weekends. **Green fees:** £10 per round weekdays, £14 per day. £14 per round weekends, £18 per day.
Catering: Yes. Bar. **Facilities:** Trolley hire, putting green, pro shop.
Accommodation: Mill House Hotel.

BURNTISLAND
BURNTISLAND GOLF HOUSE CLUB

Address: Dodhead, Kirkcaldy Road, Burntisland KY3 9EW (Manager: 01592-874093).
Location: One mile east on B923.
Professional: Jacky Montgomery (01592-873247).
Description: Inland hill course with good sea views. 18 holes, 5,965 yards. Par 70 (SSS 69). Course record 62.
Visitors: Weekend play restricted. Book with pro. **Green fees:** £15 per round weekdays, £25 per day. £23 per round weekends, £35 per day.
Catering: Full service. Bar.
Facilities: Trolley hire, putting green, pro shop, practice ground, driving range.
Accommodation: Inchview Hotel.

BUTE (Isle of)
BUTE GOLF CLUB

Address: Kingarth, Isle of Bute PA20 9PF (01700-831648).
Location: Eight miles from Rothesay, off A845.
Description: Flat links course with a number of natural hazards and gorse bushes. Nine holes, 4,994 yards. SSS 64.
Visitors: Any time. **Green fees:** £6 per day.
Accommodation: Kingarth Hotel.

PORT BANNATYNE GOLF CLUB

Address: Port Bannatyne, Isle of Bute PA20 0PH (01700-504544).
Location: West side of village off A844.
Secretary: D. Grant (01700-505073).
Description: Built on the side of a hill but no steep climbs. 13 holes (the first five holes are played twice). Small greens. Beautiful views. 13 holes, 5,085 yards. Par 68 (SSS 65). Amateur record 63 (Jim O'Donnell).
Visitors: Very welcome on weekdays and at weekends. **Green fees:** £10 per day.
Catering: May to September.
Accommodation: Port Royal Hotel.
Signature hole: FIRST (362 yards, par four) – Longest hole on the course. A blind tee shot with 270 yards to the burn. From the yellow markers, the green is driveable (256 yards). Out of bounds on the right, slope of the hill runs towards out of bounds. Easiest way to play from yellow markers is seven-iron short of burn and another iron to green.

CARD OF THE COURSE

Hole	Yds	Par	Hole	Yds	Par
1	362	4	10	164	3
2	304	4	11	274	4
3	330	4	12	296	4
4	187	3	13	362	4
5	320	4	14	304	4
6	289	4	15	330	4
7	297	4	16	187	3
8	287	4	17	320	4
9	253	4	18	219	3
Out	2,629	35	In	2,456	33
Total	**5,085**		**Par**	**68**	

ROTHESAY GOLF CLUB

Address: Canada Hill, Rothesay, Isle of Bute PA20 PHN (01700-502244).
Location: Off road to Kingarth.
Professional: James Dougal.
Description: Moorland course with magnificent views to the Kyles of Bute and the Clyde coast. A fairly hilly course, designed by James Braid and Ben Sayers. Two par fives are challenging when the wind blows. 18 holes, 5,370 yards. Par 69 (SSS 66). Course record 62.
Visitors: Yes, but pre-book for weekends.
Green fees: £14 per day weekdays, £23 per day weekends.
Catering: Bar. **Facilities:** Trolley hire, putting green, practice ground.
Accommodation: Ardmory House Hotel.

CARD OF THE COURSE

Hole	Yds	Par	Hole	Yds	Par
1	265	4	10	262	4
2	401	4	11	145	3
3	342	4	12	304	4
4	200	3	13	170	3
5	273	4	14	254	4
6	514	5	15	276	4
7	359	4	16	515	5
8	204	3	17	372	4
9	268	4	18	246	3
Out	2,826	35	In	2,544	34
Total	**5,370**		**Par**	**69**	

CALLANDER

CALLANDER GOLF CLUB

Address: Aveland Road, Callander FK17 8EN (01877-330090).
Location: 16 miles north-west of Stirling on A84.
Secretary: Ian Scott. **Professional:** William Kelly.
Description: Inland wooded parkland course with panoramic views to Ben Ledi.

Designed by Tom Morris Snr. 18 holes, 5,151 yards. Par 66 (SSS 66). Amateur record 61. Pro record 59.

Visitors: Any time but handicap certificates required on Wednesdays and Sundays.
Green fees: £20 per round weekdays, £26 per day. £26 per round weekends, £31 per day.
Catering: Full catering and bar facilities in season.
Facilities: Trolley hire, pro shop, practice ground.
Accommodation: Abbotsford Lodge, Wolseley Park Hotel.
Signature hole: FIFTEENTH (135 yards, par three) – Down a narrow avenue of trees.

CARD OF THE COURSE

Hole	Yds	Par	Hole	Yds	Par
1	348	4	10	179	3
2	199	3	11	179	3
3	329	4	12	404	4
4	321	4	13	324	4
5	183	3	14	224	3
6	372	4	15	135	3
7	250	4	16	365	4
8	296	4	17	478	5
9	232	3	18	333	4
Out	2,530	33	In	2,621	33
Total	**5,151**		**Par**	**66**	

CARDENDEN
AUCHTERDARRAN GOLF CLUB

Address: Woodend Road, Cardenden KY5 0NH (01592-721579).
Location: North of Cardenden on Kirkcaldy to Glenrothes road.
Description: Flat course. Two or three testing holes. Nine holes, 5,250 yards. Par 66 (SSS 66). Course record 63.
Visitors: Any time, except between 7 a.m. and 11 a.m. and between 1 p.m. and 3 p.m. on Saturdays, and also some Sundays in season.
Green fees: £10 per round weekdays, £19 per day. £14 per round weekends, £21 per day.
Catering: Bar.
Accommodation: Dean Park Hotel.

CARDROSS
CARDROSS GOLF CLUB

Address: Main Road, Cardross G82 5LB (01389-841754).
Location: In centre of village on A814.
Professional: Robert Farrell (01389-841350).
Description: Undulating parkland course. Testing with good views. 18 holes, 6,469 yards. Par 71 (SSS 72). Course record 65.
Visitors: Must not play at weekends unless introduced by member. Contact

professional in advance. **Green fees:** £22 per round, £32 per day.
Catering: Yes. Bar.
Facilities: Trolley/buggy hire, putting green, pro shop, practice ground.
Accommodation: Commodore Toby Hotel.

CARLUKE
CARLUKE GOLF CLUB
Address: Mauldslie Road, Hallcraig ML8 5HG (01555-771070).
Location: One mile west off A73.
Professional: Richard Forrest.
Description: Slightly hilly parkland course with views over the Clyde Valley. 18 holes, 5,853 yards. Par 70 (SSS 68). Course record 63.
Visitors: Not weekends. Must contact in advance.
Green fees: £18 per round, £25 per day.
Catering: Full service. Bar. **Facilities:** Putting green, pro shop.
Accommodation: Popinjay Hotel.

CARNOUSTIE
CARNOUSTIE GOLF LINKS
Carnoustie is back. After almost a quarter of a century, the Open Championship will in 1999 return to the links that many believe to be Britain's toughest. It is long overdue. Not since 1975 has the Open been held at Carnoustie. In that year Tom Watson came from nowhere to win and the Open took off. With demand for top-class hotels and access for thousands of cars, it was deemed that Carnoustie could not handle it.

It was nothing to do with the standard of this magnificent course. Carnoustie has been called 'the killer links' and Walter Hagen described it as the greatest course in the British Isles. When the wind blows, it changes from a sleeping giant into a terror, and at 7,240 yards it was the longest ever Open course. Even from the club's medal tees, 6,941 yards is still formidable.

Carnoustie's pedigree as an Open venue is unquestionable, producing great champions in Tommy Armour (1931), Henry Cotton (1937) , Ben Hogan (1953), Gary Player (1968) and Tom Watson (1975). Every one was a great championship.

Perhaps Player's triumph in 1968 – his second Open win – was the most spectacular. Under pressure from Billy Casper, Bob Charles and Jack Nicklaus by the par-five 14th, the little South African found himself behind 'the Spectacles', two large bunkers set in the face of a ridge that runs across the fairway less than 80 yards from the green. If ever he needed a good second shot, it was now. He struck a three-wood. From where he played, he could not see the green and, as he scrambled up the bank, he heard a roar from the crowd. It was not until he reached the green that he saw he was only two feet from the hole. That gave him an eagle three and, more importantly, the margin to win.

Armour's victory in 1931 was a popular one because he was a Scot who had emigrated to America. Henry Cotton saw off the victorious American Ryder Cup team for the second of his three Opens. The great Ben Hogan played in only one Open Championship – and won it at Carnoustie in foul weather with a final-round

68 which many regard as the true Carnoustie Open record, even though Jack Newton bettered it by three shots to force an 18-hole play-off with Watson in 1975. Each of Hogan's four rounds was lower than the one before.

So the five Opens were won by a Scot in exile, an Englishman, two Americans and a South African. Very appropriate for Carnoustie. As early as the sixteenth century, golf was played on the adjoining Barry links. There are now six clubs playing over the links but the first official club was founded in 1842 when a tract of land was bought from the Earl of Dalhousie and 10 holes were designed by Allan Robertson. In 1867 Old Tom Morris extended it to 18 holes and Willie Park Jnr improved on it. But today's great test of golf is down to James Braid, who remodelled the course in 1926.

In 1890 the population of Carnoustie was about 3,000 and the men worked in the jute mills, the chemical works, the carrot-preserving business or the local shoe factory. But the major influence was this forbidding links, and Archie Simpson was the one responsible for telling the world about it. He emigrated to the US to play and teach golf. Others followed his path. It is estimated that more than 400 left the town to earn their living as professionals around the world. Most of them went to the US and, perhaps, it can be said that they taught America, if not the world, how to play golf.

What is it that makes Carnoustie such a challenge to the very best? Basically it is a flat course, but it demands accuracy. If you are wayward, there is a heavy price to pay. The wind is a forever-changing rival, as the course is laid out in a square which means that no more than two consecutive holes, every one individual in character, run in the same direction. There are far more trees than you would expect on a links and, of course, there are the burns.

The Barry Burn and Jocky's Burn cross the fairways in the most inconvenient spots, usually just in front of greens and in areas you would like to drive to. Jocky's Burn comes into play on the second, third, fifth and sixth and the more famous Barry Burn on the first, tenth, eleventh, seventeenth and eighteenth.

But it is the finishing stretch of the final five holes that makes Carnoustie a course of the highest calibre. The famous Spectacles 14th, 483 yards from the medal tees, is the start of the run-in. Then there is the 459-yard 15th, whose green is set into a bowl. A bit of breathing space before the terrors to follow. The 245-yard 16th is a tough par three that demands a powerful, accurate tee shot to a small plateau green guarded by six bunkers. Jack Nicklaus once needed a driver followed by an eight-iron to get up. When Watson won in 1975, he never once hit the green.

Our old adversary, the Barry Burn, crosses the 17th fairway three times, earning it the name of 'The Island'. The trick is to land your drive on the 'island' between the first and second loop – not many carry both – and having done that you face a long second shot over bumps and bunkers. The burn lies in wait for you again on the home hole – 444 yards, par four – and you have to carry it with your tee shot to set up an intriguing second as the burn again guards the green. Do you go for it, or lay up? The decision is yours.

Address: Links Parade, Carnoustie DD7 7JE (Tee reservations: 01241-853789).
Location: South-west side of town off A930.
Secretary: E. Smith. **Professional:** Lee Vannet.
Catering: Contact Caledonia Golf Club (01241-852115), Carnoustie Golf Club

(01241-852480), New Taymouth Golf Club (01241-852425).
Facilities: Trolley hire, putting green.
Accommodation: Carlogie House Hotel, Glencoe Hotel, Dalhousie Hotel, Kinloch Arms Hotel, Lairds Hotel, Bayview House, Arlberg House, Station Hotel.

Championship Course
Starter: 01241-853249.
Description: 18 holes, 6,941 yards. Par 72 (SSS 75). Course record 64 (A. Tait, C. Montgomerie).
Visitors: Yes. Must have handicap certificate. Weekdays Saturdays after 2 p.m. and Sundays after 11.30 a.m.
Green fees: £50 per round. Juniors half price.
Signature hole: FOURTEENTH (483 yards, par five) – The famous Spectacles, two large and deep bunkers in the face of a ridge guarding the green about 80 yards from the flag. The tee shot is critical, for there is out of bounds on the left and a wood to the right and bunkers sited to catch and punish the smallest error. The tee shot must be long and perfectly placed to have any chance of carrying the Spectacles with the second shot. (See diagram opposite.)

CARD OF THE COURSE

Hole	Yds	Par	Hole	Yds	Par
1	401	4	10	446	4
2	435	4	11	362	4
3	337	4	12	479	5
4	375	4	13	161	3
5	387	4	14	483	5
6	520	5	15	459	4
7	394	4	16	245	3
8	167	3	17	433	4
9	413	4	18	444	4
Out	3,429	36	In	3,512	36
Total	**6,941**		**Par**	**72**	

Burnside Course
Starter: 01241-855344.
Description: 18 holes, 6,020 yards. Par 68 (SSS 69). Course record 62 (A. Tait).
Visitors: Weekdays. Saturdays after 2 p.m. Sundays after 11.30 a.m.
Green fees: £18 per round, £27 per day.

Buddon Links
Starter: 01241-853249.
Description: 18 holes, 5,420 yards. Par 66 (SSS 66).
Visitors: Weekdays. Saturdays and Sundays after 11 a.m.
Green fees: £14 per round, £21 per day.

CARNWATH
CARNWATH GOLF CLUB

Address: 1 Main Street, Carnwath ML11 8JX (01555-840251).
Location: On A70 west of village.
Secretary: W. Bruce.
Description: Hilly parkland course with small greens. 18 holes, 5,943 yards. Par 70 (SSS 69). Amateur record 63.
Visitors: Sundays, Mondays, Wednesdays and Fridays.
Green fees: £18 per day weekdays, £25 per day Sundays and public holidays.
Catering: Yes. Bar.
Facilities: Trolley hire, putting green.
Accommodation: Cartland Bridge Hotel.

CARRADALE
CARRADALE GOLF CLUB

Address: Carradale, Argyll PA28 6SG (01583-431643).
Location: South side of village.
Description: Very difficult heathland seaside course built on a promontory overlooking the Isle of Arran. Tiny greens and the terrain are the main hazards. Has been described as the most sporting nine-hole course in Scotland. Nine holes, 4,784 yards. Par 62 (SSS 64).
Visitors: Any time. **Green fees:** £7 per day.
Catering: No. **Facilities:** Trolley hire, putting green.
Accommodation: Seafield Hotel.

CARRBRIDGE
CARRBRIDGE GOLF CLUB

Address: Inverness Road, Carrbridge, Inverness-shire PH23 3AU (01479-841623, 01479-841506).
Location: Off A9. Seven miles north of Aviemore. 27 miles south of Inverness.
Secretary: Mrs Anne Baird.
Description: Short, but challenging. Part parkland, part heathland. Superb views of Cairngorm mountains. Nine holes, 5,402 yards. Par 71 (SSS 68). Amateur record 64.
Visitors: Any time except Wednesdays after 5 p.m. and Sundays.
Green fees: £10 per round weekdays, £11 per day. £12 weekends.
Catering: Tea, coffee, snacks. No bar. **Facilities:** Trolley hire, putting green.
Accommodation: Contact Carrbridge Tourist Association.
Signature hole: SEVENTH (262 yards, par four) – Elevated tee and green with large bunkers behind.

CARD OF THE COURSE

Hole	Yds	Par	Hole	Yds	Par
1	480	5	10	480	5
2	334	4	11	334	4
3	342	4	12	342	4
4	331	4	13	331	4

5	258	4	14	258	4
6	270	4	15	270	4
7	262	4	16	262	4
8	174	3	17	174	3
9	231	3	18	269	4
Out	2,682	35	In	2,720	36
Total	**5,402**		**Par**	**71**	

CASTLE DOUGLAS
CASTLE DOUGLAS GOLF CLUB
Address: Abercromby Road, Castle Douglas (01556-502099).
Location: 400 yards from town centre on A713 to Ayr.
Secretary: A. Millen.
Description: Parkland course but one very big hill. Nine holes, 5,408 yards. Par 68 (SSS 66).
Visitors: Welcome. **Green fees:** £12 per day.
Catering: During May to September. Bar.
Facilities: Trolley hire, putting green, practice ground.
Accommodation: Douglas Arms Hotel, Kings Arms Hotel, Imperial Hotel.

CARD OF THE COURSE

Hole	Yds	Par	
1	101	3	
2	261	4	
3	367	4	
4	314	4	
5	296	4	
6	443	4	
7	173	3	
8	438	4	
9	311	4	
Out	2,704	34	
Total	**5,408**	**Par**	**68**

CLYDEBANK
CLYDEBANK AND DISTRICT GOLF CLUB
Address: Glasgow Road, Hardgate G81 5QY (01389-873289).
Location: Two miles east of Erskine Bridge.
Professional: David Pirie (01389-878686).
Description: Undulating parkland course with tree-lined fairways and well-bunkered greens. Established in 1905. 18 holes, 5,823 yards. Par 68 (SSS 68). Course record 64.
Visitors: Weekdays only before 4 p.m. Round only. Contact pro.
Green fees: £13 per round.
Catering: Yes. Bar. **Facilities:** Putting green, pro shop, practice ground.
Accommodation: Patio Hotel.

CLYDEBANK MUNICIPAL COURSE

Address: Overtoun Road, Dalmuir G81 3RE (Starter: 0141-952-8698).
Location: Two miles north-west of town centre.
Professional: Stewart Savage (0141-952-6372).
Description: Hilly parkland course with burn. 18 holes, 5,349 yards. Par 67 (SSS 67).
Visitors: Any time. **Green fees:** £6.55 weekdays, £7 weekends.
Catering: No. **Facilities:** Trolley hire, pro shop.
Accommodation: Patio Hotel.

COATBRIDGE

COATBRIDGE GOLF CLUB

Address: Townhead Road, Coatbridge ML5 2HX (01236-428975; Pro shop: 01236-421492).
Location: One and a half miles west of town centre.
Description: Wooded course. 18 holes, 6,026 yards. SSS 69.
Visitors: Any time, except before 2.30 p.m. weekends and after 5.30 p.m. weekdays. **Green fees:** £4.80 per round weekdays, £7.20 weekends.
Catering: Yes. **Facilities:** Pro shop.

DRUMPELLIER GOLF CLUB

Address: Drumpellier Avenue, Coatbridge ML5 1RX (01236-424139).
Location: Eight miles east of Glasgow on A89.
Secretary: William Brownlie. **Professional:** David Ross.
Description: Undulating parkland course. 18 holes, 6,227 yards. Par 71 (SSS 71). Amateur record 65. Pro record 62.
Visitors: Yes, weekdays. **Green fees:** £22 per round, £30 per day.
Catering: Yes. Bar.
Facilities: Trolley hire, putting green, pro shop, practice ground.
Accommodation: Georgian Hotel.
Signature hole: TWELFTH (158 yards, par three) – Slightly uphill. Named 'The Copse' and, as you would expect, the green is guarded by trees.

CARD OF THE COURSE

Hole	Yds	Par	Hole	Yds	Par
1	464	4	10	325	4
2	493	5	11	370	4
3	345	4	12	158	3
4	399	4	13	376	4
5	158	3	14	160	3
6	363	4	15	478	5
7	173	3	16	379	4
8	440	4	17	270	4
9	494	5	18	382	4
Out	3,329	36	In	2,898	35
Total	**6,227**		**Par**	**71**	

COLDSTREAM
HIRSEL GOLF CLUB

Address: Kelso Road, Coldstream TD12 4 NJ (01890-882678).
Location: On A697 at west end of Coldstream.
Secretary: John Balfour (01890-882233).
Description: Beautifully situated parkland course with panoramic views of the Cheviot Hills. Truly a course not to be missed on a Borders visit. Each hole offers a different challenge and a scenic view. 18 holes, 6,092 yards. Par 70 (SSS 70).
Visitors: Yes. No restrictions. **Green fees:** £18 weekdays, £25 weekends.
Catering: Bar snacks and full restaurant.
Facilities: Trolley/buggy hire, putting green, pro shop, practice ground.
Accommodation: Cross Keys Hotel, Collingwood Arms, Tillmouth Park Hotel.
Signature hole: SEVENTH (170 yards, par three) – Demanding accuracy of flight and length from the tee to ensure carrying the water and stand a chance of a par.

CARD OF THE COURSE

Hole	Yds	Par	Hole	Yds	Par
1	304	4	10	125	3
2	290	4	11	345	4
3	246	3	12	531	5
4	320	4	13	440	4
5	372	4	14	180	3
6	357	4	15	438	4
7	170	3	16	314	4
8	345	4	17	375	4
9	420	4	18	520	5
Out	2,824	34	In	3,268	36
Total	**6,092**		**Par**	**70**	

COLONSAY (Isle of)
COLONSAY GOLF CLUB

Address: Scalasaig, Isle of Colonsay PA61 7YP (01951-200316).
Location: Two miles west on A870.
Description: Challenging traditional links course. 18 holes, 4,775 yards. Par 72 (SSS 72).
Visitors: Any time. **Green fees:** £5 per year.
Catering: Colonsay Hotel, two miles from course.
Accommodation: Colonsay Hotel.

COLVEND
COLVEND GOLF CLUB

Address: Sandyhills, Colvend, Dalbeattie, Dumfries and Galloway DG5 4PY (01556-630398).
Location: Six miles from Dalbeattie on A710 Solway coast road from Dumfries.
Secretary: J. Henderson (01556-610878).

Description: Extension to existing nine holes opens April 1997, making it a challenging 18-hole scenic parkland course with superb views over the Galloway hills and Solway Firth. 18 holes, 4,720 yards. Par 68 (SSS 67).
Visitors: Almost any time. Club competitions most Sundays.
Green fees: £15 per day, £50 per week.
Catering: All day every day throughout season. Weekends November to March. Bar.
Facilities: Trolley/buggy hire, putting green.
Accommodation: Clonyard House Hotel, Cairngill Hotel, Barons Craig Hotel, Pheasant Hotel.
Signature hole: THIRTEENTH (Par three) – Downhill with the green between two trees. Ponds either side of green.

COMRIE
COMRIE GOLF CLUB

Address: Laggan Braes, Comrie PH6 2LR (01764-670055).
Location: Seven miles west of Crieff on A75.
Secretary: G. Betty, 9 Cowden Way, Comrie PH6 2NW.
Description: Very beautiful scenery. Slightly hilly heathland course with some testing holes. Nine holes, 6,040 yards. Par 70 (SSS 70). Amateur record 62.
Visitors: Any time except Monday and Tuesdays from 4.30 p.m.
Green fees: £10 per day weekdays, £12 per day weekends.
Catering: Light snacks. **Facilities:** Trolley hire, putting green.
Accommodation: Comrie Hotel, Royal Hotel, Mossgeil Guest House.
Signature hole: FIFTH (173 yards, par three) – Play over rocks to an elevated green surrounded by bunkers.

CARD OF THE COURSE

Hole	Yds	Par	
1	340	4	
2	261	4	
3	175	3	
4	408	4	
5	173	3	
6	492	5	
7	372	4	
8	361	4	
9	438	4	
Out	3,020	35	
Total	**6,040**	**Par**	**70**

COWDENBEATH
COWDENBEATH GOLF CLUB

Address: Seco Place, Cowdenbeath KY4 8PD (01383-511918).
Location: Six miles east of Dunfermline.
Description: Parkland course. Nine holes, 6,552 yards. Par 72 (SSS 71). Course record 68.

Visitors: Any time. **Green fees:** £5 weekdays, £10.50 weekends.
Catering: Bar. **Facilities:** Putting green, practice ground.
Accommodation: Woodside Hotel.

CRAIL
CRAIL GOLFING SOCIETY

Address: Balcomie Clubhouse, Fifeness, Crail KY10 3XN.
Location: 11 miles south-east of St Andrews on A917, then two miles from Crail to Fifeness.
Manager: J. Horsfield (01333-450686).
Professional: Graeme Lennie (01333-450960).
Description: Testing links with good greens. On the edge of the North Sea, it is one of the most picturesque courses. The Crail Golfing Society was founded in 1786. 18 holes, 5,922 yards. Par 69 (SSS 69).
Visitors: Any time between 10 a.m. and 12 noon, and between 2 p.m. and 2.30 p.m.
Green fees: £19 per round weekdays, £30 per day. £24 per round weekends, £38 per day.
Catering: Yes. Bar.
Facilities: Trolley/buggy hire, putting green, pro shop, practice ground.
Accommodation: Golf Hotel, Balcomie Hotel, Craws Nest Hotel.
Signature hole: FIFTH (459 yards, par four) – Dogleg right into prevailing wind across North Sea.

CARD OF THE COURSE

Hole	Yds	Par	Hole	Yds	Par
1	328	4	10	336	4
2	494	5	11	496	5
3	184	3	12	528	5
4	346	4	13	219	3
5	459	4	14	150	3
6	186	3	15	270	4
7	349	4	16	163	3
8	442	4	17	463	4
9	306	4	18	203	3
Out	3,094	35	In	2,828	34
Total	**5,922**		**Par**	**69**	

CRIEFF
CRIEFF GOLF CLUB LTD

Address: Ferntower, Perth Road, Crieff PH7 3LR (01764-652909).
Location: On A85 between Stirling and Perth.
Managing Secretary: J. Miller. **Professional:** David Murchie.
Description: Parkland with a panoramic view of the Strathearn Valley. Ferntower course is the more challenging. Dornock has a water hazard.
Ferntower: 18 holes, 6,402 yards. SSS 71. Course record 65.
Dornock: Nine holes, 4,772 yards. Par 64 (SSS 63).

Visitors: Any time. **Green fees:** £19 per round.
Catering: Yes. Bar.
Facilities: Trolley/buggy hire, putting green, pro shop, practice ground.
Accommodation: Crieff Hydro.

CROSSHILL
LOCHORE MEADOWS GOLF CLUB
Address: Lochore Meadows Country Park, Crosshill KY5 8BA (01592-414300).
Location: Two miles north of B920.
Description: Inland, wooded lochside course with stream. Nine holes, 5,554 yards. Par 72 (SSS 71).
Visitors: Any time. **Green fees:** £7.50 weekdays, £10 weekends.
Catering: No. **Facilities:** putting green, practice ground.
Accommodation: Green Hotel.

CRUDEN BAY
CRUDEN BAY GOLF CLUB
Address: Aulton Road, Cruden Bay, Peterhead AB42 0NN (01779-812285).
Location: Seven miles south of Peterhead, 23 miles north-east of Aberdeen, just off A92.
Secretary: Mrs Rosemary Pittendrigh.
Professional: Robbie Stewart (01779-812414).
Description: Traditional Scottish links course featuring the most beautiful views. Slightly shorter than most championship courses but makes up for it by offering a good, fun test of golf. 18 holes, 6,395 yards. Par 70 (SSS 74). Amateur record 67. Pro record 65.
St Olaf course: Nine holes, 5,106 yards. SSS 65.
Visitors: Welcome. Parties on weekdays only. **Green fees:** £30 per day weekdays, £40 per day weekends. *St Olaf:* £10 weekdays, £15 weekends.
Catering: Full bar and catering facilities.
Facilities: Trolley hire, putting green, pro shop, practice ground, driving range.
Accommodation: Red House Hotel, Udny Arms Hotel, Linsmohr Hotel, Waterside Inn, Ythan Hotel, St Olaf Hotel.
Signature hole: FOURTH (193 yards, par three) – One of the most challenging as well as one of the most picturesque. Water and out of bounds on left. Long shot to a plateau green.

CARD OF THE COURSE

Hole	Yds	Par	Hole	Yds	Par
1	416	4	10	385	4
2	339	4	11	149	3
3	286	4	12	320	4
4	193	3	13	550	5
5	454	4	14	397	4
6	529	5	15	239	3
7	392	4	16	182	3

8	258	4	17	428	4
9	462	4	18	416	4
Out	3,329	36	In	3,066	34
Total	**6,395**		**Par**	**70**	

CULLEN
CULLEN GOLF CLUB
Address: The Links, Cullen, Buckie, Banffshire AB56 2UU (01542-840685).
Location: On west boundary of burgh off A98, midway between Aberdeen and Inverness on Moray Firth coast.
Secretary: Ian Findlay, 15 Queens Drive, Cullen AB56 4XF (01542-840174).
Description: Traditional seaside links course with elevated section. Natural rock landscaping coming into play at several holes. Beach (out of bounds) on several holes. On elevated section of course panoramic views of coastline and rural hinterland. Several tricky par threes. 18 holes, 4,610 yards. Par 63 (SSS 62). Amateur record 58 (B. Main 1979).
Visitors: Welcome. May be restrictions on Wednesdays due to club competitions.
Green fees: £7 per round weekdays, £12 per day. £9 per round weekends, £15 per day.
Catering: Full catering April to October. Other months by arrangement with caterer. **Facilities:** Putting green, practice ground.
Accommodation: Cullen Bay Hotel, Royal Oak Hotel, Bayview Hotel, Three Kings Inn, Grant Arms Hotel, Seafield Arms Hotel, Waverley Hotel.
Signature hole: SEVENTH (231 yards, par three) – Elevated tee to green some 80–100 feet below. Subject to wind and weather, this hole can play havoc with your score. Club selection can vary from driver to a mid-iron.

CARD OF THE COURSE

Hole	Yds	Par	Hole	Yds	Par
1	344	4	10	309	4
2	130	3	11	245	3
3	236	3	12	182	3
4	129	3	13	149	3
5	360	4	14	207	3
6	172	3	15	510	5
7	231	3	16	348	4
8	275	4	17	262	4
9	194	3	18	327	4
Out	2,071	30	In	2,539	33
Total	**4,610**		**Par**	**63**	

CUMBERNAULD
PALACERIGG GOLF CLUB
Address: Palacerigg Country Park, Cumbernauld G67 3HU (01236-734969; Starter John Murray: 01236-721461).
Location: Two miles south of Cumbernauld on Palacerigg road, off B8054 Lenziemill Road.

Secretary: David Cooper.
Description: Well-wooded parkland course. 18 holes, 6,444 yards. Par 72 (SSS 71). Amateur record 65. Pro record 66.
Visitors: Any time. Societies weekdays. **Green fees:** £10.
Catering: Yes. Bar. **Facilities:** Putting green, practice ground.
Accommodation: Castlecary Hotel, Cumbernauld Travel Inn, Moodiesburn House Hotel, Westerwood Hotel.
Signature hole: FIFTEENTH (409 yards, par four) – Player must decide to either carry burn or lay up short with drive. Second shot is uphill to sloping green with bunkers left, right and over the green.

CARD OF THE COURSE

Hole	Yds	Par	Hole	Yds	Par
1	426	4	10	383	4
2	405	4	11	338	4
3	394	4	12	344	4
4	349	4	13	308	4
5	503	5	14	314	4
6	161	3	15	409	4
7	540	5	16	222	3
8	157	3	17	342	4
9	360	4	18	489	5
Out	3,295	36	In	3,149	36
Total	**6,444**		**Par**	**72**	

WESTERWOOD HOTEL GOLF AND COUNTRY CLUB

Address: 1 St Andrews Drive, Cumbernauld G68 0EW (01236-725281).
Location: From Edinburgh, take M9 heading for Glasgow. Take M876 exit then on to A80. Take exit marked Service/Dullatur/Ward Park.
Secretary: Tom Faichnie Snr. **Professional:** Steve Killin.
Description: Undulating wooded, American-style parkland/heathland course with many water hazards. Designed by Seve Ballesteros and Dave Thomas. 18 holes, 6,601 yards. Par 72 (SSS 72). Amateur record 65. Pro record 67.
Visitors: Any time.
Green fees: £22.50 per round weekdays, £27.50 per round weekends.
Catering: Yes. Bar.
Facilities: Trolley/buggy hire, putting green, pro shop, driving range.
Accommodation: Westerwood Hotel.
Signature hole: FIFTEENTH (170 yards, par three) – 'The Waterfall'. Over a burn with a 50-foot quarry wall behind the green. A single bunker to the right of the green and beyond that a pond.

CARD OF THE COURSE

Hole	Yds	Par	Hole	Yds	Par
1	505	5	10	362	4
2	231	3	11	187	3
3	329	4	12	385	4
4	470	5	13	197	3
5	383	4	14	518	5

6	368	4	15	170	3
7	408	4	16	414	4
8	176	3	17	403	4
9	548	5	18	547	5
Out	3,418	37	In	3,183	35
Total	**6,601**		**Par**	**72**	

CUMBRAE (Isle of)
MILLPORT GOLF CLUB
Address: Golf Road, Millport, Isle of Cumbrae KA28 0HB (01475-531311).
Location: Seven-minute ferry ride from Largs on Ayrshire coast.
Secretary: John McGill CPM (01475-530306).
Professional: Ken Docherty (01475-530305).
Description: Island heathland course. Excellent test of golf with outstanding views over the Firth of Clyde. Established in 1888. 18 holes, 5,828 yards. Par 68 (SSS 69). Amateur record 64.
Visitors: At any time by arrangement with pro or secretary. **Green fees:** £12 per round weekdays, £16 per day. £16 per round weekends, £21 per day.
Catering: Full catering during bar hours.
Facilities: Trolley hire, putting green, pro shop, practice ground.
Accommodation: Brisbane House.
Signature hole: TWELFTH (159 yards, par three) – From elevated tee down to a wide but difficult green. Generally plays into the wind. Spectacular views over the Firth of Clyde.

CARD OF THE COURSE
Hole	Yds	Par	Hole	Yds	Par
1	307	4	10	345	4
2	323	4	11	384	4
3	402	4	12	159	3
4	162	3	13	449	4
5	227	3	14	342	4
6	312	4	15	418	4
7	373	4	16	160	3
8	303	4	17	449	4
9	313	4	18	400	4
Out	2,722	34	In	3,106	34
Total	**5,828**		**Par**	**68**	

CUPAR
CUPAR GOLF CLUB
Address: Hilltarvit, Cupar, Fife KY15 5NZ (01334-653549).
Location: Follow Kirkcaldy to Glenrothes road out of Cupar. Left on to Ceres Road. Car park on right after quarter of a mile on Ceres Road. Nine miles from St Andrews.
Secretary: J. Houston.

Description: Tricky, hilly, parkland course. Established 1855. Nine holes, 5,074 yards. Par 68 (SSS 65). Course record 62.
Visitors: Any time, except Saturdays.
Green fees: £10 weekdays, £12 Sundays, £5 juveniles.
Catering: Full catering available. Contact stewardess. Bar.
Facilities: Trolley hire, putting green.
Accommodation: Eden House Hotel.
Signature hole: EIGHTH (335 yards, par four) – Good positional drive required down and across side of hill to set up approach shot to small plateau green. Dogleg left cut into hillside. Tricky sloping green protected by large bunker and out of bounds at rear.

CARD OF THE COURSE

Hole	Yds	Par	
1	184	3	
2	259	4	
3	277	4	
4	319	4	
5	391	4	
6	142	3	
7	373	4	
8	335	4	
9	257	4	
Out	2,537	34	
Total	**5,074**	**Par**	**68**

DALKEITH
NEWBATTLE GOLF CLUB

Address: Abbey Road, Dalkeith EH22 3AD (0131-663-2123; 0131-660-1631).
Location: South-west of town off A68.
Professional: David Torrance.
Description: Undulating wooded parkland course. Beware the River Esk, which comes into play on the second and 17th holes. 18 holes, 6,005 yards. Par 69 (SSS 70). Course record 61.
Visitors: Weekdays before 4 p.m., except public holidays. Societies welcome.
Green fees: £16 per round, £24 per day.
Catering: Yes. Bar.
Facilities: Trolley hire, putting green, pro shop, practice ground.
Accommodation: Eskbank Hotel.

DALMAHOY
MARRIOTT DALMAHOY HOTEL GOLF AND COUNTRY CLUB

Address: Kirknewton, Midlothian EH27 8EB (0131-333-1845).
Location: South-west of Edinburgh off A71. Travelling from Glasgow, leave M8 at Junction 3, using A599 to link with A71.
Director of Golf and Country Club: Brian Anderson.

Secretary: Jennifer Bryans.
Description: Set in over 1,000 acres of fine Scottish woodland and almost in the shadow of the Pentland Hills, Dalmahoy offers something special for every golfer. A regular European Tour venue, it is only seven miles from Edinburgh. There are two outstanding courses, meandering around the lake and across picturesque streams. The West Course is the easier of the two and features some spectacular crossings of the Gogar Burn. The trickier East Course is a greater challenge.
East Course: 18 holes, 6,677 yards. Par 72 (SSS 72). Amateur record 65 (M. Backhausen, F. Jacobsen). Pro record 62 (Brian Barnes).
West Course: 18 holes, 5,185 yards. Par 68 (SSS 66). Amateur record 66 (D. Brown, H. McConkey, J. Still).
Visitors: Weekdays.
Green fees: *East Course*: £48 per round. *West Course*: £32 per round.
Catering: Excellent facilities in Country Club (Terrace Restaurant and Club Bar).
Facilities: Trolley/buggy hire, putting green, pro shop, practice ground, driving range (floodlit).
Accommodation: Marriott Dalmahoy Hotel and Country Club.
Signature hole: FIFTEENTH (149 yards, par three) – called 'The Wee Wrecker' – and not without reason.

CARD OF THE EAST COURSE

Hole	Yds	Par	Hole	Yds	Par
1	495	5	10	505	5
2	406	4	11	435	4
3	431	4	12	416	4
4	145	3	13	430	4
5	306	4	14	461	4
6	390	4	15	149	3
7	206	3	16	423	4
8	356	4	17	309	4
9	480	5	18	334	4
Out	3,215	36	In	3,462	36
Total	**6,677**		**Par**	**72**	

DALMALLY

DALMALLY GOLF CLUB

Address: Dalmally, Argyll PA33 1AS (01838-200370).
Location: Two miles west of village on A85 Oban to Tyndrum road.
Secretary: A. Burke.
Description: Flat parkland course alongside River Orchy. Lots of water hazards. Course surrounded by mountains. Nine holes, 4,514 yards. Par 64 (SSS 63). Course record 64.
Visitors: Any time. **Green fees:** £10.
Catering: By arrangement.
Accommodation: Glen Orchy Lodge Hotel.
Signature hole: THIRD (158 yards, par three) – 120-yard carry over loop in River Orchy. Trees tight left from tee and close to right of green.

CARD OF THE COURSE

Hole	Yds	Par
1	166	3
2	360	4
3	158	3
4	294	4
5	135	3
6	284	4
7	147	3
8	311	4
9	402	4
Out	2,257	32
Total	**4,514**	**Par**	**64**

DOLLAR
DOLLAR GOLF CLUB

Address: Brewlands House, Dollar FK14 7EA (01259-742400).
Location: North of village off A91.
Secretary: J. Brown.
Description: Hillside course designed by Ben Sayers in 1907. No bunkers. 18 holes, 5,242 yards. Par 69 (SSS 66). Course record 63.
Visitors: Seven days a week. Weekends by prior booking.
Green fees: £10 per round weekdays, £14 per day. £18.50 weekends.
Catering: Full service, except Tuesdays. Bar. **Facilities:** Practice ground.
Accommodation: Castle Campbell Hotel, Strathallan Hotel.
Signature hole: SECOND (97 yards, par three)
– Wedge shot to elevated green. (See diagram opposite.)

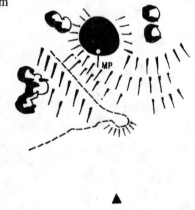

CARD OF THE COURSE

Hole	Yds	Par	Hole	Yds	Par
1	196	3	10	153	3
2	97	3	11	449	4
3	254	4	12	519	5
4	331	4	13	320	4
5	307	4	14	302	4
6	331	4	15	288	4
7	306	4	16	296	4
8	308	4	17	303	4
9	200	3	18	282	4
Out	2,330	33	In	2,912	36
Total	**5,240**		**Par**	**69**	

DORNOCH
THE CARNEGIE CLUB (SKIBO CASTLE)

Address: Skibo Castle, Dornoch, Sutherland IV25 3RQ (01862-894600).

Location: A9 towards Wick. After crossing Dornoch Firth take first left, signposted Meikle ferry.

Secretary: Alan Grant. **Professional:** Willie Milne.

Description: Billionaire Andrew Carnegie first constructed a private links course at Skibo in 1898. Donald Steel reconstructed the original course to provide an outstanding championship links. Sited in a 7,500-acre estate offering spectacular scenery with views of the Struie Hills, the course is bounded on three sides by the estuarial waters of the Firth. The course has a wide range of tees to suit all standards of play. Typical Scottish links course. Voted No. 1 new golf course by *Golf World*. 18 holes, 6,671 yards. Par 71 (SSS 72).

Visitors: Weekdays preferably, only between 11 a.m. and 12 noon.

Green fees: £100 per round.

Catering: Lunch £35, soup and sandwiches £12.50. Bar.

Facilities: Trolley/buggy hire, putting green, pro shop.

Accommodation: Skibo Castle.

Signature hole: SEVENTEENTH (267 yards, par four) – A teasing short par four which rewards accuracy and severely punishes poor shots. It takes a 250-yard drive to reach the front of the green, which is in range on a good day. The angled green rewards anyone who plays tight to the beach on the left. Large fairway bunkers must be carried and a deep greenside bunker is to be avoided. The scenery is magnificent. (See diagram opposite.)

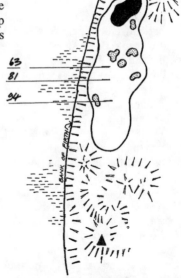

CARD OF THE COURSE

Hole	Yds	Par	Hole	Yds	Par
1	449	4	10	509	5
2	412	4	11	155	3
3	152	3	12	555	5
4	311	4	13	217	3
5	359	4	14	461	4
6	215	3	15	189	3
7	398	4	16	468	4
8	448	4	17	267	4
9	549	5	18	557	5
Out	3,293	35	In	3,378	36
Total	**6,671**		**Par**	**71**	

ROYAL DORNOCH GOLF CLUB

As five-times Open champion, Tom Watson knows a thing or two about golf, and when he says of a course 'It was the most fun I've had playing golf in my whole life', quickly endorsing that with 'It is one of the great courses of the five continents', you listen. No surprise to an international panel who rated Royal Dornoch – the third oldest in the world after St Andrews and Leith – 13th amongst the world's top courses. No surprise either to its devotees who make regular pilgrimages to the 'Star of the North', where golf was first played as early as 1616.

Originally the work of Old Tom Morris, Royal Dornoch is a classic links, with the first eight holes following the natural grades of the old dune embankments while the 10 coming back skirt the sandy beaches of Dornoch Bay. Large plateau greens are one of its main characteristics alongside raised tees. On the par threes, these crowned, inverted saucer-shaped targets are quick and deadly for anything but the most accurate of shots. Although the front nine is delightful, it is the back stretch where the real tests lie, but it is a fair course and like all the great links gives pleasure equally to the high-handicapper and the champion.

Royal Dornoch is a championship course of the highest order. Only its remoteness has stopped it hosting a series of major championships, although the Amateur Championship was staged here in 1985, when it was won by Garth McGimpsey. That remoteness adds to its charisma, and while golfers often kick themselves for sharing the secret of Dornoch with acquaintances, they can console themselves with the fact that its distance of 600 miles from London and 49 miles from Inverness, Britain's most northerly city, prevents many from sharing its delights.

Not too far from the Arctic Circle, the northerly latitude allows play until nearly midnight in midsummer, and the climate is mild. Early in summer the yellow gorse is in full bloom and for once an object of beauty rather than despair. The course is bordered by the Dornoch Firth with views of the mountains of Sutherland, and the quality of the course, including its fine turf and natural greens, and the purity of the air ensure that a round at Royal Dornoch makes you feel good, no matter your score.

As you would expect, the club is steeped in history. It was founded in 1877 by the Sutherland Golfing Society and 10 years later Old Tom Morris arrived from St Andrews to redesign a nine-hole layout, extending the course to a full 18 holes. He used the natural contours of the terrain to create the plateau greens which are the hallmark of Dornoch. Thirty years later the club secretary John Sutherland, who was the club's guiding light for 50 years, aided by J.H. Taylor, made major alterations to the links which winds between sandhills and consists of hummocks, knolls and swales.

The first mention of golf at Dornoch was in 1616 when the 13th Earl of Sutherland was recorded in household accounts as spending money on 'bows, arrows, golf clubs and balls'. At this time, Sir Robert Gordon described the links thus: 'About this town along the sea coast are the fairest and largest links or green fields of any pairt of Scotland. Fitt for archery, golfing, ryding and all other exercises, they doe surpass the fields of Montrose or St Andrews.' The first subscription was two shillings and sixpence and the club's annual income the grand total of three pounds, 18 shillings and sixpence.

As with many great courses, the start is gentle enough to lull the least proficient of players. The first is a quite short par four of 331 yards. The degree of difficulty increases progressively without ever being severe. The fifth, a favourite of Tom Watson's, starts a run of four tricky holes and is played from an elevated tee. Ahead some 170 yards away is a great mound which has to be carried. A bunker awaits the shot to the right and gorse the shot to the left. Naturally, it has a plateau green.

The sixth has been described as one of the hardest par threes in the world. It is not its length of 163 yards that makes it so. To the left are bunkers and thick grass, but miss it on the right and there is a steep slope to contend with. 'Pier', the seventh, a 463-yard par four, is rated the hardest hole on the course. But it is not as interesting as the eighth, the last of the outward stretch. You drive over a precipice about 200 yards out and the second shot has to negotiate a series of humps.

At the ninth (496 yards, par five) you turn for the clubhouse. The beach is down the left and there is long grass and gorse to the right, and the wind is probably in your face. The last is a long par four, 456 yards. Bunkers 30 yards out await the under-hit approach shot to the green, which has a grassy swale in front.

The influence of Royal Dornoch can be seen in many American courses. Donald Ross, who was born in Dornoch in 1872 and learned his golf there and his trade as a greenkeeper and professional under Old Tom at St Andrews, emigrated to America in 1898 and became one of the greatest architects of golf courses. He designed more than 500 courses, including the famous Pinehurst No. 2 Course and the Seminole Course in Florida, using much of what he had learned at Dornoch. Now many American courses have features which are reminiscent of Dornoch at its best.

The American writer Herbert Warren Wind wrote in the *New Yorker* many years ago: 'It is the most natural course in the world. We, in America, are just beginning to appreciate that no golfer has completed his education until he has played and studied Royal Dornoch. It conveys to the modern golfer the evocation of golf at its best.' Tom Watson would wholeheartedly agree.

Address: Golf Road, Dornoch IV25 3LW (01862-810219; 01862-811220).
Location: 49 miles north of Inverness off A9, north of Dornoch. Signposted from square in Dornoch.
Secretary/Manager: John Duncan.
Professional: W. Skinner.
Description: *Championship Course*: 18 holes, 6,514 yards. Par 70 (SSS 73). Amateur record 66 (C. Christie). Pro record 65 (K. Stables).
Struie Course: 18 holes, 5,438 yards. Par 69 (SSS 66).
Visitors: Yes. Gentlemen must have handicap of 24 and ladies 35 for Championship Course.
Green fees: £40 per round weekdays, £50 weekends.
Catering: Full service daily. Bar.
Facilities: Trolley hire, buggy hire for those with medical requirements, putting green, pro shop, practice ground.
Accommodation: Burghfield House Hotel, Royal Golf Hotel, The Castle Hotel, Mallin House Hotel.
Signature hole: FOURTEENTH (445 yards, par four) – 'Foxy', on the championship course, was reckoned by Harry Vardon to be the most natural hole in golf. There are no man-made obstacles; instead, on your right, there is a succession of hillocks running up to a raised narrow green of subtle contours. (See diagram opposite.)

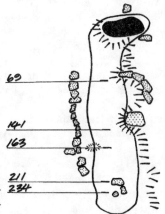

CARD OF THE CHAMPIONSHIP COURSE

Hole	Yds	Par	Hole	Yds	Par
1	331	4	10	147	3
2	177	3	11	446	4
3	414	4	12	507	5

4	427	4	13	166	3
5	354	4	14	445	4
6	163	3	15	319	4
7	463	4	16	402	4
8	396	4	17	405	4
9	496	5	18	456	4
Out	3,221	35	In	3,293	35
Total	**6,514**		**Par**	**70**	

DOUGLAS WATER
DOUGLAS WATER GOLF CLUB
Address: Old School, Ayr Road, Rigside ML11 9NP (01555-880361).
Location: Junction 11 from M74.
Secretary: Robert Paterson (01698-792249).
Description: Hilly course with small greens and undulating fairways. Nine holes, 5,894 yards. Par 72 (SSS 69).
Visitors: Any time weekdays and Sundays. Competitions on Saturdays, normal restrictions. **Green fees:** £6 weekdays, £10 Sundays and public holidays.
Facilities: Putting green.
Catering: Bar by prior arrangement. Snacks.
Accommodation: Tinto Hotel.

DRYMEN
BUCHANAN CASTLE GOLF CLUB
Address: Drymen G63 0HY (01360-660307).
Location: One mile west of village.
Professional: Keith Baxter (01360-660330).
Description: Parkland course. Easy walking and good views. 18 holes, 6,086 yards. Par 70 (SSS 69).
Visitors: Contact in advance. Restricted at weekends.
Green fees: £25 per round, £35 per day.
Catering: Yes. Bar.
Facilities: Trolley hire, putting green, pro shop, practice ground.
Accommodation: Buchanan Arms Hotel.

STRATHENDRICK GOLF CLUB
Address: Glasgow Road, Drymen G63 (01360-660695).
Location: One mile south of village on Glasgow Road.
Description: Inland hilly course. Nine holes, 4,962 yards. SSS 65.
Visitors: Only with a member. **Green fees:** On application.

DUFFTOWN
DUFFTOWN GOLF CLUB
Address: Methercluny, Tomintoul Road, Dufftown, Keith, Banffshire AB55 4BX (01340-820325).

Location: One mile south of Dufftown on Tomintoul road (B9009).
Secretary: David Smith.
Description: A scenic course with superb views of surrounding countryside with small hills in parts. The highest section of the course is 1,000 feet above sea level. 18 holes, 5,308 yards. Par 67 (SSS 67). Amateur record 65. Pro record 69.
Visitors: Any time. **Green fees:** £10 per round, £15 per day.
Catering: By arrangement. Bar. **Facilities:** Trolley hire, putting green.
Accommodation: Fife Arms Hotel, Commercial Hotel, Craigellachie Hotel.
Signature hole: TENTH (462 yards, par four) – Very impressive view from its high plateau tee. A daunting drive to start the inward nine.

CARD OF THE COURSE

Hole	Yds	Par	Hole	Yds	Par
1	288	4	10	462	4
2	285	4	11	290	4
3	333	4	12	222	3
4	367	4	13	359	4
5	143	3	14	397	4
6	345	4	15	200	3
7	103	3	16	325	4
8	276	4	17	411	4
9	305	4	18	197	3
Out	2,445	34	In	2,863	33
Total	**5,308**		**Par**	**67**	

DUMBARTON

DUMBARTON GOLF CLUB

Address: Broadmeadow, Dumbarton G82 2BQ (01389-732830).
Location: Quarter of a mile north of A814.
Description: Flat parkland course with some interesting holes, namely the 356-yard seventh aptly called 'The Punchbowl' because of its sunken green. 18 holes, 6,027 yards. Par 71 (SSS 69). Course record 64.
Visitors: Not weekends and public holidays. **Green fees:** £16 per day.
Catering: Yes. Bar. **Facilities:** Putting green, practice ground.
Accommodation: Dumbuck Hotel.
Signature hole: EIGHTEENTH (339 yards, par four) – Played over water to a generous sloping green.

CARD OF THE COURSE

Hole	Yds	Par	Hole	Yds	Par
1	337	4	10	422	4
2	376	4	11	510	5
3	332	4	12	155	3
4	158	3	13	334	4
5	355	4	14	310	4
6	267	4	15	307	4
7	356	4	16	489	5
8	186	3	17	386	4

9	408	4	18	339	4
Out	2,775	34	In	3,252	37
Total	**6,027**		**Par**	**71**	

DUMFRIES
CRICHTON GOLF CLUB
Address: Bankend Road, Dumfries DG1 4TH.
Location: Dumfries, follow signs to hospital.
Description: Inland parkland course. Nine holes, 5,952 yards. Par 70 (SSS 69). Amateur record 64 (W. Herd Jnr).
Visitors: Yes, weekdays. Societies on application.
Green fees: £12 per round.
Catering: Yes. **Facilities:** Putting green, small shop, practice ground.
Accommodation: Cairndale Hotel.
Signature hole: FIFTH (199 yards, par three) – Out of bounds on right. A sharp fall right to left provides just one line to the green, which is surrounded by mature specimen trees. (See diagram opposite.)

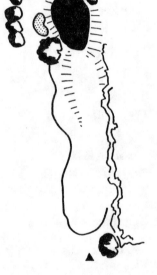

CARD OF THE COURSE

Hole	Yds	Par
1	350	4
2	380	4
3	339	4
4	323	4
5	199	3
6	494	5
7	455	4
8	253	4
9	183	3
Out	2,976	35
Total	**5,952**	**Par** 70

DUMFRIES AND COUNTY GOLF CLUB
Address: Nunfield, Edinburgh Road, Dumfries DG1 1JX (01387-253585).
Location: One mile north-east off A701.
Professional: Gordon Gray.
Description: Parkland course alongside River Nith. 18 holes, 5,928 yards. Par 69 (SSS 68).
Visitors: Must contact in advance. May not play most weekends between 9.30 a.m. and 11 a.m., and between 2 p.m. and 3.30 p.m.
Green fees: £22 per day/round weekdays, £25 weekends.
Catering: Full services. Bar.
Facilities: Trolley hire, putting green, pro shop, practice ground.
Accommodation: Station Hotel.

DUMFRIES AND GALLOWAY GOLF CLUB

Address: 2 Laurieston Avenue, Dumfries DG2 7NY (01387-263848).
Location: West of town centre on A75.
Professional: Joe Fergusson.
Description: Parkland course. 18 holes, 5,803 yards. Par 68 (SSS 68).
Visitors: May not play on competition days. Weekends restricted.
Green fees: £21 per round weekdays, £25 weekends.
Catering: Full service. Bar.
Facilities: Trolley hire, putting green, pro shop, practice ground.
Accommodation: Station Hotel.

DUNBAR
DUNBAR GOLF CLUB

Address: East Links, Dunbar EH42 1LT (01368-862317).
Location: 27 miles east of Edinburgh. Off the A1.
Secretary: Colin McWhannell.
Professional: Derek Small (01368-862086).
Description: Championship links course. Became an Open qualifying course in 1992. Club dates back to 1856 but some records suggest it may have been founded in 1794. Old Tom Morris designed the first 15 holes. The sea is a lateral water hazard on some holes, and when the wind gets up it is a formidable test for even the best of golfers. 18 holes, 6,426 yards. Par 71 (SSS 71). Course record 64.
Visitors: Yes, except Thursdays. **Green fees:** £30 weekdays, £40 weekends.
Catering: Yes. Bar.
Facilities: Trolley hire, putting green, pro shop, practice ground.
Accommodation: Royal Mackintosh Hotel, Hillside Hotel.

CARD OF THE COURSE

Hole	Yds	Par	Hole	Yds	Par
1	477	5	10	202	3
2	494	5	11	417	4
3	172	3	12	459	4
4	349	4	13	378	4
5	148	3	14	433	4
6	350	4	15	343	4
7	386	4	16	166	3
8	369	4	17	339	4
9	507	5	18	437	4
Out	3,252	37	In	3,174	34
Total	**6,426**		**Par**	**71**	

WINTERFIELD GOLF CLUB

Address: North Road, Dunbar EH42 1AY (01368-863562).
Location: West of town, off A1087.
Description: Seaside course, relatively flat but undulating. Links-like greens are quite fast. 18 holes, 5,220 yards. SSS 64.

Visitors: Contact in advance.
Green fees: £11.50 per round weekdays, £13.75 weekends.
Catering: Bar.
Accommodation: Bayswell Hotel.

DUNBLANE
DUNBLANE NEW GOLF CLUB

Address: Perth Road, Dunblane FK15 0LJ (01786-823711).
Location: One mile off M9 at Fourways Roundabout.
Secretary: John Dunsmore. **Professional:** R. Jamieson.
Description: Undulating parkland course. 18 holes, 5,957 yards. Par 69 (SSS 69). Amateur record 64. Pro record 66.
Visitors: Yes. **Green fees:** £18 per round, £27 per day.
Catering: Full. Bar.
Facilities: Trolley hire, putting green, pro shop, practice ground.
Accommodation: Stirling Arms, Dunblane Hotel, Stakis Dunblane Hydro.
Signature hole: ELEVENTH (182 yards, par three) – From tee down to green, which is guarded by bunkers front and right with out of bounds on the left. (See diagram opposite.)

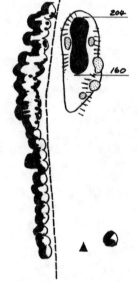

CARD OF THE COURSE

Hole	Yds	Par	Hole	Yds	Par
1	330	4	10	400	4
2	425	4	11	182	3
3	190	3	12	378	4
4	300	4	13	375	4
5	357	4	14	161	3
6	503	5	15	320	4
7	164	3	16	196	3
8	422	4	17	370	4
9	386	4	18	498	5
Out	3,077	35	In	2,880	34
Total	**5,957**		**Par**		**69**

DUNDEE
CAIRD PARK GOLF CLUB

Address: Mains Loan, Dundee DD4 9BX (01382-453606; Starter: 01382-438871).
Location: One and a half miles north of city centre, off A972.
Professional: J. Black.
Description: Municipal inland wooded course. 18 holes, 5,494 yards. Par 69 (SSS 68).
Visitors: Any time. Societies contact Dundee Council (01382-223141).
Green fees: £13.30 per round.
Catering: Bar. **Facilities:** Pro shop.
Accommodation: The Queen's Hotel.

CAMPERDOWN GOLF CLUB

Address: Camperdown House, Dundee DD2 4TF (01382-623398; Starter: 01382-432688).
Location: Three miles north-west of city centre off A923.
Secretary: Ronald Gordon. **Professional:** Roddy Brown.
Description: Public parkland course. 18 holes, 6,561 yards. Par 71 (SSS 72). Course record 67 (J. Flynn Jnr).
Visitors: Yes, all week. **Green fees:** £13.30 per round.
Catering: On request.
Facilities: Trolley hire, putting green, pro shop, practice ground.
Accommodation: Swallow Hotel, Park Hotel.
Signature hole: ELEVENTH (505 yards, par five) – Narrow, tree-lined fairway. Dogleg. Spectacular view of River Tay and Fife.

CARD OF THE COURSE

Hole	Yds	Par	Hole	Yds	Par
1	410	4	10	403	4
2	513	5	11	505	5
3	377	4	12	392	4
4	156	3	13	193	3
5	361	4	14	358	4
6	523	5	15	300	4
7	216	3	16	469	4
8	413	4	17	160	3
9	399	4	18	413	4
Out	3,368	36	In	3,193	35
Total	**6,561**		**Par**	**71**	

DOWNFIELD GOLF CLUB

Address: Turnberry Avenue, Dundee D22 3QP (01382-825595).
Location: North of Dundee off A923.
Managing Secretary: Barrie Liddle. **Professional:** Kenny Hutton.
Description: Championship undulating parkland course. Wooded with medium-paced greens. The Gelly Burn provides a hazard for a number of holes. 18 holes, 6,822 yards. Par 73 (SSS 73). Pro record 65 (Andy Crerar 1995).
Visitors: Yes, weekdays. No pre-bookings at weekends.
Green fees: £30 per round, £45 per day. **Catering:** Yes. Bar.
Facilities: Trolley/buggy hire, putting green, pro shop, practice ground.
Accommodation: Swallow Hotel, Invercarse Hotel, Earl Grey Hotel.
Signature hole: ELEVENTH (498 yards, par five) – Tree-lined, slightly downhill with water in front of green.

CARD OF THE COURSE

Hole	Yds	Par	Hole	Yds	Par
1	425	4	10	434	4
2	408	4	11	498	5
3	228	3	12	182	3
4	538	5	13	480	5
5	412	4	14	515	5

6	177	3	15	326	4
7	491	5	16	352	4
8	407	4	17	151	3
9	414	4	18	384	4
Out	3,500	36	In	3,322	37
Total	**6,822**		**Par**	**73**	

MONIFIETH GOLF LINKS

Address: The Links, Monifieth, Angus DD5 4AW (Starter: 01382-532767).
Location: Six miles east of Dundee on A930.
Secretary: H. Nicoll (01382-535553).
Professional: Ron McLeod (01382-532945).
Description: Two courses. The Medal Course has been the venue for Open qualifying. Seaside links course with tree plantations. A railway line provides the main hazard over the first few holes.
Medal Course: 18 holes, 6,655 yards. Par 71 (SSS 72). Amateur record 63. Pro record 64.
Ashludie Course: 18 holes, 5,123 yards. Par 68 (SSS 67).
Visitors: Yes, after 9.32 a.m. weekdays; after 2 p.m. Saturdays; after 10 a.m. Sundays.
Green fees: *Medal*: £24 per round weekdays, £34 per day. £28 per round weekends, £40 per day. *Ashludie*: £14 per round weekdays, £20 per day. £15 per round weekends, £22 per day. Composite ticket (one round on each course): £28 weekdays, £32 weekends.
Catering: Yes. Bar.
Facilities: Trolley hire, putting green, pro shop, practice ground.
Accommodation: Panmure Hotel, overlooking first tee.

CARD OF THE MEDAL COURSE

Hole	Yds	Par	Hole	Yds	Par
1	338	4	10	369	4
2	414	4	11	183	3
3	429	4	12	374	4
4	456	4	13	432	4
5	191	3	14	158	3
6	382	4	15	376	4
7	417	4	16	340	4
8	284	4	17	435	4
9	547	5	18	530	5
Out	3,458	36	In	3,197	35
Total	**6,655**		**Par**	**71**	

DUNECHT

DUNECHT GOLF CLUB

Address: Dunecht House, Aberdeenshire.
Description: Inland wooded course. Nine holes, 6,270 yards. SSS 70.
Visitors: No, private club.

DUNFERMLINE
CANMORE GOLF CLUB

Address: Venturefair Avenue, Dunfermline KY12 0PF (01383-724969).
Location: One mile north on A823.
Description: Undulating parkland course. 18 holes, 5,474 yards. Par 67 (SSS 66).
Visitors: Any time, but restrictions on Saturdays. **Green fees:** £12 per round weekdays, £18 per day. £18 per round weekends, £25 per day.
Catering: Bar. **Facilities:** Pro shop.
Accommodation: King Malcolm Thistle.

DUNFERMLINE GOLF CLUB

Address: Pitfirrane, Crossford, Dunfermline, Fife KY12 8QW (01383-723534).
Location: Three miles west of Dunfermline on A994.
Secretary: R. De Rose. **Professional:** Steve Craig.
Description: Undulating parkland course with 16th-century clubhouse, a category 'A' listed building. Five par threes, five par fives. 18 holes, 6,126 yards. Par 72 (SSS 70). Course record 65.
Visitors: Yes. Casual visitors Sunday to Friday; societies Monday to Friday. Members' guests all week. **Green fees:** £20 per round weekdays, £28 per day. £25 per round Sundays, £35 per day.
Catering: Full catering all week. Bar.
Facilities: Trolley hire, putting green, pro shop, practice ground.
Accommodation: Pitfirrane Arms Hotel.
Signature hole: SIXTH (374 yards, par four) – Out of bounds right. Dogleg right.

CARD OF THE COURSE

Hole	Yds	Par	Hole	Yds	Par
1	287	4	10	383	4
2	213	3	11	285	4
3	466	5	12	345	4
4	375	4	13	163	3
5	170	3	14	383	4
6	374	4	15	489	5
7	466	5	16	161	3
8	341	4	17	501	5
9	191	3	18	533	5
Out	2,883	35	In	3,243	37
Total 6,126			**Par**	**72**	

PITREAVIE GOLF CLUB

Address: Queensferry Road, Dunfermline KY11 5PR (01383-722591).
Location: South-east of town on A823.
Professional: Jim Forrester.
Description: Woodland course with undulating fairways and fairly fast greens. Panoramic view of River Forth valley. Testing golf. 18 holes, 6,086 yards. Par 70 (SSS 69). Course record 65.
Visitors: Welcome, except on competition days.
Green fees: £18 per round weekdays, £24 per day. £35 per day weekends.

Catering: Full service. Bar.
Facilities: Trolley hire, putting green, pro shop, practice ground.
Accommodation: King Malcolm Thistle Hotel.

DUNKELD
DUNKELD AND BIRNAM GOLF CLUB

Address: Fungarth, Dunkeld PH8 0HU (01350-727524).
Location: Take A923 one mile north of Dunkeld.
Secretary: Mrs Winifred Sinclair (01350-727564).
Description: Heathland course with panoramic views. Nine holes, 5,240 yards. Par 68 (SSS 66). Amateur record 65.
Visitors: Welcome, on application. **Green fees:** On application.
Catering: Full bar and catering facilities available.
Facilities: Trolley hire, putting green, shop, practice ground.
Accommodation: Stakis Dunkeld House Resort Hotel, Royal Dunkeld Hotel.

CARD OF THE COURSE

Hole	Yds	Par	
1	275	4	
2	284	4	
3	400	4	
4	377	4	
5	301	4	
6	271	4	
7	396	4	
8	193	3	
9	123	3	
Out	2,620	34	
Total	**5,240**	**Par**	**68**

DUNNING
DUNNING GOLF CLUB

Address: Rollo Park, Dunning PH2 0RH (01764-684372; 01764-684747).
Location: Off A9, nine miles south-west of Perth.
Description: Parkland course. Nine holes, 4,836 yards. Par 66 (SSS 64).
Visitors: Not Saturdays before 4 p.m. or Sundays before 1 p.m. With member only after 5 p.m. weekdays.
Green fees: £10 per round weekdays, £14 weekends.
Accommodation: Duchally House Hotel.

DUNOON
COWAL GOLF CLUB

Address: Ardenslate Road, Dunoon, Argyll PA23 8NL (01369-705673).
Location: One mile north of town.
Secretary: Mrs W. Fraser. **Professional:** Russell Weir.

Description: Founded in 1891, this heathland course overlooks the Firth of Clyde and the town of Dunoon. Redesigned in 1934 by James Braid, it is an enjoyable test of golf. Wonderful views of the Isle of Arran and Ailsa Craig. 18 holes, 6,063 yards. Par 70 (SSS 70). Amateur record 64. Pro record 63.

Visitors: Any time.

Green fees: £17 per round weekdays, £27 per round weekends.

Catering: Full, all day. Bar.

Facilities: Trolley/buggy hire, putting green, pro shop, practice ground.

Accommodation: Enmore Hotel.

Signature hole: FIFTH (191 yards, par three) – 'The Clumps'. Tricky tee shot to a well-bunkered green with a dyke to be carried. (See diagram opposite.)

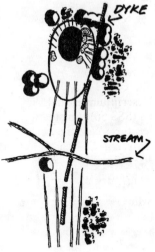

CARD OF THE COURSE

Hole	Yds	Par	Hole	Yds	Par
1	430	4	10	320	4
2	422	4	11	333	4
3	376	4	12	336	4
4	380	4	13	483	5
5	191	3	14	165	3
6	295	4	15	381	4
7	308	4	16	341	4
8	296	4	17	371	4
9	171	3	18	464	4
Out	2,869	34	In	3,194	36
Total	**6,063**			**Par**	**70**

DUNS

DUNS GOLF CLUB

Address: Hardens Road, Duns, Berwickshire TD11 3NR (01361-882194).

Location: One mile west of Duns, off A6105 Duns to Greenlaw road.

Secretary: A. Campbell, 5 Trinity Walk, Duns, Berwickshire TD11 3HN (01361-882717).

Description: Upland course suitable for both beginners and experienced players. Slightly hilly with a burn running through the course. No bunkers. Views south over the Tweed Valley to Cheviot Hills. 18 holes, 6,209 yards. Par 70 (SSS 70). Extension to 18 holes in May 1997.

Visitors: Yes, without restriction. Ring clubhouse for bookings.

Green fees: £12 per round, £15 per day.

Catering: Light snacks available March to October. Bar.

Facilities: Trolley hire, practice ground.

Accommodation: Barniken Hotel.

Signature hole: FIFTEENTH (116 yards, par three) – Played from high tee to a tiered green. Burn in front, burn behind. Not as easy as it looks.

CARD OF THE COURSE

Hole	Yds	Par	Hole	Yds	Par
1	400	4	10	545	5
2	398	4	11	390	4
3	368	4	12	204	3
4	171	3	13	366	4
5	387	4	14	326	4
6	500	5	15	116	3
7	163	3	16	369	4
8	390	4	17	195	3
9	388	4	18	533	5
Out	3,165	35	In	3,044	35
Total	**6,209**		**Par**	**70**	

DURNESS

DURNESS GOLF CLUB

Address: Balnakeil, Durness, Sutherland IV27 4PG (01971-511364).
Location: 57 miles north-west of Lairg on A838.
Secretary: L. Mackay.
Description: The most northerly course on the British mainland. Varied links course with some inland holes. Spectacular scenery in very peaceful surroundings. Nine greens but 18 tees. Nine holes, 5,555 yards. Par 70 (SSS 69). Course record 71.
Visitors: Any time.
Green fees: £10 per day, £40 per week.
Catering: Snacks available June to September.
Facilities: Trolley hire, putting green, practice ground.
Accommodation: Cape Wrath Hotel, Parkhill Hotel.
Signature hole: EIGHTEENTH (155 yards, par three) – One of the most spectacular holes in Scottish golf. Not for the faint-hearted. You have to play across a gully about 100 yards wide. When the tide is in, you are hitting over the Atlantic Ocean. (See diagram opposite.)

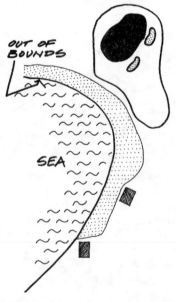

CARD OF THE COURSE

Hole	Yds	Par	Hole	Yds	Par
1	296	4	10	282	4
2	321	4	11	311	4
3	408	4	12	391	4
4	287	4	13	323	4
5	344	4	14	312	4
6	443	5	15	505	5
7	178	3	16	154	3
8	377	4	17	360	4
9	108	3	18	155	3
Out	2,762	35	In	2,793	35
Total	**5,555**		**Par**	**70**	

EAST KILBRIDE
EAST KILBRIDE GOLF CLUB

Address: Chapelside Road, Nerston, East Kilbride G74 4PE (01355-220913).
Location: Half a mile north off A749.
Professional: A. Taylor (01355-222192).
Description: Inland wooded parkland and hill course. Very windy. Some testing holes. 18 holes, 6,419 yards. Par 71 (SSS 71).
Visitors: By appointment. No weekends. Must be member of recognised golfing society.
Green fees: £20 per round, £30 per day.
Catering: Full service. Bar. **Facilities:** Pro shop.
Accommodation: Bruce Swallow Hotel.

LANGLANDS GOLF COURSE

Address: Hurlawcrook Road, Nr Auldhouse, East Kilbride (01355-224685).
Location: Two miles south of town centre.
Description: Municipal moorland course. 18 holes, 6,202 yards. SSS 70.
Visitors: Any time. **Green fees:** £7.25 weekdays, £8.50 weekends.
Facilities: Pro shop.
Accommodation: Bruce Swallow Hotel.

TORRANCE HOUSE GOLF COURSE

Address: Calderglen Country Park, Strathaven Road, East Kilbride G75 0QZ (013552-48638).
Location: One and a half miles south-east on A726.
Professional: John Dunlop.
Description: Municipal inland parkland course. 18 holes. 6,415 yards. Par 72 (SSS 69). Course record 71.
Visitors: Any time. Societies not weekends.
Green fees: £7.25 per round weekdays, £8.50 weekends.
Catering: Bar. **Facilities:** Trolley/buggy area, practice ground.
Accommodation: Bruce Swallow Hotel.

EDINBURGH
BABERTON GOLF CLUB

Address: 50 Baberton Avenue, Juniper Green, Edinburgh EH14 5DU (0131-453-4911).
Location: Five miles south-west of Edinburgh City centre off A70.
Secretary: Eric Horberry. **Professional:** Ken Kelly (0131-453-3555).
Description: Inland parkland course designed by Willie Park Jnr. 18 holes, 6,123 yards. Par 69 (SSS 70). Amateur record 64 (D. Beveridge Jnr, R. Bradly, B. Tait). Pro record 62 (B. Barnes).
Visitors: Monday to Friday 9.30 a.m. to 3.30 p.m.
Green fees: £18.50 per round, £28.50 per day.
Catering: Available. Bar.
Facilities: Trolley hire, putting green, pro shop, practice ground.
Accommodation: Braid Hills Hotel, Royal Scot Hotel.

Signature hole: THIRTEENTH (383 yards, par four) – Fine driving hole. Trees to right and left of landing area. Second shot to elevated two-tiered green.

CARD OF THE COURSE

Hole	Yds	Par	Hole	Yds	Par
1	404	4	10	342	4
2	494	5	11	212	3
3	357	4	12	472	4
4	304	4	13	383	4
5	230	3	14	125	3
6	369	4	15	487	5
7	393	4	16	464	4
8	199	3	17	152	3
9	319	4	18	417	4
Out	3,069	35	In	3,054	34
Total	**6,123**		**Par**	**69**	

BRAID HILLS GOLF CLUB

Address: Braid Hills Approach, Edinburgh EH10 6JZ (0131-447-6666).
Location: Two and a half miles south of city centre off A702.
Description: Municipal heathland course. Can be hard physically with lots of hills to climb. The No. 2 course is even higher. Good views of Edinburgh and the Firth of Forth.
Course 1: 18 holes, 6,172 yards. Par 70 (SSS 68). Course record 62.
Course 2: 18 holes, 4,832 yards. Par 65 (SSS 63).
Visitors: May not play on Saturday mornings. **Green fees:** £7.95 per round.
Facilities: Trolley hire, putting green, pro shop, practice ground.
Accommodation: Braid Hills Hotel.

THE BRUNTSFIELD LINKS GOLFING SOCIETY LTD.

Address: The Clubhouse, 32 Barnton Avenue, Edinburgh EH4 6JH (0131-336-1479).
Location: Situated at Davidsons Mains, three miles north-west of city centre. Six miles from Forth Road Bridge and airport, off A90.
Secretary: Cdr D. Sandford.
Professional: Brian Mackenzie (0131-336-4005).
Description: Fifth oldest club in the world, having been in existence since 1761. Mature parkland course, originally designed by Willie Park. Magnificently situated with views over Firth of Forth to Fife coast. A great variety of trees ensure the golfer cannot believe he is so near to the city centre. 18 holes, 6,407 yards. Par 71 (SSS 71). Course record 67.
Visitors: Yes, except on competition days. Telephone professional or secretary. Societies by prior letter, not weekends.
Green fees: £36 per round weekdays, £50 per day. £42 per round weekends, £55 per day.
Catering: Yes. Carvery lunch, high tea/dinner by arrangement. Bar.
Facilities: Trolley/buggy hire, putting green, pro shop, practice ground, driving range.
Accommodation: The Barnton Thistle Hotel.

Signature hole: ELEVENTH (415 yards, par four) – Scenic beauty and historic value. The prevailing westerly wind is very challenging. Tricky contoured green. Dogleg left with out of bounds on left and trees on right. (See diagram opposite.)

CARD OF THE COURSE

Hole	Yds	Par	Hole	Yds	Par
1	419	4	10	339	4
2	381	4	11	415	4
3	487	5	12	168	3
4	549	5	13	455	4
5	205	3	14	493	5
6	332	4	15	170	3
7	157	3	16	373	4
8	382	4	17	381	4
9	354	4	18	347	4
Out	3,266	36	In	3,141	35
Total	**6,407**		**Par**	**71**	

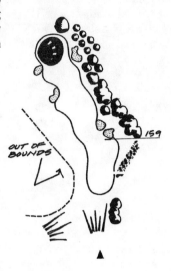

CARRICK KNOWE COURSE

Address: Glendevon Park, Edinburgh EH12 5UZ (0131-337-1096).
Location: Three miles west of city centre, south of A8.
Description: Municipal flat parkland course. 18 holes, 6,299 yards. Par 71 (SSS 70).
Visitors: May be restricted at weekends. **Green fees:** £7.95 per round.
Catering: No. **Facilities:** Trolley hire, small practice ground.
Accommodation: Forte Posthouse.

CRAIGENTINNY GOLF COURSE

Address: Fillyside Road, Lochend EH7 6RG (0131-554-7501).
Location: North-east side of city between Leith and Portobello.
Description: Municipal course. Generally flat, although some hillocks with gentle slopes. Good views of Arthur's Seat. 18 holes, 5,418 yards. Par 67 (SSS 65).
Visitors: Any time. **Green fees:** £7.95 per round.
Facilities: Trolley hire, practice ground.
Accommodation: King James Thistle Hotel.

CRAIGMILLAR PARK GOLF CLUB

Address: 1 Observatory Road, Edinburgh EH9 3HG (0131-667-0047).
Location: 10 minutes from city centre. A71 to Cameron Toll roundabout, right up Esslemont Road, past King's Buildings and course is on left.
Secretary: Tom Lawson. **Professional:** Brian McGhee.
Description: Founded in 1896 and designed by James Braid. Parkland course, set around Blackford Hill, the site of the Royal Observatory, with panoramic views over Edinburgh. 18 holes, 5,851 yards. Par 70 (SSS 69). Course record 64.
Visitors: Weekdays. **Green fees:** £17 per round, £25 per day.
Catering: Bar lunches, high teas, à la carte available.

Facilities: Trolley hire, putting green, pro shop, practice ground.
Accommodation: Iona Hotel
Signature hole: SIXTEENTH (402 yards, par four) – Played into prevailing west wind and requires an accurate tee shot and a well-hit second to a well-trapped green.

CARD OF THE COURSE

Hole	Yds	Par	Hole	Yds	Par
1	351	4	10	351	4
2	269	4	11	128	3
3	254	4	12	411	4
4	465	4	13	150	3
5	424	4	14	505	5
6	284	4	15	168	3
7	206	3	16	402	4
8	297	4	17	493	5
9	331	4	18	362	4
Out	2,881	35	In	2,970	35
Total	**5,851**		**Par**	**70**	

DUDDINGSTON GOLF CLUB

Address: Duddingston Road West, Duddingston EH15 3QD (0131-661-7688).
Location: Two and a half miles south-east of city centre off A1.
Professional: Alastair McLean.
Description: Undulating parkland, semi-seaside course with stream. Easy walking and windy. 18 holes, 6,647 yards. Par 72 (SSS 72).
Visitors: May not play weekends. Societies Tuesdays and Thursdays only.
Green fees: £26 per round, £34 per day.
Catering: Bar. **Facilities:** Pro shop.

KINGSKNOWE GOLF CLUB

Address: 326 Lanark Road, Edinburgh EH14 2JD (0131-441-1144).
Location: South-west outskirts of Edinburgh on A70.
Secretary: R. Wallace (0131-441-1145).
Professional: Andrew Marshall (0131-441-4030).
Description: Well-kept undulating parkland course. 18 holes, 5,979 yards. Par 69 (SSS 69). Course record 69.
Visitors: Yes.
Green fees: £18 per round weekdays, £23 per day. £25 per round weekends.
Catering: Opening hours, not Tuesdays. Bar.
Facilities: Trolley hire, putting green, pro shop, practice ground, driving nets.
Accommodation: Orwell Lodge, Royal Ettrick Hotel, Forte Posthouse.
Signature hole: SIXTEENTH (460 yards, par four) – Slight dogleg down valley. Long drive required to get home in two. Tree plantations both sides. Green well bunkered.

CARD OF THE COURSE

Hole	Yds	Par	Hole	Yds	Par
1	168	3	10	392	4

2	303	4	11	149	3
3	488	5	12	316	4
4	364	4	13	422	4
5	432	4	14	307	4
6	326	4	15	230	3
7	345	4	16	460	4
8	416	4	17	335	4
9	223	3	18	303	4
Out	3,065	35	In	2,914	34
Total	**5,979**		**Par**	**69**	

LIBERTON GOLF CLUB

Address: Kingston Grange, 297 Gilmerton Road, Edinburgh EH16 5OJ (0131-664-3009).
Location: Three miles from city centre on A7.
Secretary: Peter Long. **Professional:** Iain Seath.
Description: Parkland course, wooded and undulating. 18 holes, 5,299 yards. Par 67 (SSS 66). Course record 61.
Visitors: No societies at weekends.
Green fees: £15 per round weekdays, £17 per round weekends.
Catering: Full catering facilities. **Facilities:** Practice ground.
Accommodation: Eskbank Hotel.
Signature hole: EIGHTH (par three) – Played alongside clubhouse from elevated tee.

LOTHIANBURN GOLF CLUB

Address: 106A Biggar Road, Fairmilehead EH10 7DU (0131-445-2206; 0131-445-5067).
Location: Four and a half miles south of city centre on A702.
Professional: Kurt Mungall.
Description: Wooded hillside course in the Pentland foothills. Sheep on course. Testing when windy. 18 holes, 5,750 yards. Par 71 (SSS 68). Course record 66.
Visitors: Weekends after 3.30 p.m. Weekdays until 4 p.m. Contact professional.
Green fees: £14 per round weekdays, £20 per day. £20 per round weekends, £25 per day.
Catering: Full service. Bar.
Facilities: Trolley hire, putting green, pro shop, practice ground.
Accommodation: Braid Hills Hotel.

MERCHANTS OF EDINBURGH GOLF CLUB

Address: 10 Craighill Gardens, Edinburgh EH10 5PY (0131-447-1219).
Location: Two miles south-west of city centre off A702.
Secretary: A. Montgomery.
Professional: Neil Colquhoun (0131- 447-8709)
Description: Shot-testing course, a mixture of hills and parkland. Some hidden greens. 18 holes, 4,889 yards. Par 65 (SSS 64). Course record 59.
Visitors: Yes, but not weekends or after 4 p.m. on weekdays.
Green fees: £15 per round/day.
Catering: Yes, but not Wednesday afternoons or all day Thursdays.

Facilities: Trolley hire, putting green, pro shop.
Accommodation: Braid Hills Hotel.
Signature hole: THIRTEENTH (208 yards, par three) – Elevated tee with shot to well-bunkered green below. Splendid views.

CARD OF THE COURSE

Hole	Yds	Par	Hole	Yds	Par
1	244	3	10	289	4
2	246	4	11	175	3
3	174	3	12	163	3
4	400	4	13	208	3
5	253	4	14	328	4
6	406	4	15	254	4
7	118	3	16	369	4
8	406	4	17	160	3
9	414	4	18	282	4
Out	2,661	33	In	2,228	32
Total	**4,889**		**Par**	**65**	

MORTONHALL GOLF CLUB

Address: 231 Braid Road, Mortonhall EH10 6PB (0131-447-6974).
Location: Three miles south of city centre off A702.
Professional: Douglas Horn.
Description: Moorland course with views over Edinburgh. 18 holes, 6,557 yards. Par 72 (SSS 72). Course record 66.
Visitors: Contact in advance. Societies may not play at weekends.
Green fees: £23 per round weekdays, £28 per day. £28 per round weekends, £38 per day.
Catering: Full service. Bar.
Facilities: Trolley hire, putting green pro shop, practice ground.
Accommodation: Braid Hills Hotel.

MURRAYFIELD GOLF CLUB LTD

Address: 43 Murrayfield Road, Edinburgh EH12 6EU (0131-337-3478).
Professional: J.J. Fisher.
Description: Parkland course. 18 holes, 5,725 yards. Par 70 (SSS 69).
Visitors: No, private club.

PORTOBELLO GOLF CLUB

Address: Stanley Street, Portobello EH15 1JJ (0131-669-4361).
Location: Three miles east of city centre off A1.
Description: Municipal parkland course. Easy walking. Nine holes, 4,800 yards. Par 64 (SSS 64).
Visitors: May not play Saturdays between 8.30 a.m. and 10 a.m., and between 12.30 p.m. and 2 p.m., and on competition days.
Green fees: £3.95 for nine holes. **Facilities:** Trolley hire.
Accommodation: Donmaree Hotel.

PRESTONFIELD GOLF CLUB

Address: 6 Priestfield Road North, Edinburgh EH16 5HS (0131-667-9556).
Location: One mile south of city centre on A7.
Secretary: A. Robertson.
Professional: Graham MacDonald (0131-667-8597).
Description: Parkland course with good views. 18 holes, 6,212 yards. Par 70 (SSS 70). Amateur record 62 (A. Dun 1976).
Visitors: Yes, unrestricted weekdays. Saturdays not available between 8 a.m. and 10.30 a.m., and between 12 noon and 1.30 p.m. Sundays not available before 11 a.m.
Green fees: £20 per round weekdays, £30 per day. £30 per round weekends, £40 per day.
Catering: Full range. Bar. **Facilities:** Trolley hire, putting green, pro shop.
Accommodation: Prestonfield House Hotel, Arthur View Hotel.

CARD OF THE COURSE

Hole	Yds	Par	Hole	Yds	Par
1	290	4	10	366	4
2	151	3	11	440	4
3	551	5	12	436	4
4	451	4	13	145	3
5	179	3	14	353	4
6	377	4	15	370	4
7	508	5	16	256	4
8	432	4	17	436	4
9	146	3	18	325	4
Out	3,085	35	In	3,127	35
Total	**6,212**		**Par**	**70**	

RAVELSTON GOLF CLUB

Address: 24 Ravelston Dykes Road, Edinburgh EH4 5NZ (0131-315-2486).
Location: Three miles west of city centre off A90.
Secretary: H. Houston.
Description: Parkland course designed by James Braid in 1912. Nine holes, 5,400 yards. Par 66 (SSS 65). Amateur record 64. Pro record 67.
Visitors: Parties of no more than 12 accepted. Weekdays, no weekends.
Green fees: £15 per round/day.
Catering: Snacks.
Accommodation: Holiday Inn.
Signature hole: SECOND – long uphill par three to plateau green.

ROYAL BURGESS GOLFING SOCIETY OF EDINBURGH

Address: 181 Whitehouse Road, Edinburgh EH4 6BY (0131-339-2075).
Location: Five miles west of city centre off A90.
Professional: George Yuille.
Description: Instituted in 1735, it is the oldest golfing society in the world. If you are interested in the history of golf, you should visit. A pleasant parkland course. 18 holes, 6,494 yards. Par 71 (SSS 71). Visitors: 6,111 yards. Par 68 (SSS 69). Course record 66.
Visitors: On request. **Green fees:** On request.

Catering: Yes. Bar.
Facilities: Trolley hire, putting green, pro shop, practice ground.
Accommodation: Barnton Hotel.

CARD OF THE COURSE

Hole	Yds	Par	Hole	Yds	Par
1	391	4	10	380	4
2	326	4	11	348	4
3	421	4	12	314	4
4	465	4	13	201	3
5	176	3	14	386	4
6	485	5	15	413	4
7	442	4	16	481	5
8	168	3	17	443	4
9	407	4	18	247	4
Out	3,281	35	In	3,213	36
Total	**6,494**		**Par**		**71**

SILVERKNOWES GOLF CLUB

Address: Parkway, Silverknowes EH4 5ET (0131-336-3843).
Location: Four miles north-west of city centre. North of A902.
Description: Municipal parkland course. Reasonably new, having been opened in 1947. Little trouble off tees but accurate second shots needed. On coast overlooking Firth of Forth. 18 holes, 6,216 yards. Par 71 (SSS 70).
Visitors: Restricted Saturdays and Sundays. **Green fees:** £7.95 per round.
Facilities: Trolley hire, putting green, pro shop, practice ground.
Accommodation: Murrayfield Hotel.

SWANSTON GOLF CLUB

Address: 111 Swanston Road, Fairmilehead EH10 7DS (0131-445-2239).
Location: Four miles south of city centre, off B701.
Description: Hillside course with banked greens. Steep climb at 12th and 13th holes. 18 holes, 5,024 yards. Par 66 (SSS 65).
Visitors: Contact in advance. **Green fees:** £12 per round weekdays, £18 per day. Weekends and public holidays £17 per round, £22 per day.
Catering: Full service. Bar. **Facilities:** Pro shop.
Accommodation: Braid Hills Hotel.

TORPHIN HILL GOLF CLUB

Address: Torphin Road, Colinton EH13 0PG (0131-441-1100).
Location: Five miles south-west of city centre, south of A720.
Professional: Jamie Browne.
Description: Hillside heathland course with fine views of Edinburgh and the Forth estuary. 18 holes, 5,030 yards. Par 67 (SSS 66). Course record 64.
Visitors: Contact in advance. **Green fees:** £15 per day, £25 weekends.
Catering: Full service. Bar.
Facilities: Putting green, pro shop, practice ground.
Accommodation: Braid Hills Hotel.

TURNHOUSE GOLF CLUB
Address: 154 Turnhouse Road, Edinburgh EH12 0AD (0131-339-1014).
Location: West of city on A9080 near airport.
Secretary: A Hay. **Professional:** John Murray.
Description: Parkland course with some hills. 18 holes, 6,171 yards. Par 69 (SSS 70). Amateur record 64. Professional record 63.
Visitors: Yes, certain times during week. Not at weekends.
Green fees: £16 per round, £24 per day.
Catering: Available. Bar.
Facilities: Trolley hire, putting green, pro shop, practice ground.
Accommodation: Royal Scot Hotel.

CARD OF THE COURSE
Hole	Yds	Par	Hole	Yds	Par
1	400	4	10	450	4
2	278	4	11	106	3
3	380	4	12	455	4
4	478	5	13	347	4
5	234	3	14	373	4
6	440	4	15	160	3
7	445	4	16	340	4
8	405	4	17	250	3
9	145	3	18	485	5
Out	3,205	35	In	2,966	34
Total	**6,171**		**Par**	**69**	

EDZELL
THE EDZELL GOLF CLUB
Address: High Street, Edzell, Angus DD9 7TF (01356-648235).
Location: Take B966 off A9 at north end of Brechin bypass. Midway between Dundee and Aberdeen.
Secretary: J. Hutchison (01356-647283).
Professional: A. Webster (01356-648462).
Description: Located in the foothills of the Grampian mountains, the course is basically heathland, certainly with regard to the fine turf. A major tree-planting 25 years ago has given a parkland appearance. 18 holes, 6,348 yards. Par 71 (SSS 71). Amateur record 65.
Visitors: Welcome all week. Societies weekdays by arrangement.
Green fees: £20 per round weekdays, £30 per day. £26 per round weekends, £39 per day.
Catering: Full meal service. Bar.
Facilities: Trolley hire, putting green, pro shop, practice ground, driving range.

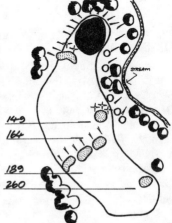

Accommodation: Glenesk Hotel, Central Hotel.

Signature hole: NINTH (478 yards, par five) – Aptly named 'The Deep End'. River to the right. Three difficult cross bunkers. Picturesque views. (See diagram on previous page.)

CARD OF THE COURSE

Hole	Yds	Par	Hole	Yds	Par
1	312	4	10	369	4
2	446	4	11	433	4
3	310	4	12	361	4
4	370	4	13	415	4
5	429	4	14	155	3
6	178	3	15	338	4
7	385	4	16	316	4
8	354	4	17	191	3
9	478	5	18	508	5
Out	3,262	36	In	3,086	35
Total	**6,348**		**Par**	**71**	

ELDERSLIE
ELDERSLIE GOLF CLUB

Address: 63 Main Road, Elderslie PA5 9AZ (01505-323956).

Location: Three miles from Glasgow Airport. Two miles from M8 on A737.

Secretary: Mrs A. Anderson.

Professional: Richard Bowman (01505-320032).

Description: Undulating parkland course. 18 holes, 6,300 yards. Par 70 (SSS 70). Course record 61.

Visitors: Yes, weekdays. **Green fees:** £18 per round, £24 per day.

Catering: Yes. Bar.

Facilities: Trolley/buggy hire, putting green, pro shop, practice ground.

Accommodation: Lynnhurst Hotel.

ELGIN
ELGIN GOLF CLUB

Address: Hardhillock, Birnie Road, Elgin, Moray IV30 3SX (01343-542338).

Location: South of Elgin on A941.

Secretary: David Black. **Professional:** Ian Rodger (01343-542884).

Description: Parkland course with some tree-lined holes. Rated by many as the best inland course in the North. Undulating greens and tight holes that demand accuracy. Panoramic views. 18 holes, 6,411 yards. Par 69 (SSS 71). Amateur record 65 (N. Grant). Pro record 64 (Kevin Stables).

Visitors: Any day usually after 9.30 a.m. Telephone secretary for details.

Green fees: £20 per round weekdays, £27 per day. £26 per round weekends, £34 per day.

Catering: Yes, every day. Limited on Tuesdays. Bar.

Facilities: Trolley hire, putting green, pro shop, practice ground, driving range.

Accommodation: Mansefield House Hotel, Sunninghill Hotel, Craigellachie Hotel, Hotel St Leonard's, Eight Acres Hotel, Laichmoray Hotel, Rothes Glen, The Mansion House Hotel.

Signature hole: SIXTH (222 yards, par three) – Standing on the elevated tee, the challenge is easy to see. Any shot which lacks height and which is short will be swept to the right of target. Too strong and a quarry, dwarfed by towering pine trees, awaits.

CARD OF THE COURSE

Hole	Yds	Par	Hole	Yds	Par
1	459	4	10	438	4
2	438	4	11	375	4
3	368	4	12	278	4
4	155	3	13	325	4
5	484	5	14	462	4
6	222	3	15	188	3
7	167	3	16	417	4
8	453	4	17	334	4
9	408	4	18	440	4
Out	3,154	34	In	3,257	35
Total	**6,411**		**Par**	**69**	

ELIE

GOLF HOUSE CLUB (ELIE)

Address: Elie KY9 1AS (01333-330301).
Location: West side of village, off A917.
Professional: Robin Wilson.
Description: The Golf House Club was founded in 1875, but golf was first played here in 1750 and there are claims that its history went back almost 300 years earlier. The first official layout was around 1770. It is a delightful holiday course with panoramic views over the Firth of Forth. The course is open and almost entirely lacking in bushes and trees. The legendary James Braid learned to play here. 18 holes, 6,273 yards. Par 70 (SSS 69). Course record 62.
Visitors: Contact in advance. Limited availability at weekends between May and September. **Green fees:** £28.50 per round weekdays, £40 per day. £36 per round weekends, £50 per day.
Catering: Full service. Bar.
Facilities: Trolley hire, putting green, pro shop, practice ground, driving range.
Accommodation: Old Manor Hotel.
Signature hole: THIRTEENTH (380 yards, par four) – James Braid called it 'the finest hole in all the country'. Drive right to avoid a grassy hollow. Accurate approach needed to a long and narrow elevated green.

ELIE SPORTS CLUB

Address: Golf Place, Elie KY9 1AS (01333-330955).
Location: 10 miles south of St Andrews on A917.
Description: Links course. Nine holes, 5,310 yards. SSS 64.

Visitors: Any time. **Green fees:** £4 per round, £7 per day.
Catering: Snacks only.
Facilities: Pro shop, driving range.

ELLON
MCDONALD GOLF CLUB

Address: Hospital Road, Ellon, Aberdeenshire AB41 9AW (01358-720576).
Location: 16 miles north of Aberdeen on A90.
Secretary: George Ironside. **Professional:** Ronnie Urquhart (01358-722891).
Description: Tight tree-lined parkland course with streams and a pond. 18 holes, 5,991 yards. Par 70 (SSS 69). Amateur record 65. Pro record 63.
Visitors: At all times. **Green fees:** £14 per round weekdays, £20 per day. Saturdays: £16 per round, £24 per day. Sundays: £20 per round, £30 per day.
Catering: Full service except on Mondays. Bar.
Facilities: Trolley hire, putting green, pro shop.
Accommodation: Mercury Hotel, Buchan Hotel, New Inn Hotel, Station Hotel.
Signature hole: SEVENTEENTH (452 yards, par four) – A dogleg to the left. Drive has to be accurately positioned to right of a gap in mature trees, otherwise the green cannot be reached in two.

CARD OF THE COURSE

Hole	Yds	Par	Hole	Yds	Par
1	291	4	10	321	4
2	329	4	11	166	3
3	379	4	12	205	3
4	484	5	13	260	4
5	378	4	14	262	4
6	389	4	15	147	3
7	201	3	16	313	4
8	403	4	17	452	4
9	580	5	18	431	4
Out	3,434	37	In	2,557	33
Total	**5,991**		**Par**	**70**	

EYEMOUTH
EYEMOUTH GOLF CLUB

Address: Gunsgreen House, Eyemouth TD14 5SF (01890-750551).
Location: East of town.
Professional: Craig Maltman.
Description: Apart from climb to first tee, flat seaside course. Compact with fast greens. Fine views. To be extended to 18 holes in August 1997. Nine holes, 5,079 yards. Par 66 (SSS 65). Course record 60.
Visitors: May not play before 10.30 a.m. on Saturdays or before noon on Sundays.
Green fees: £10 per day.
Catering: Bar in evenings. **Facilities:** Pro shop.
Accommodation: Marshall Meadows Country House Hotel.

The ninth at Turnberry – the most spectacular hole in Scottish golf, with a 50-foot drop from the championship tee (bottom left) to the rocks below. (Picture: Brian Morgan)

*With undulating fairways like the fifth, Royal
Dornoch must be one of the most beautiful
courses in the world. (Picture: Brian Morgan)*

Royal Troon's eighth, called the Postage Stamp, is perhaps the most famous par-three in the world, with a daunting tee shot to a small, well-guarded green.
(Picture: Brian Morgan)

The Home of Golf. The Royal and Ancient clubhouse provides the perfect backdrop to John Daly's Open Championship victory in 1995. (Picture: Andy Hooper, Daily Mail*)*

St Andrews' Road Hole 17th is for many the most difficult hole in golf. If you come up short of the green, you face the dilemma of getting over a cavernous bunker with not a lot of green to play with. Jack Nicklaus opted for putting around the bunker (right). Too strong and you're on the infamous road, faced with a similar shot knowing you could run through and into the bunker at the front.
(Top picture: Andy Hooper, Daily Mail; *right picture: Stanley Hunter)*

The Spectacles, the bunkers on the 14th green at Carnoustie. Many a round has come to grief here. (Picture: Brian Morgan)

Jack Nicklaus regards the 146-yard 13th at Muirfield as a golfing gem. (Picture: Brian Morgan)

FALKIRK
FALKIRK GOLF CLUB

Address: Carmuirs, 136 Stirling Road, Camelon, Falkirk FK2 7YP (01324-611061).

Location: One and a half miles north-west of Falkirk on A9.

Secretary: John Elliott.

Description: Parkland course with streams and gorse. Golfers are surprised by the degree of difficulty and the variety of holes. Several Roman burial plots have been found, the latest in 1975 – a sandstone grave below the seventh green containing the remains of a Centurion, a spearhead and the centre part of a shield. 18 holes, 6,230 yards. Par 71 (SSS 70). Course record 66.

Visitors: Weekdays. Societies Sunday only.

Green fees: £15 per round weekdays, £20 per day. £30 Sundays.

Catering: Yes. Bar.

Facilities: Trolley/buggy hire, putting green, pro shop, practice ground.

Accommodation: Inchyra Grange Hotel.

Signature hole: SIXTH (351 yards, par four) – Stroke Index 1. Dogleg left to an elevated green with out of bounds behind. (See diagram opposite.)

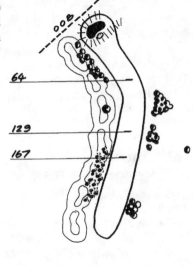

CARD OF THE COURSE

Hole	Yds	Par	Hole	Yds	Par
1	493	5	10	367	4
2	363	4	11	150	3
3	326	4	12	516	5
4	388	4	13	205	3
5	172	3	14	357	4
6	351	4	15	387	4
7	192	3	16	181	3
8	477	5	17	452	4
9	353	4	18	500	5
Out	3,115	36	In	3,115	35
Total	**6,230**		**Par**	**71**	

POLMONT GOLF CLUB LTD

Address: Manuelrigg, Maddiston, Falkirk FK2 0LS (01324-711277).

Location: Four miles south of Falkirk on the B805 into Maddiston village.

Description: Hilly with tree-lined fairways. Small, tricky greens, well bunkered. Nine holes, 6,062 yards. Par 72 (SSS 69). Course record 68.

Visitors: Welcome any time, except Saturdays.

Green fees: £7 per round weekdays, £12 per round Sundays.

Catering: Available if booked in advance.

Facilities: Putting green, practice ground.

Accommodation: Inchyra Grange Hotel.

Signature hole: THIRD (187 yards, par three) – Requires a good tee shot to make the green, which is small and well bunkered. Later in 1997 new medal tee will be 30 yards longer.

CARD OF THE COURSE

Hole	Yds	Par	
1	340	4	
2	318	4	
3	187	3	
4	455	5	
5	376	4	
6	318	4	
7	197	3	
8	368	4	
9	482	5	
Out	3,031	36	
Total	**6,062**	**Par**	**72**

FALKLAND
FALKLAND GOLF CLUB

Address: The Myre, Falkland KY7 7AA (01337-857404).
Location: North of town on A192.
Description: Well-kept flat course with fast greens. Nine holes, 5,216 yards. Par 68 (SSS 65). Course record 62.
Visitors: Contact in advance. **Green fees:** £8 per round weekdays, £12 weekends.
Catering: Bar.
Accommodation: Lomond Hills Hotel.

FAULDHOUSE
GREENBURN GOLF CLUB

Address: 6 Greenburn Road, Fauldhouse, West Lothian EH47 9HG (01501-770292).
Location: Five miles south of Bathgate junction off M8.
Secretary: Jim Irvine, 65 East Main Street, Blackburn, West Lothian (01506-635309). **Professional:** Malcolm Leighton (01501-771187).
Description: Set in moorland. Features include railway, which bisects the course, and water hazards. 18 holes, 6,046 yards. Par 71 (SSS 71). Course record 64.
Visitors: Yes, casual by arrangement with pro. Parties by arrangement with secretary. No visitors on competition days.
Green fees: £10 per round weekdays, £12 weekends.
Catering: Yes. Bar.
Facilities: Trolley/buggy hire, putting green, pro shop, practice ground.
Accommodation: Dreadnought Hotel.

FORFAR
FORFAR GOLF CLUB

Address: Cunninghill, Arbroath Road, Forfar DD8 2RL (01307-462120).
Location: One and a half miles east of Forfar on A932.

Secretary: William Baird (01307-463773).
Professional: Peter McNiven (01307-465683).
Description: Heathland course with tree-lined, undulating fairways. 18 holes, 6,052 yards. Par 69 (SSS 70). Amateur record 61. Pro record 65.
Visitors: Yes. 10 a.m. to 11.30 a.m. and 2.30 p.m. to 4 p.m., except on Saturdays.
Green fees: £16 per round weekdays, £24 per day. £20 per round weekends, £32 per day.
Catering: Yes. Bar.
Facilities: Trolley/buggy hire, putting green, pro shop, practice ground.
Accommodation: Idvies House Hotel.
Signature hole: FIFTEENTH (412 yards, par four) – 'Braid's Best'. Dogleg right. Accurate drive required. Second shot over bunkers. Ground slopes right to left.

CARD OF THE COURSE

Hole	Yds	Par	Hole	Yds	Par
1	341	4	10	359	4
2	354	4	11	352	4
3	381	4	12	444	4
4	393	4	13	154	3
5	200	3	14	478	5
6	376	4	15	412	4
7	404	4	16	153	3
8	395	4	17	344	4
9	164	3	18	348	4
Out	3,008	34	In	3,044	35
Total	**6,052**		**Par**	**69**	

FORRES
FORRES GOLF CLUB

Address: Muiryshade, IV36 0RD (01309-672250).
Location: South-east of town centre, off B9010.
Professional: Sandy Aird.
Description: All-year parkland course in wooded countryside. Some holes flat, others gently undulating. Easy walking despite some hilly holes. 18 holes, 6,240 yards. Par 70 (SSS 70). Course record 64.
Visitors: Welcome, but club competitions take priority. Weekends may be restricted in summer. Societies must telephone two to three weeks in advance.
Green fees: £16 per round weekdays, £22 per day. £18 per round weekends, £24 per day.
Catering: Bar. **Facilities:** Trolley/buggy hire, putting green, pro shop.
Accommodation: Ramnee Hotel.

FORT AUGUSTUS
FORT AUGUSTUS GOLF CLUB

Address: Markethill, Fort Augustus, Inverness-shire PH32 4AU (01320-366660).
Location: One mile west of Fort Augustus on A82.

Secretary: Hugh Fraser.

Description: Moorland course set in the beauty and quiet of the countryside and bordered by the Caledonian Canal. Its tight fairways provide a good challenge to golfers of all standards. Nine holes (18 tees), 5,454 yards. Par 67 (SSS 67). Amateur record 67 (P. MacDonald).

Visitors: At all times, except Saturday afternoons and occasional Sunday afternoons. **Green fees:** £10 per day, £35 per week (5 days).

Catering: Lounge bar, but no meals. **Facilities:** Trolley hire.

Accommodation: Lovat Arms Hotel.

Signature hole: FIRST (321 yards, par four) – Drive towards picturesque Ben Teigh, but the scenery is forgotten if you are wayward – out of bounds to left and water hazard on right. If second shot to elevated green is short, it runs downhill into bunker. A short but testing par four.

CARD OF THE COURSE

Hole	Yds	Par	Hole	Yds	Par
1	321	4	10	313	4
2	438	4	11	455	4
3	349	4	12	363	4
4	172	3	13	150	3
5	160	3	14	193	3
6	550	5	15	493	5
7	233	3	16	253	4
8	352	4	17	336	3
9	131	3	18	192	3
Out	2,706	33	In	2,748	34
Total	**5,454**		**Par**	**67**	

FORTROSE

FORTROSE AND ROSEMARKIE GOLF CLUB

Address: Ness Road East, Fortrose IV10 8SE (01351-620529).

Location: A832 to Fortrose off A9 at Tore roundabout. North of Inverness.

Secretary: Margaret Collier.

Description: Seaside links course, set on a peninsula with sea on three sides. Designed by James Braid and founded in 1888. Easy walking, good views. 18 holes, 5,858 yards. Par 71 (SSS 69). Course record 64 (N. Hampton).

Visitors: Yes, by arrangement with secretary. **Green fees:** £16 per round weekdays, £22 per day. £22 per round weekends, £30 per day.

Catering: Yes. Bar. **Facilities:** Driving range.

Accommodation: Royal Hotel.

CARD OF THE COURSE

Hole	Yds	Par	Hole	Yds	Par
1	331	4	10	322	4
2	412	4	11	381	4
3	303	4	12	394	4
4	455	5	13	308	4
5	132	3	14	267	4

6	469	5	15	293	4
7	303	4	16	336	4
8	389	4	17	355	4
9	196	3	18	212	3
Out	2,990	36	In	2,868	35
Total	**5,858**		**Par**	**71**	

FORT WILLIAM
FORT WILLIAM GOLF CLUB

Address: Torlundy, Fort William, Inverness-shire PH33 6SN (01397-704464).
Location: Two miles north of Fort William on A82.
Secretary: Gordon Bales (01397-702404).
Description: Sitting at the foot of Ben Nevis, Britain's highest mountain, this parkland course, which was built in 1975, is ideal for both the beginner and the experienced golfer. Major improvements to the course were made in 1995. 18 holes, 6,217 yards. Par 72 (SSS 71). Course record 67.
Visitors: Very welcome at all times including Saturdays and Sundays.
Green fees: £12, including weekends.
Catering: Limited. Bar. **Facilities:** Trolley hire, putting green.
Accommodation: Moorings Hotel.
Signature hole: SIXTH (125 yards, par three) – A wide, inviting green surrounded by a highland burn, with trees flanking the hole. Trouble if you are short.

CARD OF THE COURSE

Hole	Yds	Par	Hole	Yds	Par
1	339	4	10	479	5
2	385	4	11	387	4
3	110	3	12	183	3
4	566	5	13	284	4
5	482	5	14	407	4
6	125	3	15	262	4
7	464	4	16	156	3
8	372	4	17	357	4
9	527	5	18	332	4
Out	3,370	37	In	2,847	35
Total	**6,217**		**Par**	**72**	

FRASERBURGH
FRASERBURGH GOLF CLUB

Address: Philorth Road, Fraserburgh, Aberdeenshire AB43 8TL (01346-516616; Pro shop: 01346-517898).
Location: One mile south-east on B9033.
Secretary: Alasdair Stewart.
Description: Testing natural seaside links course. *Corbie*: 18 holes, 6,278 yards. Par 70 (SSS 70). Course record 66. *Rosehill*: Nine holes, 6,760 yards. Par 70 (SSS 71).

Visitors: Yes, but some weekend restrictions.
Green fees: £14 per round weekdays, £17 per day.
Catering: Yes. Bar.
Facilities: Trolley hire, putting green, pro shop, practice ground.
Accommodation: Tufted Duck Hotel, Royal Hotel, Station Hotel.
Signature hole: FOURTH (328 yards, par four) – Short, but a difficult approach to the green.

CARD OF THE COURSE

Hole	Yds	Par	Hole	Yds	Par
1	434	4	10	322	4
2	391	4	11	357	4
3	332	4	12	389	4
4	328	4	13	315	4
5	183	3	14	198	3
6	528	5	15	508	5
7	165	3	16	378	4
8	368	4	17	189	3
9	458	4	18	435	4
Out	3,187	35	In	3,091	35
Total	**6,278**		**Par**	**70**	

GAIRLOCH
GAIRLOCH GOLF CLUB

Address: Gairloch, Ross-shire IV21 2BE (01445-712407).
Location: 80 miles west of Inverness. Alongside A832.
Secretary: A. Shinkins (01445-781346).
Description: Seaside links course. A good test of golf, particularly in windy conditions. Superb views. Nine holes, 4,514 yards. Par 62 (SSS 64). Course record 61.
Visitors: Most welcome any time. Societies by arrangement.
Green fees: £12.50 per day, £45 per week. Senior citizens £7.50 per day.
Catering: Light refreshments only.
Facilities: Trolley hire, shop, practice net.
Accommodation: The Old Inn. Also, self-catering accommodation within easy reach of course.
Signature hole: EIGHTH (526 yards, par five) – Asks many questions of the average club golfer. Accuracy required as there is deep rough on the left along with Gairloch Sands for the really wild hook. Trouble awaits the wayward second shot, too.

CARD OF THE COURSE

Hole	Yds	Par	Hole	Yds	Par
1	320	4	10	327	4
2	185	3	11	182	3
3	184	3	12	162	3
4	244	3	13	233	3
5	423	4	14	317	4
6	194	3	15	194	3

7	91	3	16	143	3
8	526	5	17	526	5
9	119	3	18	144	3
Out	2,286	31	In	2,228	31
Total	4,514		Par	62	

GALASHIELS
GALASHIELS GOLF CLUB
Address: Ladhope Recreation Ground, Galashiels TD1 2NJ (01896-753724).
Location: Half a mile from town centre off A7 to Edinburgh.
Description: A parkland course of two halves with a climb connecting them. 18 holes, 5,185 yards. Par 67 (SSS 66). Course record 61.
Visitors: Any time, but weekends must be arranged through secretary.
Green fees: £13 per round weekdays, £18 per day. £15 per round weekends, £20 per day.
Catering: Full service available. Bar. **Facilities:** Trolley hire.
Accommodation: Kingsknowe Hotel, Abbotsford Arms.
Signature hole: FIRST (170 yards, par three) – Teeing off towards town to a bunkered green with panoramic views.

CARD OF THE COURSE

Hole	Yds	Par	Hole	Yds	Par
1	170	3	10	272	4
2	244	4	11	121	3
3	524	5	12	376	4
4	460	5	13	230	3
5	150	3	14	359	4
6	432	4	15	277	4
7	246	3	16	304	4
8	357	4	17	275	4
9	217	3	18	171	3
Out	2,800	34	In	2,385	33
Total	5,185		Par	67	

TORWOODLEE GOLF CLUB
Address: Edinburgh Road, Galashiels, Selkirkshire TD6 9SR (01896-752260).
Location: Two miles from town centre on main Galashiels to Edinburgh A7 road.
Description: Wooded parkland course, designed by James Braid, running alongside River Gala. 18 holes, 6,087 yards. Par 70 (SSS 69). Course record 70.
Visitors: All week, except during competitions. **Green fees:** £16 per round weekdays, £20 per day. £22 per round weekends, £27 per day.
Catering: Yes, except on Tuesdays.
Facilities: Trolley/buggy hire, putting green, pro shop, practice ground.
Accommodation: Burts Hotel, Kingsknowe Hotel.
Signature hole: FOURTEENTH (546 yards, par five) – Elevated tee. Out of bounds on right. Hole doglegs right with tight approach to the green. (See diagram overleaf.)

CARD OF THE COURSE

Hole	Yds	Par	Hole	Yds	Par
1	378	4	10	176	3
2	401	4	11	425	4
3	124	3	12	139	3
4	293	4	13	420	4
5	484	5	14	546	5
6	355	4	15	336	4
7	152	3	16	325	4
8	512	5	17	234	3
9	367	4	18	420	4
Out	**3,066**	**36**	**In**	**3,021**	**34**
Total	**6,087**		**Par**	**70**	

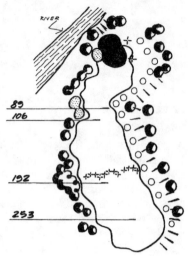

GALSTON
LOUDOUN GOWF CLUB

Address: Edinburgh Road, Galston KA4 8PA
(01563-821993).
Location: North-east of town on A71.
Description: Testing parkland course. 18 holes, 5,844 yards. Par 67 (SSS 68).
Course record 61.
Visitors: Not at weekends. Contact in advance.
Green fees: £17 per round, £29 per day.
Catering: Yes. Bar.
Facilities: Trolley hire, putting green, pro shop, practice ground.
Accommodation: Strathaven Hotel.

GARMOUTH
GARMOUTH AND KINGSTON GOLF CLUB

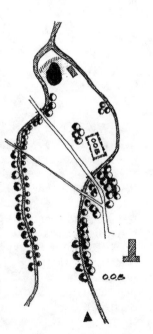

Address: Spey Street, Garmouth, Fochabers IV32 7NJ
(01343-870388).
Location: Three miles north from A96 at Mosstodloch.
West bank at mouth of River Spey.
Secretary: A. Robertson (01343-870231).
Description: Links/parkland. Flat. Every green within
500 yards of clubhouse. Course will change in 1998
when three extra holes will be ready for play. 18 holes,
5,395 yards. Par 66 (SSS 66). Amateur record 64. Pro
record 70.
Visitors: At all times except during club competitions.
Green fees: £11 per round weekdays, £17 per day. £15
per round weekends, £20 per day.
Catering: Snacks at bar. Catering can be arranged prior
to course booking.
Facilities: Trolley hire.
Accommodation: Garmouth Hotel.

Signature hole: EIGHTH (338 yards, par four) – Double dogleg with out of bounds at right and left of drive, and at left of green. Water is in play at right of drive and around green. (See diagram on previous page.)

CARD OF THE COURSE

Hole	Yds	Par	Hole	Yds	Par
1	368	4	10	384	4
2	373	4	11	239	4
3	417	4	12	269	4
4	419	4	13	126	3
5	420	4	14	386	4
6	106	3	15	406	4
7	332	4	16	217	3
8	338	4	17	282	4
9	166	3	18	147	3
Out	2,939	34	In	2,456	32
Total	**5,395**		**Par**	**66**	

GATEHOUSE OF FLEET

GATEHOUSE OF FLEET GOLF CLUB

Address: Gatehouse of Fleet, Dumfries and Galloway.
Location: Quarter of a mile north of town.
Hon. Secretary: John McConchie. **Administrator:** Keith Cooper (01644-450260).
Description: Undulating course in excellent condition all year round. In an idyllic location with stunning views over Wigtown Bay. Nine holes, 4,796 yards. Par 66 (SSS 64).
Visitors: All year round, except Sunday mornings.
Green fees: £10 per day or per round.
Catering: No. **Facilities:** Putting green.
Accommodation: Murray Arms Hotel.
Signature hole: NINTH (162 yards, par three) – An extremely intimidating finishing hole which drops almost 100 feet from tee to green. Out of bounds to left of green, rough to the right and bunkers below green.

CARD OF THE COURSE

Hole	Yds	Par
1	214	3
2	293	4
3	251	4
4	328	4
5	137	3
6	545	5
7	283	4
8	185	3
9	162	3
Out	2,398	33
Total	**4,796**	**Par**	66

GIFFORD
GIFFORD GOLF CLUB

Address: Edinburgh Road, Gifford EH41 4JE (01620-810267).
Location: Four miles from A1, Haddington exit.
Secretary: Pete Blyth.
Description: Gently undulating parkland course in the foothills of the Lammermuir Hills. Maintained to the highest standards with first-class greens. The Speedyburn meanders through the course and comes into play on four holes. Nine holes, 6,243 yards. Par 71 (SSS 70). Amateur record 64.
Visitors: Yes, but not after 4 p.m. Tuesdays, Wednesdays and Saturdays, and midday Sundays. **Green fees:** £10 per round, £15 per day.
Catering: Two hotels 500 yards from club.
Facilities: Trolley hire, putting green, practice ground.
Accommodation: Goblin Ha' Hotel, Tweeddale Arms Hotel.

CARD OF THE COURSE

Hole	Yds	Par	Hole	Yds	Par
1	362	4	10	172	3
2	365	4	11	365	4
3	324	4	12	324	4
4	365	4	13	365	4
5	153	3	14	216	3
6	412	4	15	412	4
7	319	4	16	319	4
8	407	4	17	407	4
9	478	5	18	478	5
Out	3,185	36	In	3,058	35
Total	**6,243**		**Par**	**71**	

GIGHA (Isle of)
ISLE OF GIGHA GOLF CLUB

Address: Argyll PA41 7AA.
Location: Ferry from Tayinloan to Gigha. Course half a mile north from PO.
Secretary: M. Tart (01583-505287).
Description: Meadowland course with wide fairways but very heavy rough. Scenic views over the Sound of Gigha. Nine holes, 5,042 yards. Par 66 (SSS 65).
Visitors: Any time. **Green fees:** £10 per round.
Catering: At Gigha Hotel.
Accommodation: Gigha Hotel.
Signature hole: FOURTH (300 yards, par four) – Narrow fairway with out of bounds on right. Heavy rough to left.

GIRVAN
GIRVAN GOLF COURSE

Address: Golf Course Road, Girvan KA26 9HW (01465-714272; Starter: 01465-714346).

Location: North of town, off A77.

Professional: David Gemmell.

Description: Municipal course in two sections. The first eight holes run along the shore and the rest are inland, dissected by the river. Lush with wide fairways and minimal rough. Although only two holes are more than 400 yards, five of the par threes are in excess of 200 yards to small greens. Not as easy as it might look. 18 holes, 5,095 yards. Par 64 (SSS 64).

Visitors: Any time. **Green fees:** £11 per round, £18 per day.

Catering: Bar. **Facilities:** Putting green.

Accommodation: King's Arms Hotel, Malin Court Hotel.

Signature hole: SEVENTEENTH (220 yards, par three) – Uphill. It needs an accurate and powerful tee shot to a small green.

CARD OF THE COURSE

Hole	Yds	Par	Hole	Yds	Par
1	360	4	10	105	3
2	419	4	11	356	4
3	223	3	12	378	4
4	322	4	13	384	4
5	171	3	14	210	3
6	295	4	15	427	4
7	223	3	16	277	4
8	245	3	17	220	3
9	344	4	18	136	3
Out	2,602	32	In	2,493	32
Total	**5,095**		**Par**	**64**	

BRUNSTON CASTLE GOLF CLUB

Address: Bargany, Dailly KA26 9RH (01465-811471).

Location: Six miles south-east of Turnberry

Professional: Derek McKenzie.

Description: Sheltered, inland parkland course. Course is bisected by River Girvan and includes a man-made lake. 18 holes, 6,858 yards. Par 72 (SSS 73). Course record 69.

Visitors: Reserved for members at weekends between 8 a.m. and 10 a.m. and between 12.30 p.m. and 1.30 p.m. **Green fees:** £22.50 per round weekdays, £35 per day. £27.50 per round weekends, £39 per day.

Catering: Full service. Bar. **Facilities:** Trolley/buggy hire, putting green, pro shop, practice ground, driving range.

Accommodation: Malin Court Hotel.

GLASGOW

ALEXANDRA PARK GOLF COURSE

Address: Sannox Gardens, Glasgow G31 8SE.

Location: Two miles east of city centre off M8/A8.

Secretary: G. Campbell (0141-556-1294).

Description: A hilly parkland course with lots of trees. Nine holes, 4,016 yards. Par 60 (SSS 61).

Visitors: Any time. **Green fees:** On application.
Facilities: Practice ground.
Accommodation: Courtyard Hotel.
Signature hole: SEVENTH (217 yards, par three) – Attractive views of surrounding parkland.

CARD OF THE COURSE

Hole	Yds	Par	
1	351	4	
2	221	3	
3	212	3	
4	132	3	
5	155	3	
6	146	3	
7	217	3	
8	244	4	
9	330	4	
Out	2,008	30	
Total	**4,016**	**Par**	60

BEARSDEN GOLF CLUB

Address: Thorn Road, Bearsden, Glasgow G61 4BP (0141-942-2351).
Location: Six miles north-west of Glasgow off A809.
Secretary: J. Mercer.
Description: Started off as a parkland nine-hole course. Now has 16 greens (play to alternate greens at seven of the holes) and 11 teeing areas. 6,014 yards. Par 68 (SSS 69). Course record 67.
Visitors: Due to being basically a nine-hole course, very few societies can be accommodated. Visitors usually introduced by a member.
Green fees: £10 per round, £15 per day.
Catering: Full. **Facilities:** Putting green, practice ground.
Accommodation: Burnbrae Hotel, Black Bull Thistle.

CARD OF THE COURSE

Hole	Yds	Par	Hole	Yds	Par
1	304	4	10	304	4
2	428	4	11	455	4
3	366	4	12	350	4
4	455	4	13	449	4
5	206	3	14	137	3
6	398	4	15	391	4
7	170	3	16	156	3
8	327	4	17	327	4
9	373	4	18	418	4
Out	3,027	34	In	2,987	34
Total	**6,014**		**Par**	**68**	

BISHOPBRIGGS GOLF CLUB

Address: Brackenbrae Road, Bishopbriggs G64 2DX (0141-772-1810).

Location: Half a mile north-west off A803.
Description: Inland wooded parkland course. 18 holes, 6,041 yards. Par 69 (SSS 69). Course record 63.
Visitors: Must be accompanied by member, contact in advance and have introduction from own club. Societies apply in writing to the committee one month in advance. **Green fees:** On application.
Catering: Bar. **Facilities:** Pro shop.
Accommodation: Black Bull Thistle Hotel.

BLAIRBETH GOLF CLUB

Address: Fernbrae Avenue, Rutherglen, Glasgow G73 4SF (0141-634-3355).
Location: One mile south of Rutherglen off Stonelaw Road.
Secretary: F. Henderson.
Description: Hilly parkland course. 18 holes, 5,518 yards. Par 70 (SSS 68). Amateur record 64 (D. Orr). Pro record 69 (W. Cunningham).
Visitors: By arrangement with secretary. **Green fees:** On application.
Catering: Available. **Facilities:** Putting green.
Accommodation: Kings Park Hotel.
Signature hole: ELEVENTH (452 yards, par five).

CARD OF THE COURSE

Hole	Yds	Par	Hole	Yds	Par
1	268	4	10	228	3
2	356	4	11	452	5
3	264	4	12	167	3
4	186	3	13	223	3
5	383	4	14	299	4
6	377	4	15	541	5
7	501	5	16	303	4
8	277	4	17	122	3
9	247	4	18	324	4
Out	2,859	36	In	2,659	34
Total	**5,518**		**Par**	**70**	

BONNYTON GOLF CLUB

Address: Kirktonmore Road, Eaglesham G76 0QA (01355-302781).
Location: Quarter of a mile south-west, off B764.
Professional: Kendal McWade.
Description: Windy moorland course. 18 holes, 6,255 yards. Par 72 (SSS 71).
Visitors: Welcome weekdays only, except Tuesdays. Contact in advance.
Green fees: £20 per round, £30 for two rounds.
Catering: Full service. Bar.
Facilities: Trolley/buggy hire, putting green, pro shop, practice ground.
Accommodation: Bruce Swallow Hotel.

CAMBUSLANG GOLF CLUB

Address: 30 Westburn Drive, Cambuslang G72 7NA (0141-641-3130).
Secretary: R. Dunlop.

Description: Sparsely wooded inland course. Nine holes, 6,072 yards.
Visitors: No, private club.

CAMPSIE GOLF CLUB

Address: Crow Road, Lennoxtown G65 7HX (01360-310244).
Location: On B822 on north side of Lennoxtown.
Secretary: D. Barbour. **Professional:** Mark Brennan (01360-310920).
Description: Hillside course with open views to south. Sporting, short, energetic and welcoming. 18 holes, 5,509 yards. Par 70 (SSS 68). Amateur record 70 (M. Howat).
Visitors: Weekdays. **Green fees:** £12 per round, £20 per day.
Catering: Meals and snacks available April to October.
Facilities: Putting green, pro shop, practice ground.
Accommodation: Glazert Country Hotel.
Signature hole: THIRTEENTH (278 yards, par four) In play since 1897. Chance for birdie if luck is in, otherwise has reduced strong men to despair. (See diagram opposite.)

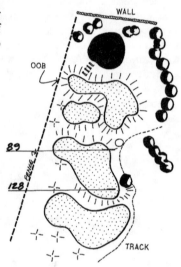

CARD OF THE COURSE

Hole	Yds	Par	Hole	Yds	Par
1	262	4	10	250	4
2	182	3	11	252	4
3	330	4	12	194	3
4	355	4	13	278	4
5	386	4	14	191	3
6	478	5	15	380	4
7	380	4	16	477	5
8	245	4	17	165	3
9	291	4	18	413	4
Out	2,909	36	In	2,600	34
Total	**5,509**		**Par**		**70**

CATHCART CASTLE GOLF CLUB

Address: Mearns Road, Clarkston G76 7YL (0141-638-0082).
Location: Three-quarters of a mile south-west, off A726.
Professional: David Naylor.
Description: Undulating, tree-lined parkland course. 18 holes, 5,832 yards. Par 68 (SSS 68).
Visitors: Must have letter of introduction from own club. Not weekends unless with member. Societies Tuesdays and Thursdays only.
Green fees: £25 per round, £28 per day.
Catering: Full service. Bar. **Facilities:** Pro shop.
Accommodation: Macdonald Thistle Hotel.

CATHKIN BRAES GOLF CLUB

Address: Cathkin Road, Burnside G73 4SE (0141-634-6605).
Location: One mile south on B759.

Professional: Stephen Bree (0141-634-0650).
Description: Inland moorland course. Loch at fifth hole. 18 holes, 6,208 yards. Par 69 (SSS 69).
Visitors: Contact in advance and have handicap certificate. Not weekends.
Green fees: £25 per round weekdays, £35 per day.
Catering: Bar. **Facilities:** Trolley hire, putting green, pro shop, practice ground.
Accommodation: Macdonald Thistle Hotel.

CAWDER GOLF CLUB

Address: Cadder Road, Bishopbriggs G64 3QD (0141-772-5167; Pro shop: 0141-772-7102).
Location: One mile north-east off A803.
Description: Two parkland courses.
Cawder: Hilly with some testing holes. 18 holes, 6,295 yards. Par 70 (SSS 71).
Keir: Flat. 18 holes, 5,877 yards. Par 68 (SSS 68).
Visitors: Contact in advance. Weekdays only.
Green fees: £25 per round weekdays, £30 per day.
Catering: Bar. **Facilities:** Pro shop.
Accommodation: Black Bull Thistle Hotel.

CLOBER GOLF CLUB

Address: Craigton Road, Milngavie, Glasgow G62 7HP (0141-956-1685).
Location: From Milngavie Cross, proceed along Clober Road for more than half a mile. Turn left into Craigton Road. Club is on left after 500 yards.
Secretary: T. Arthur.
Professional: No professional but Miss M. Myers runs shop (0141-956-6963).
Description: Parkland course, fairly short with eight par threes. 18 holes, 5,098 yards. Par 66 (SSS 65). Amateur record 62.
Visitors: Weekdays before 4 p.m. **Green fees:** £12 per round.
Catering: Yes. **Facilities:** Trolley hire, putting green, pro shop.
Accommodation: Black Bull Hotel, Burnbrae Hotel.
Signature hole: FIFTH (119 yards, par three) – The Burn Hole is short but has out of bounds to the left and to the right so the tee shot has to be accurate. There are trees left and right.

CARD OF THE COURSE

Hole	Yds	Par	Hole	Yds	Par
1	378	4	10	485	5
2	348	4	11	349	4
3	189	3	12	181	3
4	214	3	13	196	3
5	119	3	14	280	4
6	311	4	15	161	3
7	364	4	16	192	3
8	490	5	17	380	4
9	156	3	18	305	4
Out	2,569	33	In	2,529	33
Total	**5,098**		**Par**	**66**	

COWGLEN GOLF CLUB

Address: Barrhead Road, Cowglen G43 1AU (0141-632-0556).
Location: Four and a half miles south-west of city centre on B762.
Professional: John McTear.
Description: Parkland course with good views over Clyde Valley to Campsie Hills. 18 holes, 5,976 yards. Par 69 (SSS 69). Course record 63.
Visitors: Play on shorter course. Contact in advance. Handicap certificate. No weekends. **Green fees:** On application.
Catering: Bar. **Facilities:** Putting green, pro shop, practice ground, driving range.
Accommodation: Macdonald Thistle Hotel

CROW WOOD GOLF CLUB

Address: Garnkirk House, Cumbernauld Road, Muirhead, Glasgow G69 9JF.
Location: Take M80 from Glasgow towards Stirling. At end of motorway, entrance is first left after 200 yards. Driveway is approximately half a mile on.
Secretary: Ian McInnes (0141-779-4954).
Professional: Brian Moffat (0141-779-1043).
Description: James Braid-designed, tree-lined parkland course. Rolling fairways enjoy the scenic backdrop of the Campsie Fells. Good greens and fairways. Ideal for the budding star and high handicapper alike. 18 holes, 6,261 yards. Par 71 (SSS 71). Amateur record 62 (Dean Robertson). Pro record 66 (Colin Gillies).
Visitors: Midweek, excluding public holidays and medal days.
Green fees: £20 per round, £28 per day.
Catering: Bar snacks and full meals.
Facilities: Trolley hire, putting green, pro shop, practice ground.
Accommodation: Crow Wood House Hotel, Garfield Hotel, Moodiesburn House Hotel.
Signature hole: TENTH (291 yards, par four) – One of the most picturesque holes you could find. Although short, it has trees on either side and the Garnkirk Burn only some 100 yards from the tee. It can yield many birdies but also some horrific scores.

CARD OF THE COURSE

Hole	Yds	Par	Hole	Yds	Par
1	146	3	10	291	4
2	530	5	11	402	4
3	362	4	12	277	4
4	344	4	13	453	4
5	197	3	14	349	4
6	378	4	15	167	3
7	421	4	16	336	4
8	372	4	17	386	4
9	333	4	18	517	5
Out	3,083	35	In	3,178	36
Total	**6,261**		**Par**	**71**	

DOUGALSTON GOLF CLUB

Address: Strathblane Road, Milngavie, Glasgow G62 8HJ (0141-956-5750).

Location: Seven miles from Glasgow city centre on the A81 out of Milngavie.
Manager: Mrs Sandra Currie.
Description: Very picturesque wooded course with some tree-lined fairways and three ponds. 18 holes, 6,354 yards. Par 71 (SSS 72).
Visitors: Weekdays 8 a.m. to 4.30 p.m.
Green fees: £12 per round, £20 per day.
Catering: Bar and dining-room. Varied menu.
Facilities: Trolley hire, putting green, practice ground.
Accommodation: Burnbrae Hotel, Black Bull Hotel.
Signature hole: SEVENTEENTH (368 yards, par four) – Left-to-right sloping fairway means you have to be accurate with your tee shot or you end up in the trees.

CARD OF THE COURSE

Hole	Yds	Par	Hole	Yds	Par
1	443	4	10	187	3
2	348	4	11	425	4
3	187	3	12	430	4
4	500	5	13	377	4
5	326	4	14	342	4
6	163	3	15	393	4
7	383	4	16	480	5
8	367	4	17	368	4
9	478	5	18	157	3
Out	3,195	36	In	3,159	35
Total	**6,354**		**Par**	**71**	

DOUGLAS PARK GOLF CLUB

Address: Hillfoot G61 2TJ (0141-942-2220).
Location: East of town on A81.
Secretary: Norman Nicholson (0141-942-1899).
Professional: David Scott (0141-942-1482).
Description: Parkland course with wide variety of holes. 18 holes, 5,957 yards. Par 69 (SSS 69).
Visitors: Must be accompanied by member. Contact in advance. Societies Wednesdays and Thursdays. **Green fees:** £23 per day.
Catering: Bar. **Facilities:** Trolley hire, pro shop.
Accommodation: Black Bull Thistle Hotel.

DULLATUR GOLF CLUB

Address: 1a Glen Douglas Drive, Dullatur G68 0DW (01236-723230).
Location: One and a half miles north of Cumbernauld.
Professional: Duncan Sinclair.
Description: Parkland course with natural hazards. 18 holes, 6,219 yards. Par 70 (SSS 70). Course record 65.
Visitors: Telephone for availability. May not play at weekends.
Green fees: £15 per round, £25 per day.
Catering: Full service. Bar.
Facilities: Trolley/buggy hire, putting green, pro shop, practice ground.
Accommodation: Westerwood Hotel Golf and Country Club.

THE EAST RENFREWSHIRE GOLF CLUB

Address: Ayr Road, Pilmuir, Newton Mearns, Glasgow G77 6RT.
Location: Travel south along A77 past Mearns Cross and club is on the left.
Secretary: A. Gillespie (0141-333-9989).
Professional: Gordon Clarke (01355-500206).
Description: Designed by James Braid, this magnificent course is one of the finest in the West of Scotland, enjoying magnificent scenery and panoramic views over Glasgow and the Clyde Valley to the Campsie Fells to the north. 18 holes, 6,097 yards. Par 70 (SSS 70). Course record 64.
Visitors: Most Tuesdays and Thursdays throughout the year.
Green fees: £25 per round, £30 per day.
Catering: Yes. **Facilities:** Putting green, pro shop, practice ground, driving range.
Accommodation: Macdonald Thistle Hotel.

CARD OF THE COURSE

Hole	Yds	Par	Hole	Yds	Par
1	367	4	10	280	4
2	346	4	11	213	3
3	436	4	12	360	4
4	151	3	13	124	3
5	392	4	14	496	5
6	352	4	15	348	4
7	204	3	16	353	4
8	503	5	17	394	4
9	324	4	18	454	4
Out	3,075	35	In	3,022	35
Total	**6,097**		**Par**	**70**	

THE EASTWOOD GOLF CLUB

Address: Muirshield, Loganswell, Newton Mearns, Glasgow G77 6RX (01355-500280).
Location: Three miles south of Mearns Cross, just off the A77. Turn left at monument on road to Mearnskirk.
Professional: Alan McGinness.
Description: Scenic moorland course. 18 holes, 5,864 yards. Par 68 (SSS 69). Amateur record 62.
Visitors: Weekdays only.
Green fees: £20 per round, £30 per day.
Catering: Available.
Facilities: Trolley hire, putting green, pro shop, practice ground.
Accommodation: Fenwick Hotel.
Signature hole: EIGHTH (480 yards, par five) – Called 'Muckle Dicht', it is the hardest hole on the course. (See diagram opposite.)

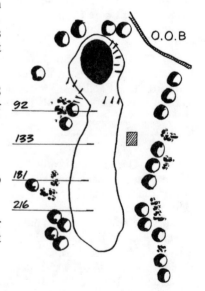

CARD OF THE COURSE

Hole	Yds	Par	Hole	Yds	Par
1	385	4	10	173	3
2	247	3	11	431	4
3	360	4	12	335	4
4	153	3	13	159	3
5	233	3	14	451	4
6	325	4	15	142	3
7	383	4	16	353	4
8	480	5	17	385	4
9	481	5	18	388	4
Out	3,047	35	In	2,817	33
Total	**5,864**		**Par**	**68**	

GLASGOW GOLF CLUB

Address: Killermont G61 2TW (0141-942-2011).

Location: South-east of city, off A81.

Professional: J. Steven.

Description: Founded in 1787, it is probably the eighth oldest club in the world. One of the finest parkland courses in Scotland with wide open fairways. Designed by Old Tom Morris in 1904. Magnificent clubhouse, a former stately home, houses an impressive trophy collection. The club has a second course, Glasgow Gailes, which is 35 miles away in Irvine. 18 holes, 5,968 yards. Par 70 (SSS 69).

Visitors: Must contact in advance and have handicap certificate.

Green fees: On application.

Catering: Full service. Restaurant and bar.

Facilities: Trolley hire, putting green, pro shop.

Accommodation: Black Bull Thistle Hotel.

HAGGS CASTLE GOLF CLUB

Address: 70 Dumbreck Road, Glasgow G41 4SN (0141-427-1157).

Location: First slip road off M77 from M8.

Secretary: Ian Harvey. **Professional:** Jim McAlister (0141-427-3355).

Description: A tricky wooded parkland course which has hosted a number of major championships, including the Scottish Open. 18 holes, 6,464 yards. Par 72 (SSS 72). Amateur record 64. Pro record 62.

Visitors: By arrangement only. **Green fees:** £27 per round, £38 per day.

Catering: Yes. **Facilities:** Trolley hire, putting green, pro shop, practice ground.

Accommodation: Sherbrooke Castle Hotel.

HAYSTON GOLF CLUB

Address: Campsie Road, Kirkintilloch G66 1RN (0141-776-1244).

Location: One mile north-west off A803.

Professional: Steven Barnett.

Description: Undulating tree-lined course. 18 holes, 6,042 yards. Par 70 (SSS 70). Course record 62.

Visitors: Not at weekends. Contact in advance. Societies Tuesdays and Thursdays.

Green fees: £18 per round, £25 per day.

Catering: Full service. Bar.
Facilities: Trolley hire, putting green, pro shop, practice ground.
Accommodation: Kirkhouse Inn.

HILTON PARK GOLF CLUB

Address: Stockiemuir Road, Milngavie, Glasgow G62 7HB (0141-956-4657).
Location: A809 approximately five miles north-west of Glasgow.
Secretary: Mrs J. Warnock (0141- 956-5124).
Professional: William McCondichie (0141-956-5125).
Description: Two moorland courses set in extremely scenic surroundings.
Hilton: 18 holes, 6,054 yards. Par 70 (SSS 70). Amateur record 65 (A. McDonald, R. Fraser, B. Reid).
Allander: 18 holes, 5,374 yards. Par 69 (SSS 66). Amateur record 66 (I. Weir).
Visitors: Weekdays by arrangement.
Green fees: £20 per round, £26 per day.
Catering: Full catering.
Facilities: Trolley/buggy hire, putting green, pro shop, practice ground.
Accommodation: Black Bull, Kirkhouse Inn.
Signature hole: *Hilton*: FIFTH (422 yards, par four) – Stroke Index 1.
Allander: FIFTH (372 yards, par four) – Particularly scenic.

CARD OF THE HILTON COURSE

Hole	Yds	Par	Hole	Yds	Par
1	496	5	10	340	4
2	386	4	11	373	4
3	403	4	12	157	3
4	177	3	13	415	4
5	422	4	14	329	4
6	220	3	15	363	4
7	306	4	16	498	5
8	307	4	17	184	3
9	314	4	18	364	4
Out	3,031	35	In	3,023	35
Total	**6,054**		**Par**	**70**	

KIRKHILL GOLF CLUB

Address: Greenlees Road, Cambuslang, Glasgow G72 8YN (0141-641-8499).
Location: Quarter of a mile north of A749, Rutherglen to East Kilbride road.
Description: Hilly parkland course designed by James Braid. 18 holes, 5,889 yards. Par 69 (SSS 69). Course record 63.
Visitors: Yes, midweek.
Green fees: £15 per round, £22 per day.
Catering: Yes. **Facilities:** Putting green, pro shop, practice ground.
Accommodation: Burnside Hotel.
Signature hole: FIRST (445 yards, par four) –

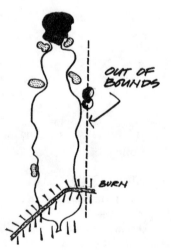

116

Drive over Kirk Burn, avoiding out of bounds on right. Fairway narrows to mouth of green guarded by bunkers right and left. (See diagram on previous page.)

KNIGHTSWOOD GOLF CLUB

Address: Lincoln Avenue, Glasgow G71 5QZ (Starter: 0141-959-6358).
Location: Four miles west of city centre off A82.
Secretary: J. Dean (0141-954-6495).
Description: Flat parkland course. Nine holes, 5,584 yards. Par 68 (SSS 67).
Visitors: Yes, without restriction.
Green fees: £2.80 for nine holes, £5.60 for 18.
Catering: None.
Accommodation: Jurys Glasgow Hotel.
Signature hole: FIRST (442 yards, par four) – Out of bounds on right. Approach must be accurate. Bunkers front left, right and behind green, which slopes away severely.

CARD OF THE COURSE

Hole	Yds	Par	
1	442	4	
2	309	4	
3	410	4	
4	280	4	
5	116	3	
6	215	3	
7	321	4	
8	203	3	
9	496	5	
Out	2,792	34	
Total	**5,584**	**Par**	**68**

LENZIE GOLF CLUB

Address: 19 Crosshill Road, Lenzie G66 5DA (Club Master David Galbraith: 0141-776-1535).
Location: South side of Lenzie on B819.
Secretary: Scott Davidson (0141-776-6020).
Professional: Jim McCallum (0141-777-7748).
Description: Founded in 1889. Parkland course. Prominent features include the old beech trees which line some of the fairways, together with thorn hedges and shallow ditches. Extensive larch and fir plantations have also been created. A substantial practice area lies to the west of the 18th and beside a small loch. Course is relatively flat apart from a steep hill to the fifth green. From there is a fine view of the Campsie Hills to the north and beyond to Ben Lomond. 18 holes, 5,984 yards. Par 69 (SSS 69). Amateur record 64. Pro record 63.
Visitors: Yes. Weekdays. **Green fees:** £16 per round, £24 per day.
Catering: Yes. Clubhouse refurbished in 1996. Two dining-rooms. Bar snacks to à la carte dinners.
Facilities: Trolley/buggy hire, putting green, pro shop, practice ground.
Accommodation: Garfield Hotel, Moodiesburn House Hotel.
Signature hole: FIFTH (343 yards, par four) – Small green on hilltop with out of bounds on left.

CARD OF THE COURSE

Hole	Yds	Par	Hole	Yds	Par
1	307	4	10	500	5
2	286	4	11	431	4
3	433	4	12	462	4
4	350	4	13	400	4
5	343	4	14	159	3
6	140	3	15	370	4
7	363	4	16	425	4
8	205	3	17	152	3
9	286	4	18	372	4
Out	2,713	34	In	3,271	35
Total	**5,984**		**Par**	**69**	

LETHAMHILL GOLF COURSE

Address: 1,240 Cumbernauld Road, Millerston G33 1AH (0141-770-6220).
Location: Three miles north-east of city centre on A80.
Description: Municipal parkland course. 18 holes, 5,859 yards. Par 70 (SSS 68).
Visitors: Must have introduction from own club. **Green fees:** £6 per round/day.
Accommodation: The Copthorne Hotel.

LINN PARK GOLF CLUB

Address: Simshill Road, Glasgow G44 5EP (0141-637-5871).
Location: South Glasgow. Near Castlemilk.
Secretary: R. Flanagan.
Description: Municipal parkland course with six par threes in outward half. Medium greens. 18 holes, 5,132 yards. Par 66 (SSS 65). Amateur record 61.
Visitors: Yes, any time. **Green fees:** £5.40. Book 24 hours in advance.
Catering: No. Soft drink machine only.
Accommodation: Bruce Swallow Hotel.
Signature hole: TENTH (400 yards, par four) – Dogleg left. Out of bounds behind green. Blind approach. Tree trouble left and right from tee.

LITTLEHILL GOLF CLUB

Address: Auchinairn Road, Glasgow (0141-772-1916).
Location: Three miles north of city centre.
Description: Inland course. 18 holes, 6,100 yards. SSS 70.
Visitors: Yes. **Green fees:** £6 per round.
Catering: Snacks only.

MILNGAVIE GOLF CLUB

Address: Laighpark, Milngavie, Glasgow G62 8EP (0141-956-1619).
Location: Glasgow to Anniesland Cross then to Bearsden. Three-quarters of a mile through Bearsden Cross follow sign to Drymen. Through two roundabouts, then at Craigton Village turn right.
Secretary: Ms S. McInnes.
Description: Moorland. Short in yardage but plays its distance. Very scenic. 18 holes, 5,818 yards. Par 68 (SSS 68). Course record 59.

118

Visitors: Yes. Weekdays by prior arrangement with secretary.
Green fees: £20 per round, £30 per day.
Catering: Yes, by prior arrangement with clubmaster.
Facilities: Putting green, practice ground.
Accommodation: Burnbrae Hotel, Black Bull Hotel.
Signature hole: FIRST – One of the most challenging anywhere. From elevated tee, you have to drive over a burn and whins to a plateau fairway with out of bounds on right and trees on left. The fairway then doglegs left to a plateau green.

MOUNT ELLEN GOLF CLUB

Address: Johnstone Road, Gartcosh, Glasgow G69 8EY (01236-872277).
Location: Two miles off Stirling road through Muirhead Cryston.
Secretary: J. Docherty. **Professional:** 01236-872632.
Description: Short but tricky parkland course suitable for all handicaps. Four par threes. No par fives. 18 holes, 5,525 yards. Par 68 (SSS 68). Amateur record 63. Pro record 61.
Visitors: Yes. Weekdays 9 a.m. to 4 p.m.
Green fees: £12 per round, £20 per day.
Catering: Full service.
Accommodation: Garfield House, Moodiesburn House Hotel.

CARD OF THE COURSE

Hole	Yds	Par	Hole	Yds	Par
1	355	4	10	156	3
2	331	4	11	166	3
3	282	4	12	233	3
4	285	4	13	300	4
5	328	4	14	405	4
6	308	4	15	434	4
7	461	4	16	292	4
8	191	2	17	307	4
9	265	4	18	426	4
Out	2,806	35	In	2,719	33
Total	**5,525**		**Par**	**68**	

POLLOK GOLF CLUB

Address: 90 Barrhead Road, Glasgow G43 1BG (0141-632-4351; 0141-632-1080).
Location: M77 to Pollok or Haggs Castle. On north side of B762.
Secretary: A. Mathison Boyd.
Description: Founded in 1892. Wooded parkland course. The holes are agreeably flat with subtle undulations, making a choice of shot always available, and sculpted between magnificent oaks and chestnuts. More than 70 bunkers. 18 holes, 6,257 yards. Par 71 (SSS 70). Course record 62.
Visitors: Mondays, Wednesdays and Thursdays. Write to secretary.
Green fees: £30 per round, £40 per day.
Catering: Yes. **Facilities:** Trolley hire, putting green, practice ground.
Accommodation: Eglington Hotel, Macdonald Thistle Hotel, Forte Crest Hotel, Hilton Hotel.

CARD OF THE COURSE

Hole	Yds	Par	Hole	Yds	Par
1	384	4	10	395	4
2	329	4	11	388	4
3	350	4	12	166	3
4	335	4	13	336	4
5	371	4	14	407	4
6	174	3	15	476	5
7	487	5	16	321	4
8	361	4	17	150	3
9	430	4	18	397	4
Out	3,221	36	In	3,036	35
Total	**6,257**		**Par**	**71**	

RUCHILL GOLF COURSE

Address: Maryhill.
Description: Inland course. Nine holes.

SANDYHILLS GOLF CLUB

Address: 223 Sandyhills Road G32 9NA (0141-778-1179).
Location: On east boundary of city.
Description: Inland course, slightly hilly. Excellent greens. 18 holes, 6,354 yards. SSS 70.
Visitors: Yes, but only with a member. **Green fees:** On application.
Catering: Yes.

WHITECRAIGS GOLF CLUB

Address: 72 Ayr Road, Newton Mearns G46 6SW (0141-639-4530).
Location: One and a half miles north-east on A77.
Secretary: A. Keith. **Professional:** Alistair Forrow (0141-639-2140).
Description: Beautiful parkland course. 18 holes, 6,230 yards. Par 70 (SSS 70). Course record 65.
Visitors: Contact pro in advance and have handicap certificate. With member only at weekends and bank holidays. **Green fees:** £28 per round, £35 per day.
Catering: Full service. Bar.
Facilities: Trolley hire, putting green, pro shop, practice ground.
Accommodation: Macdonald Thistle Hotel.

WILLIAMWOOD GOLF CLUB

Address: Clarkston Road G44 3YR (0141-637-1783).
Location: Five miles south of city centre on B767.
Professional: Jack Gardner (0141-637-2715).
Description: Inland course, fairly hilly with wooded areas. Small lake and pond. 18 holes, 5,878 yards. SSS 69. Course record 61.
Visitors: Apply in writing to secretary. No weekends. Societies midweek only.
Green fees: £20 per round, £30 per day.
Catering: Full service. Bar. **Facilities:** Trolley hire, pro shop, practice ground.
Accommodation: Macdonald Thistle Hotel.

WINDYHILL GOLF CLUB

Address: Baljaffray Road, Bearsden, Glasgow G61 4QQ (0141-942-2349).
Location: From Bearsden, take A809 to Baljaffray roundabout, then B8050.
Secretary: Andrew Miller. **Professional:** Gary Collinson.
Description: Undulating open parkland course with splendid views of Glasgow. 18 holes, 6,254 yards. Par 71 (SSS 70). Amateur record 64. Pro record 67.
Visitors: Weekdays. **Green fees:** £20 per day.
Catering: Yes. Bar.
Facilities: Trolley hire, putting green, pro shop, practice ground.
Accommodation: Burnbrae Hotel, Black Bull Hotel.
Signature hole: TWELFTH (450 yards, par four) – Two-tier fairway and an elevated plateau green.

CARD OF THE COURSE

Hole	Yds	Par	Hole	Yds	Par
1	362	4	10	178	3
2	162	3	11	292	4
3	425	4	12	450	4
4	368	4	13	500	5
5	386	4	14	154	3
6	421	4	15	479	5
7	193	3	16	380	4
8	480	5	17	295	4
9	420	4	18	309	4
Out	3,217	35	In	3,037	36
Total	**6,254**		**Par**	**71**	

GLEDDOCH

GLEDDOCH GOLF AND COUNTRY CLUB

Address: Langbank PA14 6YE (01475-540304).
Location: B789 Old Greenock road.
Professional: Keith Campbell.
Description: Parkland and heathland course. Good views over Firth of Clyde. 18 holes, 5,661 yards. Par 68 (SSS 67).
Visitors: Contact in advance. **Green fees:** £30 per round.
Catering: Full service. Bar. **Facilities:** Pro shop.
Accommodation: Gleddoch House Hotel.

GLENROTHES

GLENROTHES GOLF CLUB

Address: Golf Course Road, Glenrothes KY6 2LA (01592-754561; 01592-758686).
Location: 35 miles north-east of Edinburgh. Junction 3 on M90, then A92 to Glenrothes.
Secretary: Mrs P. Landells.
Description: Testing parkland course with burn which comes into play on the 11th,

121

12th, 13th and 18th holes. Wide fairways. Back nine hilly. Pleasant outlook to Lomond Hills and Firth of Forth. 18 holes, 6,444 yards. Par 71 (SSS 71). Course record 67.

Visitors: Any time. Telephone in advance. **Green fees:** £11 per round weekdays, £19 per day. £14 per round weekends, £21 per day.

Catering: Full service. Bar. **Facilities:** Practice ground.

Accommodation: Balgeddie House Hotel.

Signature hole: THIRD (151 yards, par three) – Elevated tee to raised green, 50 feet below and surrounded by bunkers. Anything from wedge to two-iron depending on wind direction.

GLENSHEE
DALMUNZIE GOLF CLUB

Address: Dalmunzie Estate, Glenshee PH10 7QG (01250-885226).

Location: Two miles north-west of Spittal of Glenshee.

Description: Challenging hilly upland course. Reasonably small greens. Well maintained. Nine holes, 4,070 yards. Par 60 (SSS 60).

Visitors: Restricted Sundays between 10.30 a.m. and 11.30 a.m.

Green fees: £5 per round, £8.50 per day, £34 weekly.

Catering: Full service. Bar. **Facilities:** Pro shop.

Accommodation: Dalmunzie House Hotel.

GOLSPIE
GOLSPIE GOLF CLUB

Address: Ferry Road, Golspie KW10 6ST (01408-633266).

Location: 10 miles north of Dornoch on A9. One hour north of Inverness.

Secretary: Mrs Marie Macleod.

Description: Founded in 1889, Golspie is a mixture of links, heath and parkland, offering a challenge to all standards of golfer. When the wind blows, the course offers a true test of shot-making. Stunning views over the Dornoch Firth on one side and majestic Ben Bhraggie on the other, an easy-walking course and a friendly relaxed atmosphere in the clubhouse. 18 holes, 5,890 yards. Par 68.

Visitors: Parties must pre-book.

Green fees: £18 per day weekdays, £20 per days weekends.

Catering: Yes. **Facilities:** Trolley hire, putting green, pro shop, practice ground.

Accommodation: Golf Link Hotel, Sutherland Arms.

Signature hole: 'The Lochy' (148 yards, par three) with water hazard.

GOREBRIDGE
VOGRIE COUNTRY PARK GOLF CLUB

Address: Vogrie Estate Country Park, Gorebridge EH23 4NU (01875-821716).

Location: Off B6372.

Description: Municipal course with wide fairways. Nine holes, 5,060 yards. Par 66.

Visitors: Book 24 hours in advance. **Green fees:** £5.40 per round.

Accommodation: Johnstounburn House Hotel.

GOUROCK

GOUROCK GOLF CLUB

Address: Cowal View, Gourock PA19 6HD (01475-631001).
Location: South-west of town off A770.
Professional: A. Green.
Description: Moorland course with hills and dells. Magnificent views of Firth of Clyde. 18 holes, 6,492 yards. Par 73 (SSS 73). Course record 64.
Visitors: By introduction or with member. Societies welcome weekdays.
Green fees: £16 per round weekdays, £23 per round weekends.
Catering: Full service. Bar.
Facilities: Trolley hire, putting green, pro shop, practice ground.
Accommodation: Manor Park Hotel.

GRANGEMOUTH

GRANGEMOUTH GOLF CLUB

Address: Polmont Hill, Grangemouth FK2 0YE (01324-711500; Pro shop: 01324-714355).
Location: On unclassed road half a mile north of M9 Junction 4.
Description: Undulating parkland course. 18 holes, 6,314 yards. Par 71 (SSS 71).
Visitors: Contact in advance.
Green fees: £8.20 per round weekdays, £10.40 per round weekends.
Catering: Bar. **Facilities:** Pro shop.
Accommodation: Inchyra Grange Hotel.
Signature hole: SEVENTH (216 yards, par three) – Tee shot over reservoir to elevated green.

GRANTOWN-ON-SPEY

GRANTOWN-ON-SPEY GOLF CLUB

Address: Golf Course Road, Grantown-on-Spey, Morayshire PH26 3HY (01479-872079).
Location: South-east side of town centre.
Secretary: J. Matheson. **Professional:** Bill Mitchell.
Description: Parkland/woodland course with generally easy walking, providing a fair test for every calibre of golfer. Scenically beautiful. 18 holes, 5,710 yards. Par 70 (SSS 68). Amateur record 60 (G. Bain). Pro record 62 (D. Webster).
Visitors: Any time except weekends before 10 a.m. Essential to book in advance.
Green fees: £16 per day weekdays, £21 per day weekends.
Catering: Full service available April to October.
Facilities: Trolley hire, putting green, pro shop, practice ground.
Accommodation: All types of accommodation available within easy reach of the course.
Signature hole: NINTH (275 yards, par four) – Downhill, which tempts the longer hitters. Fairway is lined with heather and pine trees and the Cromdale Hills provide a backdrop. Even if you are expert enough to hit the green with your tee shot, you may not get your birdie because the surface is severely undulating.

CARD OF THE COURSE

Hole	Yds	Par	Hole	Yds	Par
1	287	4	10	367	4
2	441	4	11	191	3
3	401	4	12	413	4
4	308	4	13	295	4
5	359	4	14	388	4
6	475	5	15	265	4
7	380	4	16	137	3
8	161	3	17	277	4
9	275	4	18	290	4
Out	3,087	36	In	2,623	34
Total	**5,710**		**Par**	**70**	

GREENOCK

GREENOCK GOLF CLUB

Address: Forsyth Street, Greenock PA16 8RE (01475-720793).
Location: South-west of town off A770.
Professional: Graham Ross (01475-787236).
Description: Testing moorland course with panoramic views of Clyde estuary. 18 holes, 5,838 yards. Par 69 (SSS 69). Nine holes, 4,320 yards. Par 64.
Visitors: May not play Saturdays. Contact in advance and have handicap certificates. **Green fees:** £15 per round weekdays, £20 per day. £20 per round weekends, £25 per day. Nine-hole course: £7.50 per round, £10 per day.
Catering: Bar. **Facilities:** Trolley hire, putting green, pro shop.
Accommodation: Manor Park Hotel.

GREENOCK WHINHILL GOLF CLUB

Address: Beith Road, Greenock PA16 9LN (01475-724694).
Location: Upper Greenock, off Dunlop Street towards old Largs Road. Off B7054.
Secretary: Raymond Kirkpatrick.
Description: Public heathland course with private clubhouse and members. Well maintained but reasonably difficult. 18 holes, 5,504 yards. Par 68 (SSS 68). Course record 64.
Visitors: Most days, except Saturdays. **Green fees:** On application.
Catering: Maybe, if given plenty of time. **Facilities:** Putting green.
Accommodation: Manor Park Hotel.
Signature hole: FOURTH (459 yards, par four) – The toughest hole on the course.

CARD OF THE COURSE

Hole	Yds	Par	Hole	Yds	Par
1	187	3	10	405	4
2	297	4	11	355	4
3	275	4	12	270	4
4	459	4	13	261	4
5	370	4	14	406	4
6	363	4	15	261	4

7	292	4	16	181	3
8	201	3	17	298	4
9	176	3	18	447	4
Out	2,620	33	In	2,884	35
Total	**5,504**		**Par**	**68**	

GRETNA
GRETNA GOLF CLUB
Address: Gretna, Dumfriesshire DG16 5HD (01461-338464).
Location: Half a mile west of Gretna. Well signposted from M74 and A75.
Secretary: Mrs L. Skinner.
Description: Parkland and not too hilly, a real test for enthusiastic and social golfer alike. Two par fives. Extensive views over the Solway Firth and Cumberland Hills. Nine holes, 6,430 yards. Par 72 (SSS 71). Course record 71.
Visitors: Yes. Societies by prior arrangement.
Green fees: £5 per nine holes, £8 per day weekdays, £10 per day weekends.
Catering: For parties, by prior arrangement. **Facilities:** Trolley hire, driving range.
Accommodation: Solway Lodge Hotel.
Signature hole: FIRST (174 yards, par three) – Appears to be a nice gentle start, but do not be fooled!

CARD OF THE COURSE

Hole	Yds	Par	
1	174	3	
2	387	4	
3	370	4	
4	484	5	
5	418	4	
6	351	4	
7	514	5	
8	324	4	
9	193	3	
Out	3,215	36	
Total	**6,430**	**Par**	**72**

GULLANE
GULLANE GOLF CLUB
Address: West Links Road, Gullane, East Lothian EH31 2BB (01620-842255; Starter: 01620-843115).
Location: West end of village on A198.
Professional: Jimmy Hume.
Description: The East Lothian Golf Club first played here in 1854. All three are tough links courses but No. 1 is a real test, especially when the wind gets up. Has been used for pre-qualifying for the Open Championship.
Course No. 1: 18 holes, 6,466 yards. Par 71 (SSS 72). Course record 65.
Course No. 2: 18 holes, 6,244 yards. Par 71 (SSS 70).

Course No. 3: 18 holes, 5,251 yards. Par 68 (SSS 66).

Visitors: Advance booking recommended.

Green fees: *Course No. 1*: £47 per round weekdays, £70 per day. £58 per round weekends. *Course No. 2*: £22 per round weekdays, £33 per day. £28 per round weekends, £42 per day. *Course No. 3*: £13 per round weekdays, £20 per day. £17 per round weekends, £25 per day.

Catering: Full service. Bar.

Facilities: Trolley/buggy hire, putting green, pro shop, practice ground.

Accommodation: Greywalls Hotel.

THE HONOURABLE COMPANY OF EDINBURGH GOLFERS (MUIRFIELD)

Whenever Muirfield comes up in conversation, the first thing mentioned is its standing amongst the world's best, quickly followed by the subject of great British defeat rather than triumph. Harry Vardon, James Braid and Henry Cotton have all won the Open at Muirfield, and in recent times Nick Faldo has done so twice, playing 'the best four holes of my life' to defeat John Cook in 1992. Yet it is the Open of 1972 that most golfers remember, when the mercurial Mexican Lee Trevino edged out Tony Jacklin in one of the most dramatic Championship finales ever.

They were level going into the 550-yard, par five 17th, which doglegged left and was littered with bunkers (11, to be exact). For once Trevino didn't feel like wisecracking as he was all over the place, hooking his drive into one of those traps. He played out, then hit a three-wood into thick rough well short of the green. Jacklin was playing like a champion, lying 20 yards short of the green in two. Trevino mishit his fourth out of the rough downwind and through the dry, fast green and on to a fluffy bank several yards behind the putting surface.

'My next shot from the bank was strictly a give-up one,' he said afterwards. 'And the ball went straight in the hole.' Jacklin chipped up well short, missed his putt and missed the return. A par for Trevino and a bogey for Jacklin, who dropped another shot at the last to finish two shots away in third place.

That was just one of 14 Open Championships staged since 1892 at Muirfield, which has also hosted the Amateur Championship on numerous occasions, the Ryder Cup and the Walker and Curtis Cups. Although the thick rough and cavernous bunkers, of which there are 151, can make it a very severe test, it is a course which invokes respect from all who have tangled with it. Cotton called it 'cruelly fair'. Tom Watson said there was 'not a weak hole on the course'. Jack Nicklaus, who won in 1966, was so taken with this links in the lee of Gullane Hill, almost 20 miles from Edinburgh, that he named his golf complex in Ohio, Muirfield Village, after it.

Old Tom Morris designed Muirfield in 1891 and it received a lot of criticism in its early days, one professional calling it 'nothing but an auld watter meddie'. Today the site of only one green has survived and the present course is very much the result of Harry Colt's work in the mid-1920s. Muirfield is laid out in two separate undulating loops, with the back nine forming an 'inner circle' which ensures that the golfer will not have to contend with the same wind direction on more than a few holes.

The lushness of its turf is easily matched by the richness of the club's tradition and history. Two years before Bonnie Prince Charlie's forces were defeated at the Battle of Culloden, The Honourable Company of Edinburgh Golfers, the descendants of the gentlemen golfers who played the Leith Links from as early as the fifteenth century, were involved in more peaceful pursuits, establishing a club which is 10 years older than the Royal and Ancient of St Andrews.

On 7 March 1744, 'several Gentlemen of Honour, skillfull in the ancient and healthfull exercise of the Golf' enlisted the help of the city fathers of Edinburgh. The Council provided a silver club which was played for annually on the Leith Links, the winner being made captain of the club. Also that year they drew up the game's first rules, the 'Thirteen Articles', which were adopted by the R. and A. 10 years later.

In those days it was *de rigueur* to play over the five holes at Leith, all about 400 yards long, in the club's red uniform. Failure to do so resulted in a fine. The Company continued at Leith for almost a hundred years before moving on to a nine-hole course at Musselburgh. Musselburgh first staged the Open Championship in 1874 and it was held there every third year until 1889, but the Company moved on again to Muirfield, taking the Open with them.

From the championship tees the course stretches to a formidable 6,970 yards and still adds up to a par-70, 6,601 yards off the medal tees. There is no lulling you into a false sense of security with this course. Right from the off you have to battle for par. Nicklaus has said of the 444-yard first that it is as tough an opening hole as you will find on any championship course.

But it is perhaps its four par threes which present the biggest danger to a golfer's card. Each has raised greens, which are tight targets. Miss them and you are just as likely to end up in a seriously deep bunker, where sideways or even backwards is often the only way to escape.

You get the idea as early as the 174-yard fourth which has four bunkers in front – and is one of the costliest holes on the course. The 151-yard seventh is similar in design to the fourth but runs in the opposite direction, into the prevailing wind, and offers an exposed elevated green, guarded by four bunkers. Nicklaus regards the 146-yard 13th as a truly great par three and a golfing gem. It runs uphill to a narrow green with deep bunkers on both sides. Beware – you could spend the day here. The final par three is the 16th, at 181 yards the longest of the four short holes. There are seven bunkers to contend with, the slope of the terrain taking any shot played to the left side into the traps.

In addition to the short holes, Muirfield demands accuracy everywhere else, especially on the 436-yard par four sixth which doglegs left to a split-level fairway. You must be right to get that second shot close. Someone once said they thought Muirfield had a bunker for every day of the year, and it certainly seems that way on the eighth. This 439-yard par four has 12 bunkers and starts a run of three very challenging holes. The ninth (460 yards, par four) has out of bounds all along the left and a bunker called 'Simpson's Folly' 40 yards short of the green. The 350-yard 11th has the only blind drive at Muirfield and, of course, the tricky green is surrounded by bunkers.

It hardly needs repeating that two of the characteristics of Muirfield are the bunkers and the long grasses of the rough. When Nicklaus won in 1966, the grass had been allowed to grow so long that the philosophical Doug Sanders reportedly remarked that he didn't mind about the championship as long as he could have the hay concession.

Address: Gullane, East Lothian (01620-842123).
Location: Duncur Road, Gullane. Off A198 on north-east of village.
Secretary: Group Captain J.A. Prideaux.
Description: 18 holes, 6,601 yards (championship 6,970). Par 70 (SSS 73). Course record 63 (R. Davis, I. Aoki).
Visitors: Tuesdays and Thursdays only. Visiting groups of no more than 12 on these days. Evening clubs of no more than 40. Contact in advance. Must have handicap certificate (limits of 18 for men, 24 for women).
Green fees: £60 per round, £80 per day.
Catering: Full service (ladies may not lunch in the clubhouse). Bar.
Facilities: Trolley/ buggy hire, putting green, practice area.
Accommodation: Greywalls Hotel, Kilspindie House, The Marine Hotel, Nether Abbey Hotel, Point Garry Hotel.
Signature hole: FIRST (444 yards, par four) – One of many large bunkers dominates the left of the fairway, which is narrow. Stray off it and you are in severe rough. The green slopes from front to back. (See diagram opposite.)

CARD OF THE COURSE

Hole	Yds	Par	Hole	Yds	Par
1	444	4	10	471	4
2	345	4	11	350	4
3	374	4	12	376	4
4	174	3	13	146	3
5	506	5	14	442	4
6	436	4	15	391	4
7	151	3	16	181	3
8	439	4	17	501	5
9	460	4	18	414	4
Out	3,329	35	In	3,272	35
Total	**6,601**		**Par**		**70**

HADDINGTON
HADDINGTON GOLF CLUB

Address: Amisfield Park, Haddington EH41 4PT (01620-823627).
Location: East side, off A613.
Professional: John Sandilands (01620-822727).
Description: Inland tree-lined course. Not hilly but bunkered. 18 holes, 6,280 yards. Par 71 (SSS 70).
Visitors: May not play between 7 a.m. and 10 a.m., and between noon and 2 p.m. at weekends. Contact in advance. **Green fees:** £15.50 per round weekdays, £20 per day. £20 per round weekends, £27 per day.
Catering: Bar. **Facilities:** Pro shop.
Accommodation: Tweeddale Arms Hotel.

HAMILTON
HAMILTON GOLF CLUB

Address: Carlisle Road, Ferniegair ML3 7TU (01698-282872).
Location: One and a half miles south-east on A72.
Professional: Maurice Moir.
Description: Inland parkland wooded course. 18 holes, 6,243 yards. Par 70 (SSS 71). Course record 62.
Visitors: Not weekends. Contact in advance. Must be accompanied by member.
Green fees: On application.
Catering: Full service. Bar. **Facilities:** Pro shop.
Accommodation: Silvertrees Hotel.

STRATHCLYDE PARK GOLF COURSE

Address: Motehill, Hamilton ML3 6BY (01698-266155).
Location: M74 towards Glasgow. Exit at Hamilton/Motherwell.
Description: Municipal wooded parkland course. Race course at top side of course. Nature reserve surrounds rest of course. Small greens. Nine holes, 6,256 yards. Par 36 (SSS 70). Course record 64.
Visitors: Any time. Same-day booking system. Societies must contact in advance.
Green fees: £3 per nine holes.
Facilities: Putting green, pro shop, practice ground, driving range.
Accommodation: Travel Lodge, Holiday Inn.
Signature hole: FOURTH – Drive downhill. Out of bounds on right looking into bird sanctuary lake. Slight dogleg to right around small copse.

HARRIS (Isle of)
HARRIS GOLF CLUB

Address: Scarista Links, Isle of Harris.
Location: 15 miles south of Tarbert on west coast.
Secretary: Andrew Haddow, Cnocant-sithean, Borrisdale, Isle of Harris H55 3UE (01859-520236).
Description: Links course clinging to the side of a hill which runs down to the Atlantic Ocean and the beautiful Scarista beach. Several years ago in an effort to raise funds the club offered life memberships for £100 a head to golfers all around the world. It is an experience. Nine holes, 4,668 yards. Par 62.
Visitors: Any time. But no play on Sundays. **Green fees:** £5 per day.
Catering: No clubhouse. **Facilities:** Putting green.
Accommodation: Many local bed and breakfasts.
Signature hole: SECOND (395 yards, par four) – Drive over the rocks on to fairway sloping sharply to the sea. Then blind second shot to small green cut into the hillside.

CARD OF THE COURSE

Hole	Yds	Par
1	295	4
2	395	4
3	217	3

4	143	3
5	381	4
6	204	3
7	166	3
8	168	3
9	365	4
Out	2,334	31
Total	**4,668**	**Par**	**62**

HAWICK
HAWICK GOLF CLUB

Address: Vertish Hill, Hawick, Roxburghshire TD9 0NY (01450-372293).
Location: From north, A7 through town. Pass horse monument on left, proceed along Main Street. Turn left just before roundabout and continue uphill, then down to course. From south, A7 to roundabout then turn sharp right up hill.
Secretary: J. Harley.
Description: Well-bunkered hill course with spectacular views. 18 holes, 5,929 yards. Par 68 (SSS 69).
Visitors: Daily but usually after 3 p.m. on Saturdays.
Green fees: £18 per round, £24 per day all week.
Catering: Full service, except on Wednesdays.
Facilities: Trolley hire, putting green.
Accommodation: Elm Guest House, Buccleugh Hotel, Mansfield House Hotel, Kirklands Hotel.
Signature hole: SIXTH (445 yards, par four) – Stroke Index 1.

CARD OF THE COURSE

Hole	Yds	Par	Hole	Yds	Par
1	195	3	10	382	4
2	350	4	11	390	4
3	388	4	12	292	4
4	325	4	13	198	3
5	338	4	14	388	4
6	445	4	15	437	4
7	449	4	16	292	4
8	144	3	17	276	4
9	430	4	18	210	3
Out	3,064	34	In	2,865	34
Total	**5,929**		**Par**	**68**	

HELENSBURGH
HELENSBURGH GOLF CLUB

Address: 25 East Abercromby Street, Helensburgh G84 9JD (01436-674173).
Location: A82 through Dumbarton and Cardross to Helensburgh. Turn right at traffic lights. Follow signs.
Secretary: D. Loch. **Professional:** David Fotheringham (01436-675505).

Description: Challenging moorland course with panoramic views across Loch Lomond and the Clyde estuary. 18 holes, 6,104 yards. Par 69 (SSS 70). Amateur and pro records 64.

Visitors: Weekdays only. **Green fees:** £17 per round, £25 per day.

Catering: Yes. **Facilities:** Trolley hire, putting green, pro shop, practice ground.

Accommodation: Commodore Hotel.

Signature hole: THIRD (182 yards, par three) – A tough par three with out of bounds on left, woods beyond, wild moorland trees and a pond in front. Anything but a well-struck shot to a heavily bunkered green will be punished. (See diagram opposite.)

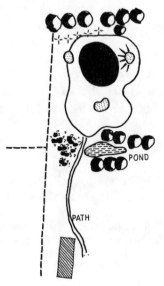

CARD OF THE COURSE

Hole	Yds	Par	Hole	Yds	Par
1	283	4	10	447	4
2	429	4	11	210	3
3	182	3	12	339	4
4	372	4	13	508	5
5	300	4	14	408	4
6	412	4	15	371	4
7	408	4	16	150	3
8	371	4	17	379	4
9	131	3	18	404	4
Out	2,888	34	In	3,216	35
Total	**6,104**		**Par**	**69**	

HELMSDALE

HELMSDALE GOLF CLUB

Address: Strath Road, Helmsdale KW8 6JA (01431-821650).

Location: From A9 junction in Helmsdale, follow A897. Course is on right on outskirts of village.

Secretary: Liz Cowie.

Description: Testing undulating course with a fair expanse of gorse and bracken, bordered by a hill on the north and the A897 on the south. Tight fairways. Nine holes, 3,720 yards. Par 62 (SSS 61).

Visitors: Any time by prior arrangement. **Green fees:** £6 per round, £12 per day, £30 per week. Country membership available on application.

Catering: No.

Accommodation: The Links Hotel.

Signature hole: NINTH (192 yards, par three) – Elevated tee, giving a panoramic view of the Moray Firth to the east and the Strath of Kildonan to the west. Misjudge this one at your peril. Numerous hazards await the wayward shot.

CARD OF THE COURSE

Hole	Yds	Par
1	256	4
2	82	3

3	137	3
4	301	4
5	179	3
6	308	4
7	238	4
8	167	3
9	192	3
Out	1,860	31
Total	**3,720**	**Par** 62

HOLLANDBUSH
HOLLANDBUSH GOLF CLUB

Address: Acretophead ML11 0JS (01555-893484).
Location: Off M74 between Lesmahagow and Coalburn.
Secretary: James Hamilton. **Professional:** Ian Rae (01555-893646).
Description: Moderately undulating municipal course. Tree-lined parkland on edge of moorland. First half flat, second half hilly. No bunkers. 18 holes, 6,200 yards. Par 72 (SSS 70). Course record 63.
Visitors: Any time. **Green fees:** £7.25 per round weekdays, £8.50 weekends.
Catering: Full service. Bar. **Facilities:** Trolley hire, pro shop, practice ground.
Accommodation: Strathaven Hotel.
Signature hole: SIXTEENTH (470 yards, par five) – Played from elevated tee to elevated green.

HOPEMAN
HOPEMAN GOLF CLUB

Address: IV30 2YA (01343-830578).
Location: A96 to Elgin. East side of village, off B9040.
Secretary: R. Johnston.
Description: Links-type course with beautiful views over the Moray Firth. 18 holes, 5,531 yards. Par 67 (SSS 67). Course record 64.
Visitors: Contact in advance. Restricted tee times at weekends.
Green fees: £10 per round weekdays, £15 per day. £15 per round weekends, £20 per day.
Catering: Available all day. Bar.
Facilities: Trolley hire, practice ground.
Accommodation: Station Hotel.
Signature hole: TWELFTH (152 yards, par three) – Green alongside shore, 100 feet below tee. (See diagram opposite.)

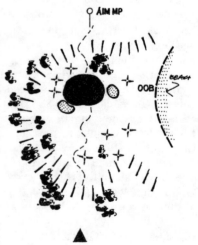

CARD OF THE COURSE

Hole	Yds	Par	Hole	Yds	Par
1	371	4	10	299	4
2	352	4	11	355	4
3	174	3	12	152	3
4	471	4	13	344	4
5	342	4	14	383	4
6	371	4	15	106	3
7	198	3	16	384	4
8	346	4	17	194	3
9	302	4	18	387	4
Ou	2,927	34	In	2,604	33
Total	**5,531**		**Par**	**67**	

HUNTLY
HUNTLY GOLF CLUB

Address: Cooper Park, Huntly, Aberdeenshire AB54 4SH (01466-792643).
Location: 39 miles north-west of Aberdeen on A96. On north side of Huntly.
Description: An inland parkland course. 18 holes, 5,399 yards. Par 67 (SSS 66).
Visitors: Any day after 8 a.m. Societies by arrangement with secretary.
Green fees: £13 weekday, £20 weekend, £65 weekly (all-day tickets).
Catering: Yes.
Accommodation: Castle Hotel, Huntly Hotel, Gordon Arms Hotel.
Signature hole: EIGHTH (406 yards, par four) – Regarded as the toughest hole on the course.

CARD OF THE COURSE

Hole	Yds	Par	Hole	Yds	Par
1	366	4	10	393	4
2	154	3	11	387	4
3	158	3	12	350	4
4	389	4	13	333	4
5	294	4	14	187	3
6	107	3	15	336	4
7	334	4	16	389	4
8	406	4	17	163	3
9	369	4	18	284	4
Out	2,577	33	In	2,822	34
Total	**5,399**		**Par**	**67**	

INNELLAN
INNELLAN GOLF CLUB

Address: Knockamillie Road, Innellan PA23 7SG (01369-830242; 01369-703327).
Location: Four miles south of Dunoon.
Description: Undulating hilltop course. Views of the Firth of Clyde. Nine holes, 4,683 yards. Par 64 (SSS 64). Course record 63.

Visitors: Welcome but may not play after 5 p.m. on Mondays.
Green fees: £8 weekdays, £10 weekends.
Catering: Snacks. Bar.
Accommodation: Enmore Hotel.

INNERLEITHEN

INNERLEITHEN GOLF CLUB

Address: Leithen Water, Leithen Road, Innerleithen EH44 6NJ (01896-830951).
Location: A72 from Peebles (south) for six miles. At Innerleithen, left into Heriot Road. Golf course approximately three-quarters of a mile.
Description: Attractive course set in a valley with a lovely view of surrounding hills. A stream meanders through six holes and offers a challenge to all standards of golfers, yet is easy walking. Nine holes, 6,056 yards. Par 70 (SSS 69). Course record 66.
Visitors: Yes, by arrangement. **Green fees:** £11 per round weekdays, £16 per day. £13 per round weekends, £19 per day.
Facilities: Putting green, practice ground.
Accommodation: Traquair Hotel.
Signature hole: FIRST (177 yards, par three) – Narrow entry to green with roadway on right, a burn on front left and the Leithen Water at the back.

CARD OF THE COURSE

Hole	Yds	Par	
1	177	3	
2	343	4	
3	474	4	
4	376	4	
5	100	3	
6	485	5	
7	177	3	
8	524	5	
9	372	4	
Out	3,028	35	
Total	**6,056**	**Par**	**70**

INSCH

INSCH GOLF CLUB

Address: Golf Terrace, Insch, Aberdeenshire AB52 6XN (01464-820363).
Location: Close to centre of village.
Outings Secretary: Jane Williams, Craigour, Templand, Culsalmond, Insch.
Description: Currently upgrading to 18 holes – opening June 1997. Original course flat, easy walking. New holes are testing. One hole steep but excellent panoramic views over local hills and village. Nine holes, 5,632 yards. Par 70 (SSS 67). Course record 65.
Visitors: Yes. **Green fees:** £12 weekdays, £15 weekends.
Catering: If booked in advance.
Accommodation: Lodge Hotel.

Signature hole: SIXTH (536 yards, par five) – An extremely long hole requiring an accurate drive into the prevailing wind. Final approach slightly uphill to a green set into the slope.

INVERALLOCHY
INVERALLOCHY GOLF CLUB

Address: Cairnbulg AB43 5YL (01346-582000).
Location: Four miles south-east of Fraserburgh.
Secretary: Ian Watt.
Description: Typical seaside links course with several tricky par threes. Runs parallel to picturesque beach. 18 holes, 5,237 yards. Par 64 (SSS 65). Course record 59.
Visitors: Any time. **Green fees:** £10 weekdays, £12 weekends.
Catering: Limited. **Facilities:** Putting green, small practice ground.
Accommodation: Tufted Duck Hotel.
Signature hole: SEVENTEENTH (418 yards, par four) – Tee shot has to be fairly long but short of burn which runs diagonally across fairway. Second shot to a small elevated green.

CARD OF THE COURSE

Hole	Yds	Par	Hole	Yds	Par
1	384	4	10	239	3
2	203	3	11	192	3
3	371	4	12	442	4
4	319	4	13	335	4
5	184	3	14	157	3
6	454	4	15	322	4
7	200	3	16	190	3
8	147	3	17	418	4
9	282	4	18	398	4
Out	2,544	32	In	2,693	32
Total	**5,237**		**Par**	**64**	

INVERARAY
INVERARAY GOLF CLUB

Address: Lochgilphead Road, Inveraray (01467-624080).
Location: One mile south of town.
Description: Parkland course. Quite testing with views over Loch Fyne. Nine holes, 5,790 yards. Par 70 (SSS 68).
Visitors: Welcome. **Green fees:** £10 per round.
Facilities: Practice ground.
Accommodation: Fernpoint Hotel.

INVERGORDON
INVERGORDON GOLF CLUB

Address: King George Street, Invergordon, Ross-shire IV18 0BD (01349-852715).

Location: A9 north from Inverness, then B817 entering town from west along the High Street. Turn left at Albany Road and left again over railway bridge (Cromlet Drive). Continue to end of road.

Secretary: N. Paterson (01349-882693).

Description: 11-hole extension completed in 1994. Parkland with moderate slopes on some holes. Mature trees/rhododendrons on old holes. Many young trees on the new. 18 holes, 6,030 yards. Par 69 (SSS 69). Amateur record 66.

Visitors: Yes. Club competitions are held on Tuesday/Thursday evenings and Saturday mornings. These should be avoided but check club noticeboard.

Green fees: £10 per day weekdays. £10 per round weekends, £15 per day.

Catering: Bar snacks/meals. Tuesday/Thursday/Friday evenings after 7 p.m. Weekends normal bar hours.

Facilities: Trolley hire, putting green, practice ground.

Accommodation: Marine Hotel, Kincraig Hotel.

Signature hole: EIGHTH (123 yards, par three) – One of the new holes created in 1994. Although the shortest of the par threes, it is often played into the prevailing wind and is all about carry. Trees and whins line the left, while on the right is a pond which cuts into the fairway and has to be carried if the pin is on the right of the green. Rhododendrons lie to the right of the pond, while there are more bushes and trees behind the green. (See diagram opposite.)

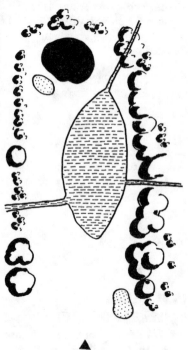

CARD OF THE COURSE

Hole	Yds	Par	Hole	Yds	Par
1	134	3	10	166	3
2	275	4	11	425	4
3	456	4	12	383	4
4	374	4	13	371	4
5	506	5	14	387	4
6	430	4	15	195	3
7	376	4	16	340	4
8	123	3	17	385	4
9	387	4	18	317	4
Out	3,061	35	In	2,969	34
Total	**6,030**		**Par**		**69**

INVERNESS

INVERNESS GOLF CLUB ✓

Address: Culcabock, Inverness IV2 3XQ (01463-239882).

Location: One mile south of town centre.

Professional: Alistair Thomson (01463-231989).

Description: Fairly flat parkland course with burn. 18 holes, 6,226 yards. Par 69 (SSS 70).

Visitors: Restricted at weekends. **Green fees:** £25 per round weekdays, £34 per day. £30 per round weekends, £40 per day.

Catering: Bar. **Facilities:** Trolley hire, putting green, pro shop, practice ground.
Accommodation: Kingsmill Hotel

TORVEAN GOLF CLUB

Address: Glenurquhart Road, Inverness IV3 6JN (01463-711434).
Location: On A82 Fort William road, approximately one mile from Inverness town centre.
Secretary: Mrs K. Gray.
Description: Municipal parkland course. Close to Loch Ness and the Caledonian Canal. Easy walking. 18 holes, 5,784 yards. Par 69 (SSS 68). Amateur record 65 (D. Walker). Pro record 70 (R. Weir).
Visitors: Yes. Book through the Highland Council (01463-239111).
Green fees: £10 weekdays, £12 weekends.
Catering: Weekends only, except by prior arrangement with the secretary.
Facilities: Trolley hire, putting green.
Accommodation: Loch Ness House Hotel.
Signature hole: SEVENTEENTH (164 yards, par three) – Carry of 164 yards over water to the green.

CARD OF THE COURSE

Hole	Yds	Par	Hole	Yds	Par
1	194	3	10	286	4
2	358	4	11	526	5
3	273	4	12	400	4
4	270	4	13	410	4
5	565	5	14	338	4
6	277	4	15	174	3
7	157	3	16	471	4
8	277	4	17	164	3
9	220	3	18	424	4
Out	2,591	34	In	3,193	35
Total	**5,784**		**Par**	**69**	

INVERURIE

INVERURIE GOLF CLUB

Address: Davah Wood, Blackhall Road, Inverurie AB51 9WB (01467-624080).
Location: Off A96, west side of town.
Secretary: John Ramage.
Description: Wooded parkland course. 18 holes, 5,711 yards. Par 69 (SSS 68). Course record 65.
Visitors: Any time, but easier weekdays.
Green fees: £18 per day weekdays, £24 per day weekends.
Catering: Full. **Facilities:** Putting green, pro shop, practice ground.
Accommodation: Strathburn Hotel.
Signature hole: THIRD (401 yards, par four) – Easy drive, precise second shot.

CARD OF THE COURSE

Hole	Yds	Par	Hole	Yds	Par
1	294	4	10	128	3
2	346	4	11	304	4
3	401	4	12	322	4
4	196	3	13	257	4
5	512	5	14	369	4
6	348	4	15	183	3
7	184	3	16	444	4
8	365	4	17	407	4
9	301	4	18	350	4
Out	2,947	35	In	2,764	34
Total	**5,711**		**Par**	**69**	

IRVINE

IRVINE GOLF CLUB

Address: Bogside, Irvine KA12 8SN (01294-275626).
Location: North of town, off A737.
Professional: Keith Erskine.
Description: Testing links course. 18 holes, 6,400 yards. Par 71 (SSS 71). Course record 65.
Visitors: May not play before 2 p.m. Saturdays and Sundays. Contact in advance. Welcome weekdays, telephone 01294-275979 to book.
Green fees: £30 per round Mondays to Thursdays, £45 per day. £45 per round weekends.
Catering: Bar. **Facilities:** Pro shop.
Accommodation: Hospitality Inn.

GLASGOW GOLF CLUB

Address: Gailes, Irvine, Ayrshire KA11 5AE (01294-311258).
Location: One mile south of Irvine off A78.
Secretary: David Deas. **Professional:** Jack Steven.
Description: Championship links course with heather-lined fairways. Established in 1787, this is the ninth-oldest course in the world and is a qualifying course for the Open. 18 holes, 6,510 yards. Par 71 (SSS 72). Amateur record 65 (G. Sherry). Pro record 64 (C. Gillies).
Visitors: By arrangement (telephone 0141-942-2011). **Green fees:** £40 per round weekdays, £50 per day. £45 per round weekends (afternoon only).
Catering: Full service available.
Facilities: Trolley hire, putting green, pro shop, practice ground.
Accommodation: Hospitality Inn.
Signature hole: FIFTH (530 yards, par five) – Stroke Index 1.

CARD OF THE COURSE

Hole	Yds	Par	Hole	Yds	Par
1	345	4	10	422	4
2	349	4	11	419	4

3	425	4	12	179	3
4	414	4	13	334	4
5	530	5	14	526	5
6	152	3	15	152	3
7	403	4	16	413	4
8	343	4	17	365	4
9	304	4	18	435	4
Out	3,265	36	In	3,245	35
Total	**6,510**		**Par**	**71**	

IRVINE RAVENSPARK GOLF CLUB

Address: 13 Kidsneuk, Irvine KA12 8SR.

Location: Irvine to Kilwinning main road, turn left at Irvine Royal Academy.

Secretary: George Robertson (01294-554617).

Professional: Peter Bond (01294-276467).

Description: Flat parkland course. Well bunkered. Hosted several national competitions. 18 holes, 6,429 yards. Par 71 (SSS 71). Amateur record 65. Pro record 67.

Visitors: Any time, except before 2 p.m. on Saturdays (April to September).

Green fees: £7 per round weekdays, £10 per day. £11 per round weekends, £15 per day.

Catering: Full. **Facilities:** Putting green, pro shop, practice ground.

Accommodation: Montgreenan Mansion House Hotel.

Signature hole: THIRD (452 yards, par four) – Stroke Index 1.

CARD OF THE COURSE

Hole	Yds	Par	Hole	Yds	Par
1	343	4	10	508	5
2	380	4	11	394	4
3	452	4	12	412	4
4	158	3	13	398	4
5	400	4	14	346	4
6	365	4	15	185	3
7	339	4	16	313	4
8	282	4	17	347	4
9	398	4	18	409	4
Out	3,117	35	In	3,312	36
Total	**6,429**		**Par**	**71**	

WESTERN GAILES GOLF CLUB

Address: Gailes, Irvine, Ayrshire KA11 5AE (01294-311649).

Location: Three miles north of Troon.

Secretary: Andrew McBean.

Description: Championship links course with views across the Firth of Clyde. Good greens and turf. Three burns cross the course. 18 holes, 6,639 yards (medal tees). Par 71 (SSS 73). Amateur record 66. Pro record 65.

Visitors: Mondays, Tuesdays, Wednesdays and Fridays. Sunday afternoons. No ladies on Tuesdays. Visitors from May 1 to September 30. Must have handicap certificate. **Green fees:** £50 per round. £80 per day.

Catering: Full service available. Contact club manager. Bar.

Facilities: Trolley/buggy hire, putting green, golf shop in bar, practice ground.
Accommodation: Marine Hotel, Hospitality Inn.
Signature hole: SIXTH (506 yards, par five) – Drive should be hit slightly across the fairway, which points towards Troon harbour, to land in a series of humps and hollows. The second is played through a gap in the dunes and runs down to the fairway at a lower level. The golfer is left with a short iron which has to be accurate because the green, nestling in a hollow in the dunes, has a pronounced hump set into the middle of the right side.

CARD OF THE COURSE

Hole	Yds	Par	Hole	Yds	Par
1	304	4	10	348	4
2	434	4	11	445	4
3	365	4	12	436	4
4	355	4	13	141	3
5	453	4	14	562	5
6	506	5	15	194	3
7	171	3	16	404	4
8	365	4	17	443	4
9	336	4	18	377	4
Out	3,289	36	In	3,350	35
Total	**6,639**		**Par**	**71**	

ISLAY (Isle of)
ISLAY GOLF CLUB

Address: Machrie Hotel and Golf Course, Port Ellen, Isle of Islay, Argyll PA42 7AN (01496-302310).
Location: A846, three and a half miles north of Port Ellen.
Secretary: Tom Dunn.
Description: Golfing history. A championship seaside links opened in 1891. 18 holes, 6,226 yards. Par 71 (SSS 70). Course record 66 (Iain Middleton).
Visitors: Yes, all year. **Green fees:** £16.50 per round, £25 per day.
Catering: Full facilities at hotel.
Facilities: Trolley/buggy hire, putting green, shop, practice ground.
Accommodation: Machrie Hotel.
Signature hole: SEVENTH – 'The Maiden'. Fearsome sandy ridge 100 yards from tee. Blind second shot to the green guarded by two bunkers.

JEDBURGH
JEDBURGH GOLF CLUB

Address: Dunion Road, Jedburgh TD8 6DQ (01835-863587).
Location: One mile west on B6358.
Description: Undulating wooded parkland course with small greens. Nine holes, 5,760 yards. Par 68 (SSS 67).
Visitors: Restricted at weekends during competitions.
Green fees: £12 per round.

Catering: Bar (April to September). **Facilities:** Pro shop.
Accommodation: Larkhall Burn Hotel.

JOHNSTONE
COCHRANE CASTLE GOLF CLUB

Address: Scott Avenue, Craigston, Johnstone PA5 0HF (01505-320146).
Location: Five miles west of Paisley. Half a mile off Beith road.
Secretary: J. Cowan. **Professional:** Stuart Campbell (01505-328465).
Description: Fairly hilly wooded parkland course. Two streams run through it. 18 holes, 6,226 yards. Par 71 (SSS 71). Amateur record 65. Pro record 71.
Visitors: Weekdays. **Green fees:** £17 per round, £25 per day.
Catering: Full, except limited on Mondays.
Facilities: Trolley hire, putting green, pro shop, practice ground.
Accommodation: Lynnhurst Hotel.

CARD OF THE COURSE

Hole	Yds	Par	Hole	Yds	Par
1	166	3	10	346	4
2	332	4	11	361	4
3	454	5	12	394	4
4	428	4	13	348	4
5	500	5	14	167	3
6	156	3	15	423	4
7	331	4	16	486	5
8	554	5	17	164	3
9	211	3	18	405	4
Out	3,132	36	In	3,094	35
Total	**6,226**		**Par**	**71**	

KEITH
KEITH GOLF CLUB

Address: Fife Park, Keith, Banffshire AB55 5DF (01542-882469).
Location: Leave A96 at Keith, taking Dufftown road. Turn first right then first left, then left again.
Secretary: Denis Shepherd.
Description: Undulating parkland course with greens renowned for their texture and consistency. Panoramic views of surrounding countryside. 18 holes, 5,802 yards. Par 69 (SSS 68).
Visitors: Any time. By appointment. **Green fees:** £10 per round weekdays, £12 per day. £12 per round weekends, £15 per day.
Catering: By arrangement. **Facilities:** Trolley hire, putting green, practice ground.
Accommodation: Grampian Hotel, Royal Hotel.
Signature hole: SEVENTH (232 yards, par three) – Out of bounds to left and behind the small green, which has a bunker to the right and slopes to the left.

KELSO
KELSO GOLF CLUB

Address: Golf Course Road, Kelso TD5 7SL (01573-223009).
Location: One mile north-east of Kelso Square, off B6461.
Secretary: J. Payne (01573-223259).
Description: Flat but testing parkland course within Kelso Racecourse. The Stank, a water hazard, crosses six holes. 18 holes, 6,046 yards. Par 70 (SSS 70). Amateur record 64 (J. Thomas).
Visitors: Yes, by arrangement. **Green fees:** £14 per round weekdays, £20 per day. £18 per round weekends, £27 per day.
Catering: Yes, except on Tuesdays. Bar.
Facilities: Trolley/buggy hire, putting green, practice ground.
Accommodation: Cross Keys Hotel, Queen's Head.
Signature hole: FIFTEENTH (176 yards, par three) – Tee shot to raised green protected by bunkers left and right.

CARD OF THE COURSE

Hole	Yds	Par	Hole	Yds	Par
1	427	4	10	268	4
2	177	3	11	439	4
3	151	3	12	215	3
4	395	4	13	369	4
5	434	4	14	350	4
6	284	4	15	176	3
7	434	4	16	330	4
8	493	5	17	298	4
9	315	4	18	491	5
Out	3,110	35	In	2,936	35
Total	**6,046**		**Par**	**70**	

THE ROXBURGHE GOLF CLUB

Address: Kelso, Roxburghshire TD5 8JZ (01573-450331).
Location: From Kelso to Jedburgh. In village of Heiton, follow signs to course.
General manager: David Webster. **Professional:** Gordon Niven.
Description: Long, demanding championship course in mature woodland. Hilly in parts. Two par threes have water hazards. 18 holes, 7,111 yards. Par 72 (SSS 74). Medal tees: par 68 (SSS 73). Opened March 1997.
Visitors: Yes. **Green fees:** £20 per round weekdays, £30 per day. £28 per round weekends, £40 per day.
Catering: Full catering. Bar.
Facilities: Trolley/buggy hire, putting green, pro shop, practice ground, driving range.
Accommodation: Sunlaws House Hotel.
Signature hole: FOURTEENTH (525 yards, par five) – Runs alongside river. From elevated tee you drive straight out towards old Roxburghe Viaduct.

KEMNAY
KEMNAY GOLF CLUB

Address: Monymusk Road, Kemnay, Aberdeenshire AB51 5RA (01467-643746;

Shop: 01467-642225).

Location: From A96 main Aberdeen to Inverness road, take B994 signposted Kemnay.

Secretary: Doug Imrie.

Description: Flat parkland course surrounded by mature trees. A stream crosses four holes. Superb views. 18 holes, 5,903 yards. Par 70 (SSS 69). Amateur record 69. Pro record 72.

Visitors: Yes. Book through shop. **Green fees:** £16 per round weekdays, £20 per day. £18 per round weekends, £22 per day.

Catering: Full catering. **Facilities:** Trolley/buggy hire, pro shop.

Accommodation: Burnett Arms.

CARD OF THE COURSE

Hole	Yds	Par	Hole	Yds	Par
1	352	4	10	308	4
2	282	4	11	326	4
3	340	4	12	208	3
4	180	3	13	498	5
5	374	4	14	403	4
6	386	4	15	420	4
7	348	4	16	356	4
8	160	3	17	170	3
9	488	5	18	304	4
Out	2,910	35	In	2,993	35
Total	**5,903**		**Par**	**70**	

KENMORE

KENMORE GOLF COURSE

Address: Kenmore, Aberfeldy, Perthshire PH15 2HN (01887-830226).

Location: On A827. West of Kenmore over bridge on right.

Manager: Robin Menzies.

Description: Mildly undulating, testing course for all abilities in magnificent Highland setting. Nine holes, 6,052 yards. Par 70 (SSS 69). Amateur record 70 (A. Cooper).

Visitors: Yes. **Green fees:** £10 per round weekdays, £12 per round weekends.

Catering: Full catering.

Facilities: Trolley/buggy hire, putting green, pro shop, practice ground.

Accommodation: Self-catering cottages by course.

CARD OF THE COURSE

Hole	Yds	Par
1	392	4
2	316	4
3	170	3
4	560	5
5	160	3
6	445	5
7	171	3

8	404	4
9	408	4
Out	3,026	35
Total	**6,052**	**Par**	**70**

TAYMOUTH CASTLE GOLF CLUB

Address: Taymouth Castle, Kenmore, Perthshire PH15 2LE (01887-830228).
Location: Six miles outside Aberfeldy on Killin road.
Description: Flat parkland course surrounded by hills and beautiful scenery. Rated as one of the most scenic courses in the UK. Easy walking. 18 holes, 6,066 yards. Par 69 (SSS 69). Course record 62.
Visitors: Any time. **Green fees:** £17 per round weekdays, £28 per day. £21 per round weekends, £38 per day.
Catering: Full service.
Facilities: Trolley/buggy hire, putting green, pro shop, practice ground.
Accommodation: Kenmore Hotel (25 per cent discount).

CARD OF THE COURSE

Hole	Yds	Par	Hole	Yds	Par
1	296	4	10	182	3
2	306	4	11	452	4
3	420	4	12	444	4
4	170	3	13	298	4
5	543	5	14	190	3
6	365	4	15	410	4
7	283	4	16	174	3
8	383	4	17	330	4
9	377	4	18	443	4
Out	3,143	36	In	2,923	33
Total	**6,066**		**Par**	**69**	

KILBIRNIE
KILBIRNIE PLACE GOLF CLUB

Address: Largs Road, Kilbirnie KA25 7AT (01505-683398).
Location: 14 miles from Paisley. One mile west of town on A760.
Description: Inland parkland course. Easy walking. 18 holes, 5,400 yards. Par 69 (SSS 67).
Visitors: Any time except Saturdays.
Green fees: £10 per round weekdays, £18 per day. £18 per round weekends.
Catering: Bar. **Facilities:** Putting green, practice ground.
Accommodation: Elderslie Hotel.

KILLIN
KILLIN GOLF CLUB

Address: Killin, Perthshire FK21 8TX (01567-820312).
Location: West end of Loch Tay on A827.

Secretary: S. Chisholm.
Description: Hilly parkland course. Very scenic. Nine holes, 5,016 yards. Par 66 (SSS 65). Course record 61.
Visitors: Yes. **Green fees:** £12 per round, £15 per day.
Catering: Yes.
Facilities: Trolley/buggy hire, putting green, pro shop, practice ground.
Accommodation: Dall Lodge Country House Hotel.
Signature hole: FIFTH (97 yards, par three) – Called 'The Dyke', the green is hidden behind a stone wall. Bunkered left, right and behind.

CARD OF THE COURSE

Hole	Yds	Par	
1	288	4	
2	211	3	
3	206	3	
4	361	4	
5	97	3	
6	327	4	
7	340	4	
8	159	3	
9	519	5	
Out	2,508	33	
Total	**5,016**	**Par**	**66**

KILMACOLM

KILMACOLM GOLF CLUB

Address: Porterfield Road, Kilmacolm, Renfrewshire PA13 4PD (01505-872139).
Location: South-east side of town off A761.
Secretary: R. McDonald. **Professional:** David Stewart.
Description: Situated on a plateau some 400 feet above sea level. Maximum use is made of natural hills and hollows, making this one of the most attractive inland courses. Course demands accurate driving and well-judged second shots. 18 holes, 5,961 yards. Par 69 (SSS 69).
Visitors: Weekdays only. Must be accompanied by a member.
Green fees: £20 per round, £30 per day.
Catering: Full facilities available.
Facilities: Trolley hire, putting green, pro shop, practice ground.
Accommodation: Gryffe Arms, Gleddoch House Hotel.

CARD OF THE COURSE

Hole	Yds	Par	Hole	Yds	Par
1	283	4	10	324	4
2	153	3	11	511	5
3	353	4	12	163	3
4	344	4	13	428	4
5	326	4	14	392	4
6	230	3	15	334	4
7	472	4	16	354	4

8	369	4	17	137	3
9	382	4	18	406	4
Out	2,912	34	In	3,049	35
Total	**5,961**		**Par**	**69**	

KILMARNOCK
ANNANHILL GOLF CLUB

Address: Irvine Road, Kilmarnock KA1 2RT (01563-521644).
Location: One mile west on A71.
Description: Municipal tree-lined parkland course. 18 holes, 6,269 yards. Par 71 (SSS 70). Course record 66.
Visitors: Book at starter's office. **Green fees:** £9 per round weekdays, £14.25 per day. £14.25 per round weekends, £17.50 per day.
Catering: By prior arrangement. Bar. **Facilities:** Putting green, practice ground.
Accommodation: Chapeltoun House Hotel.

CAPRINGTON GOLF CLUB

Address: Ayr Road, Kilmarnock KA1 4UW (01563-523702).
Location: One and a half miles south on B7038.
Description: Municipal parkland course with generous fairways and few hills. 18 holes, 5,718 yards. Par 69 (SSS 68).
Visitors: Not on Saturdays.
Green fees: £9.25 per round weekdays, £13.40 per round weekends.
Catering: Bar. **Facilities:** Pro shop.
Accommodation: Chapeltoun House Hotel.

KILSYTH
KILSYTH LENNOX GOLF CLUB

Address: Tak Ma Doon Road, Kilsyth G65 0RS (01236-824115; 01236-823089).
Location: North side of town, off A803.
Professional: R. Abercrombie.
Description: Hilly moorland course, hard walking. 18 holes, 5,912 yards. Par 70 (SSS 70). Course record 66.
Visitors: Contact in advance. No restrictions weekdays until 5 p.m. Not Saturdays but may play Sundays on application. **Green fees:** £10 per round weekdays, £16 per day. £12 per round weekends, £18 per day.
Catering: Full service. Bar. **Facilities:** Buggy hire, putting green, pro shop.
Accommodation: Kirkhouse Inn.

KINCARDINE
TULLIALLAN GOLF CLUB

Address: Alloa Road, Kincardine FK10 4BB (01259-730396).
Location: One mile north-west on A977.
Professional: Steven Kelly (01259-730798).

146

Description: Partially hilly parkland course, 18 holes, 5,982 yards. Par 69 (SSS 69).
Visitors: Yes. Restrictions on Saturdays. **Green fees:** £15 per round weekdays, £25 per day. £20 per round weekends, £30 per day.
Catering: Bar. **Facilities:** Pro shop.
Accommodation: Dall Lodge Country House Hotel.

KINGHORN
KINGHORN GOLF CLUB

Address: Macduff Crescent, Kinghorn KY3 9RE (01592-890345; Starter: 01592-890978).
Location: South side of town on A921.
Description: Municipal course 300 feet above sea level. Undulating and testing. 18 holes, 5,269 yards. Par 65 (SSS 67).
Visitors: Any time. **Green fees:** £11 per round weekdays, £14 per day. £14 per round weekends, £16 per day
Catering: Bar.
Accommodation: Dean Park Hotel.

KINGUSSIE
KINGUSSIE GOLF CLUB

Address: Kingussie PH21 1LR (01540-661600).
Location: Quarter of a mile north off A86.
Secretary: Norman MacWilliam.
Description: Hilly upland course. Very scenic. 1,000 feet above sea level at its highest point. River Gynack comes into play on five holes. 18 holes, 5,555 yards. Par 66 (SSS 68). Amateur record 63. Pro record 66.
Visitors: Yes, April to October. **Green fees:** £13.50 per round weekdays, £16.50 per day. £15.50 per round weekends, £20.50 per day.
Catering: Full. **Facilities:** Trolley/buggy hire, putting green, pro shop.
Accommodation: Columba House Hotel.

CARD OF THE COURSE

Hole	Yds	Par	Hole	Yds	Par
1	230	3	10	180	3
2	429	4	11	336	4
3	352	4	12	393	4
4	468	4	13	418	4
5	321	4	14	436	4
6	325	4	15	105	3
7	144	3	16	200	3
8	128	3	17	385	4
9	426	4	18	279	4
Out	2,823	33	In	2,732	33
Total	**5,555**		**Par**	**66**	

KINROSS
GREEN HOTEL GOLF COURSES

Address: Kinross Estate, 2 The Muirs, Kinross KY13 7AS (01577-863467).
Location: Off M90 at Junction 6. Into Kinross, turn left at mini roundabout. Golf courses are directly across.
Secretary: Mrs M. Smith. **Professional:** Stuart Geraghty (01577-865125).
Description: Two parkland courses. Easy walking. Unspoilt countryside further enhanced by planting of 15,000 additional trees.
Red Course: 18 holes, 6,245 yards. Par 72 (SSS 70).
Blue Course: 18 holes, 6,445 yards. Par 71 (SSS 71).
Visitors: Any time. **Green fees:** £15 per round weekdays, £25 per day. £25 per round weekends, £35 per day.
Catering: Clubhouse and hotel.
Facilities: Trolley/buggy hire, putting green, pro shop, practice ground.
Accommodation: Green Hotel.

KINTORE
KINTORE GOLF CLUB

Address: Balbithan Road, Kintore AB51 0UR (01467-632631).
Location: One mile from village on B977.
Description: Undulating moorland course, including mature woodland. 18 holes, 5,997 yards. Par 70 (SSS 69). Course record 64.
Visitors: Yes. **Green fees:** £10 per round weekdays, £13 per day. £15 per round weekends, £18 per day.
Catering: Yes. Bar. **Facilities:** Putting green, practice area.
Accommodation: Torryburn Hotel.

KIRKCALDY
DUNNIKIER PARK GOLF CLUB

Address: Dunnikier Way, Kirkcaldy KY1 3LP (01592-261599).
Location: From M90, join A92 for nine miles. Leave at junction marked Kirkcaldy West. On B981, one mile from A92.
Secretary: A. Waddell. **Professional:** Gregor Whyte.
Description: Municipal parkland course. Not hilly, and tree-lined. 18 holes, 6,601 yards. Par 72 (SSS 72). Course record 65.
Visitors: Societies by arrangement with secretary.
Green fees: 1996 rates: £11 per round weekdays, £19 per day. £15 per round weekends, £21 per day.
Catering: Full facilities.
Facilities: Trolley hire, putting green, pro shop, practice ground.
Accommodation: Dunnikier House Hotel, Dean Park Hotel.

CARD OF THE COURSE

Hole	Yds	Par	Hole	Yds	Par
1	423	4	10	366	4
2	385	4	11	163	3

3	201	3	12	597	5
4	358	4	13	305	4
5	501	5	14	198	3
6	157	3	15	418	4
7	371	4	16	333	4
8	383	4	17	397	4
9	547	5	18	498	5
Out	3,326	36	In	3,275	36
Total	**6,601**		**Par**	**72**	

KIRKCALDY GOLF CLUB

Address: Balwearie Road, Kirkcaldy KY2 5LT (01592-205240).
Location: South-west side of town off A910.
Secretary: Alistair Thomson. **Professional:** Scott McKay.
Description: Challenging parkland layout in lovely rural setting with good views over surrounding countryside and Firth of Forth. 18 holes, 6,004 yards. Par 71 (SSS 69).
Visitors: Weekdays and Sundays by prior arrangement (letter to secretary).
Green fees: £15 per round weekdays, £20 per day. £20 per round weekends, £30 per day.
Catering: Full service.
Facilities: Trolley/buggy hire, putting green, pro shop, practice ground.
Accommodation: Dunnikier House, Dean Park Hotel.
Signature hole: SEVENTEENTH (518 yards, par five) – A superb hole with the second shot from an elevated fairway to a green nestling across a burn. To go for it or not, that is the question.

CARD OF THE COURSE

Hole	Yds	Par	Hole	Yds	Par
1	330	4	10	275	4
2	230	3	11	385	4
3	332	4	12	542	5
4	390	4	13	153	3
5	540	5	14	430	4
6	330	4	15	310	4
7	120	3	16	369	4
8	300	4	17	518	5
9	310	4	18	140	3
Out	2,882	35	In	3,122	36
Total	**6,004**		**Par**	**71**	

KIRKCUDBRIGHT

KIRKCUDBRIGHT GOLF CLUB

Address: Stirling Crescent, Kirkcudbright DG6 4EZ (01557-330314).
Location: Enter town from A75 on A713. Take fourth road on left, and course is straight ahead.
Secretary: Norman Russell.

Description: Fairly hilly parkland course with lovely views over the historic town of Kirkcudbright and the Dee estuary. Hard walking. 18 holes, 5,696 yards (in process of being lengthened). Par 68 (SSS 68). Amateur record 63.
Visitors: Any time. Wednesday is gents' day.
Green fees: £15 per round, £20 per day.
Catering: Yes. **Facilities:** Trolley hire, putting green.
Accommodation: Selkirk Arms Hotel.
Signature hole: TWELFTH (455 yards, par five) – Dogleg. Drive from elevated tee over burn, landing area guarded by three bunkers. Elevated green with vicious gorse behind.

CARD OF THE COURSE

Hole	Yds	Par	Hole	Yds	Par
1	331	4	10	342	4
2	390	4	11	334	4
3	295	4	12	455	5
4	143	3	13	190	3
5	427	4	14	326	4
6	134	3	15	263	3
7	385	4	16	179	3
8	487	5	17	405	4
9	206	3	18	404	4
Out	2,798	34	In	2,898	34
Total	**5,696**		**Par**	**68**	

KIRKINTILLOCH
KIRKINTILLOCH GOLF CLUB

Address: Campsie Road, Kirkintilloch G66 1RN (0141-775-2387).
Location: One mile north-west, off A803.
Description: Parkland course. 18 holes, 5,269 yards. Par 70 (SSS 66).
Visitors: Must be introduced by member. **Green fees:** On application.
Facilities: Pro shop.
Accommodation: Kirkhouse Hotel.

KIRRIEMUIR
KIRRIEMUIR GOLF CLUB

Address: Shielhill Road, Northmuir DD8 4LN (01575-572144).
Location: One mile north, off B955.
Professional: Anthony Caira (01575-573317).
Description: Wooded parkland course with narrow fairways and small greens. Demands accuracy. 18 holes, 5,510 yards. Par 68 (SSS 67). Course record 62.
Visitors: Must play with member at weekends. Societies not at weekends.
Green fees: £16 per round, £22 per day.
Catering: Full service. Bar.
Facilities: Trolley hire, putting green, pro shop, practice ground.
Accommodation: Airlie Arms Hotel, Thrums Hotel.

Signature hole: SEVENTEENTH (195 yards, par three) – 'Braid's Gem', designed by James Braid. Approach shot, if landed front left, should run around on to green. (See diagram opposite.)

OUT OF BOUNDS

CARD OF THE COURSE

Hole	Yds	Par	Hole	Yds	Par
1	373	4	10	330	4
2	147	3	11	325	4
3	414	4	12	388	4
4	335	4	13	391	4
5	277	4	14	352	4
6	384	4	15	285	4
7	301	4	16	119	3
8	154	3	17	195	3
9	352	4	18	388	4
Out	2,737	34	In	2,773	34
Total	**5,510**		**Par**	**68**	

LADYBANK
LADYBANK GOLF CLUB

Address: Annsmuir, Ladybank, Cupar, Fife KY15 7RA (01337-830814).
Location: North side of village off B9129.
Professional: Martin Gray (01337-830725).
Description: Established in 1879, the course was originally six holes and designed by Old Tom Morris. It was expanded to nine holes in 1910 and 18 in 1961. The back nine remain relatively unchanged. Qualifying course for the Open. Jack Nicklaus and Seve Ballesteros are both honorary members. Inland heathland course set amongst heather, pine trees and silver birch. 18 holes, 6,641 yards. Par 71 (SSS 72). Amateur record 63 (Paul Stuart). Pro record 65 (Mark Brooks).
Visitors: Monday, Wednesday and Friday: 9.30 a.m. to 12 noon, 1.15 p.m. to 4 p.m. Tuesday and Thursday: 10 a.m. to 12 noon, 1.15 p.m. to 4 p.m. Saturday: no parties. Sunday: by arrangement.
Green fees: November to April: £19 per round weekdays, £27 per day. £25 weekends. May to October: £28 per round weekdays, £38 per day. £35 weekends.
Catering: Full service. Dining-room seats 80.
Facilities: Trolley/buggy hire, putting green, pro shop, practice ground.
Accommodation: Lundin Links Hotel, Balgeddie House Hotel, Royal Hotel.

CARD OF THE COURSE

Hole	Yds	Par	Hole	Yds	Par
1	374	4	10	165	3
2	548	5	11	407	4
3	391	4	12	243	3
4	166	3	13	528	5
5	344	4	14	417	4
6	372	4	15	390	4

7	543	5	16	398	4
8	159	3	17	387	4
9	401	4	18	408	4
Out	3,298	36	In	3,343	35
Total	**6,641**		**Par**	**71**	

LANARK
LANARK GOLF CLUB

Address: The Moor, Whitelees Road, Lanark ML11 7RX (01555-663219).
Location: East side of town off A73.
Secretary: George Cuthill. **Professional:** Alan White.
Description: Tough moorland course which is open to the prevailing wind. Club dates from 1851. 18 holes, 6,423 yards. Par 70 (SSS 71). Amateur record 64 (V. McInally). Pro record 62 (C. Maltman).
Visitors: Monday to Wednesday: 12 noon onwards.
Thursdays and Fridays: up to 12 noon.
Green fees: £23 per round, £35 per day.
Catering: Full.
Facilities: Trolley/buggy hire, putting green, pro shop, practice ground.
Accommodation: Cartland Bridge Hotel.
Signature hole: EIGHTEENTH (216 yards, par three) – Downhill to elevated green. (See diagram opposite.)

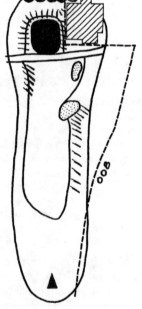

CARD OF THE COURSE

Hole	Yds	Par	Hole	Yds	Par
1	360	4	10	152	3
2	467	4	11	397	4
3	409	4	12	362	4
4	457	4	13	362	4
5	318	4	14	399	4
6	377	4	15	470	4
7	141	3	16	337	4
8	530	5	17	309	4
9	360	4	18	216	3
Out	3,419	36	In	3,004	34
Total	**6,423**		**Par**	**70**	

LANGHOLM
LANGHOLM GOLF CLUB

Address: Whitaside, Langholm, Dumfriesshire DG13 0JR (013873-81247; 013873-80673).
Location: Turn off Edinburgh to Carlisle road (A7) in Langholm at Post Office and follow signposts.
Secretary: W. Wilson.
Description: Pleasant hillside course with commanding views over the rolling

Border hills and south towards the Lake District. Nine holes, 5,744 yards. Par 70 (SSS 68). Amateur record 63 (G. Davidson).

Visitors: Any time, except Saturday and Sunday mornings.

Green fees: £10 per day.

Catering: By prior arrangement only. **Facilities:** Putting green, practice ground.

Accommodation: Eskdale Hotel, Crown Hotel, Buck Hotel.

Signature hole: SEVENTH (415 yards, par four) – Stroke Index 1. Tight drive with out of bounds on left and trees on right. Second shot needs touch of draw if you are to hit and stop on green.

CARD OF THE COURSE

Hole	Yds	Par	
1	295	4	
2	344	4	
3	180	3	
4	510	5	
5	175	3	
6	300	4	
7	415	4	
8	291	4	
9	362	4	
Out	2,872	35	
Total	**5,744**	**Par**	**70**

LARBERT

FALKIRK TRYST GOLF CLUB

Address: 86 Burnhead Road, Larbert FK5 4BD (01324-562415).

Location: West of Stenhousemuir on A88.

Secretary: R. Wallace (01324-562054).

Professional: Steven Dunsmore (01324-562091).

Description: Links course with sandy sub-soil. Mostly flat, tree-lined fairways. Large areas of gorse and whin bushes. 18 holes, 6,053 yards. Par 70 (SSS 69). Amateur record 62. Pro record 65.

Visitors: Weekdays only. **Green fees:** £15 per round, £25 per day.

Catering: Yes. Bar.

Facilities: Trolley hire, putting green, pro shop, practice ground.

Accommodation: Stakis Park Hotel, Cladman Hotel, Plough Hotel, Station Hotel, Red Lion, Commercial Hotel.

CARD OF THE COURSE

Hole	Yds	Par	Hole	Yds	Par
1	325	4	10	488	5
2	188	3	11	245	3
3	347	4	12	298	4
4	201	3	13	162	3
5	337	4	14	361	4
6	412	4	15	175	3
7	544	5	16	503	5

8	257	4	17	357	4
9	418	4	18	435	4
Out	3,029	35	In	3,024	35
Total	**6,053**		**Par**	**70**	

GLENBERVIE CLUBHOUSE

Address: Stirling Road, Larbert FK5 4SJ (01324-562605).
Location: Two miles north-west on A9.
Professional: John Chillas.
Description: Woodland parkland course with good views. 18 holes, 6,469 yards. Par 70 (SSS 70). Course record 65.
Visitors: Contact in advance. May not play at weekends. Societies Tuesdays and Thursdays only. **Green fees:** £30 per round weekdays, £45 per day.
Catering: Bar. **Facilities:** Pro shop.
Accommodation: Inchyra Grange Hotel.

LARGS

INVERCLYDE NATIONAL GOLF TRAINING CENTRE

Address: Burnside Road, Largs KA30 8RW (01475-674666).
Description: Six holes, training bunkers, driving range.
Visitors: Groups only, bookings in advance on a weekly residential basis.
Green fees: On application.

LARGS GOLF CLUB

Address: Irvine Road, Largs KA30 8EU (01475-674681).
Location: Off Irvine Road (A78), one mile south of Largs.
Secretary: D MacGillivray (01475-673594).
Professional: Bob Collinson (01475-686192).
Description: Parkland and woodland with scenic views over islands of Cumbrae and Arran. 18 holes, 6,237 yards. Par 70 (SSS 71). Amateur record 64 (Charles White). Pro record 65 (Mike McLaren).
Visitors: Any time by arrangement with secretary. Parties: Tuesdays and Thursdays. **Green fees:** £25 per round, £35 per day. Special packages for parties.
Catering: Full catering. Contact 01475-687390.
Facilities: Trolley/buggy hire, putting green, pro shop, practice nets.
Accommodation: Elderslie Hotel, Brisbane House Hotel, Queen's Hotel, Willowbank Hotel.
Signature hole: TENTH (398 yards, par four) – Spectacular avenue of trees to left on this dogleg demands a placed tee shot which opens up the green with the island of Arran as a backdrop. (See diagram opposite.)

CARD OF THE COURSE

Hole	Yds	Par	Hole	Yds	Par
1	150	3	10	398	4
2	405	4	11	416	4
3	476	5	12	496	5
4	206	3	13	378	4
5	305	4	14	152	3
6	365	4	15	469	4
7	412	4	16	340	4
8	162	3	17	350	4
9	392	4	18	365	4
Out	2,873	34	In	3,364	36
Total	**6,237**		**Par**	**70**	

ROUTENBURN GOLF CLUB

Address: Routenburn Road, Largs KA30 8QA (01475-673230).
Location: One mile north, off A78.
Professional: J. G. McQueen.
Description: Hilly heathland course with fine views over the Firth of Clyde. 18 holes, 5,675 yards. Par 68 (SSS 68).
Visitors: Any time. **Green fees:** £9 per round weekdays, £15 per day. £15 per round weekends, £20 per day.
Catering: Bar. **Facilities:** Buggy hire, pro shop.
Accommodation: Manor Park Hotel.

LARKHALL
LARKHALL GOLF CLUB

Address: Burnhead Road, Larkhall ML9 3AB (01698-881113).
Location: East side of town on B7019.
Description: Inland parkland course. Nine holes, 6,700 yards. Par 72 (SSS 71). Course record 69.
Visitors: Restricted Tuesdays and Saturdays.
Green fees: £2.90 for nine holes weekdays, £3.40 weekends.
Catering: Bar.
Accommodation: Popinjay Hotel.

LASSWADE
MELVILLE GOLF CENTRE

Address: South Melville, Lasswade, Midlothian EH18 1AN (0131-654-0224; 0131-663-8038).
Location: South of Edinburgh. Off A7 Galashiels road.
Proprietor: Colin Macfarlane. **Professional:** Garry Carter.
Description: Although nine holes has an 18-hole feel. Twisting fairways and a good test. Nine holes, 4,530 yards. Par 66. Course record 61.
Visitors: Yes. **Green fees:** £7 per nine holes weekdays, £9 weekends.
Catering: Hot and cold drinks. Snacks.

Facilities: Trolley hire, putting green, pro shop, practice ground, driving range.
Accommodation: Eskbank Hotel, Dalhousie Castle.
Signature hole: THIRD (151 yards, par three) – Steep hill to a green surrounded by bunkers.

LAUDER
ROYAL BURGH OF LAUDER GOLF CLUB

Address: Galashiels Road, Lauder TD2 6RS (01578-722526).
Location: A68 south. Turn right at Town Hall.
Secretary: D. Dickson.
Description: Undulating parkland course on hillside. Designed by Willie Park Jnr. Nine holes, 6,002 yards. Par 72 (SSS 69). Amateur record 66 (A. Lumsden). Pro record 70 (Willie Park Jnr).
Visitors: Yes, except Sunday mornings and Tuesday and Wednesday afternoons.
Green fees: £10.
Catering: No. Local hotels. **Facilities:** Putting green, practice ground.
Accommodation: Black Bull Hotel, Lauderdale Hotel, Eagle Hotel.
Signature hole: SIXTH (150 yards, par three) – Called 'The Quarry'. You have to carry to the green or end up in deep trouble.

CARD OF THE COURSE

Hole	Yds	Par	
1	374	4	
2	353	4	
3	252	4	
4	351	4	
5	405	4	
6	150	3	
7	482	5	
8	368	4	
9	266	4	
Out	3,001	36	
Total	**6,002**	**Par**	**72**

LEADHILLS
LEADHILLS GOLF CLUB

Address: Leadhills, Nr Biggar, Lanarkshire ML12 6XR.
Location: East side of village, off B797.
Description: Highest course in Scotland at 1,500 feet above sea level. Testing hilly moorland course, with high winds. Nine holes, 4,354 yards. Par 66 (SSS 64).
Visitors: Any time. **Green fees:** £6 per day.
Accommodation: Mennockfoot Lodge Hotel.

LESLIE
LESLIE GOLF CLUB

Address: Balsillie Laws, Leslie KY6 3EZ (01592-620040).

Location: 10 miles east of M90 from Junctions 5, 6 or 7.
Description: Flat parkland course. Nine holes, 4,686 yards. Par 63 (SSS 64). Course record 63.
Visitors: Contact in advance. **Green fees:** £8 per day, £10 weekends.
Catering: By prior arrangement.
Accommodation: Balgeddie House Hotel.

LEUCHARS

ST MICHAEL'S GOLF CLUB

Address: Leuchars, Fife KY16 0DX (01334-839365, 01334-838666).
Location: On A919 St Andrews to Dundee road. Five miles from St Andrews.
Secretary: R. Smith.
Description: Expanded to 18 holes in 1996. Undulating parkland course with trees and water hazard. 5,802 yards. Par 70 (SSS 68). Amateur record 69. Pro record 73.
Visitors: Any time, except Sunday mornings.
Green fees: £15 per round, £22.50 per day.
Catering: All day if required. **Facilities:** Trolley hire, putting green.
Accommodation: St Michael's Inn.
Signature hole: FIFTEENTH (157 yards, par three) – Elevated tee to raised green close to railway line.

CARD OF THE COURSE

Hole	Yds	Par	Hole	Yds	Par
1	415	4	10	352	4
2	168	3	11	360	4
3	341	4	12	156	3
4	443	4	13	391	4
5	307	4	14	486	5
6	337	4	15	157	3
7	176	3	16	337	4
8	261	4	17	265	4
9	502	5	18	348	4
Out	2,950	35	In	2,852	35
Total	**5,802**		**Par**	**70**	

LEVEN

LEVEN LINKS GOLF CLUB

Address: Balfour Street, Leven, Fife (01333-428859).
Location: On main Kirkcaldy to St Andrews road. 10 miles east of Kirkcaldy on Leven Promenade.
Secretary: J. Scott.
Description: A championship links used as a final qualifier for the Open. A traditional Scottish links with undulating fairways, hills, out of bounds and a burn. 18 holes, 6,435 yards. Par 71 (SSS 70). Amateur record 64. Pro record 63.
Visitors: Any time, except Saturdays. **Green fees:** £22 per round weekdays, £32 per day. £26 per round weekends, £38 per day.

Catering: Yes. Leven Thistle Golf Club.
Facilities: Trolley hire, putting green, pro shop, practice ground.
Accommodation: Caledonian Hotel, Old Manor Hotel, Lundin Links Hotel.
Signature hole: EIGHTEENTH (457 yards, par four) – Green fronted by burn.

CARD OF THE COURSE

Hole	Yds	Par	Hole	Yds	Par
1	413	4	10	325	4
2	381	4	11	363	4
3	343	4	12	482	5
4	449	4	13	482	5
5	158	3	14	332	4
6	567	5	15	188	3
7	184	3	16	386	4
8	348	4	17	414	4
9	164	3	18	457	4
Out	3,006	34	In	3,429	37
Total	**6,435**		**Par**	**71**	

SCOONIE GOLF CLUB

Address: North Links, Leven KY8 4SP (01333-427057).
Location: On coastal route between Kirkcaldy and St Andrews, close to Leven town centre.
Description: Pleasant inland course. Easy walking. Suitable for all ages. 18 holes, 5,456 yards. SSS 66.
Visitors: Any time. **Green fees:** £11 per round weekdays, £19 per day. £14 per round weekends, £21 per day.
Catering: Bar.
Accommodation: Caledonian Hotel.

LEWIS (Isle of)

STORNOWAY GOLF CLUB

Address: Lady Lever Park, Stornoway, Isle of Lewis H52 0XP (01851-702240).
Location: Half a mile out of town on Tarbert road.
Secretary: Huw Lloyd.
Description: Parkland course. Undulating but not too hilly. Excellent views to the north and east and to the mainland. 18 holes, 5,252 yards. Par 68 (SSS 67). Amateur record 62 (K. Galloway). Pro record 65 (J. Farmer).
Visitors: Any time, except Sundays. **Green fees:** £10 per day.
Catering: Light bar snacks available.
Facilities: Trolley/buggy hire, putting green, shop.
Accommodation: Caberfeidh Hotel.
Signature hole: ELEVENTH – A most challenging par five. Tee-shot has to be hit over a dip on to a steeply sloping fairway. Second shot has to be threaded through to two tree plantations with trees to the right and heather to the left, utilising the war memorial as a guide line.

LINLITHGOW
LINLITHGOW GOLF CLUB

Address: Braehead, Linlithgow, West Lothian EH49 6QF (01506-842585).
Location: Off Bathgate Road off A803.
Secretary: Tommy Thomson. **Professional:** Derek Smith.
Description: Undulating parkland course with panoramic views of the Forth Valley and beyond. Tricky fast greens. 18 holes, 5,729 yards. Par 70 (SSS 68).
Visitors: Yes. Not Saturdays. **Green fees:** £15 per round weekdays, £23 per day. £23 per round Sundays, £30 per day.
Catering: Yes. **Facilities:** Trolley hire, putting green, pro shop, practice ground.
Accommodation: West Port Hotel, Star and Garter Hotel.
Signature hole: SEVENTEENTH (169 yards, par three) – Downhill with difficulty in holding green. Bushes, rough and canal to contend with.

CARD OF THE COURSE

Hole	Yds	Par	Hole	Yds	Par
1	312	4	10	232	3
2	384	4	11	315	4
3	279	4	12	477	5
4	376	4	13	490	5
5	282	4	14	273	4
6	250	4	15	278	4
7	168	3	16	446	4
8	169	3	17	169	3
9	417	4	18	412	4
Out	2,637	34	In	3,092	36
Total	**5,729**		**Par**	**70**	

THE WEST LOTHIAN GOLF CLUB

Address: Airngath Hill, Linlithgow, West Lothian EH49 7RH (01506-826030).
Location: One mile south, off A706.
Professional: Neil Robertson.
Description: Undulating parkland course with superb views of Forth Valley. 18 holes, 6,406 yards. Par 71 (SSS 71). Course record 64.
Visitors: Weekends by arrangement. Contact in advance. **Green fees:** £15 per round weekdays, £20 per day. £20 per round weekends, £28 per day.
Catering: Full service. Bar.
Facilities: Trolley hire, putting green, pro shop, practice ground.
Accommodation: Earl O'Moray Inn.

LIVINGSTON
DEER PARK GOLF AND COUNTRY CLUB

Address: Golf Course Road, Livingston, West Lothian E54 8AD (01506-431037).
Location: Off M8, junction 3.
Secretary: R. Fyfe. **Professional:** Bill Yule.
Description: Championship course. Flat first nine, hilly second nine. Hosted regional qualifying for the Open and Scottish Professional Championship. 18 holes,

6,688 yards. Par 72 (SSS 72). Amateur record 67 (D. Thomson). Pro record 65 (Colin Brooks).
Visitors: Yes, any time. **Green fees:** £16 per round weekdays, £22 per day. £26 per round weekends, £35 per day.
Catering: All week.
Facilities: Trolley/buggy hire, putting green, pro shop, practice ground.
Accommodation: Deer Park Beefeater.
Signature hole: FOURTEENTH (par five) – Long uphill hole. Oxygen mask required.

LOCHCARRON
LOCHCARRON GOLF CLUB

Address: East End IV54 8YL (01520-722257).
Location: One mile east of village.
Description: Lochside links course with some parkland. Short, but great accuracy needed. Plans to extend to 18 holes. Nine holes, 3,500 yards. SSS 60.
Visitors: Restricted Friday evenings and Saturdays between 2 p.m. and 5 p.m.
Green fees: £7 per round, £10 per day.
Accommodation: Lochcarron Hotel.

LOCHGELLY
LOCHGELLY GOLF CLUB

Address: Cartmore Road, Lochgelly KY5 9PB (01592-780174).
Location: West of town, off A910.
Description: Parkland course. Easy walking. 18 holes, 5,491 yards. Par 68 (SSS 67).
Visitors: Any time. **Green fees:** £12 per round weekdays, £18 per day. £21 per round weekends, £27 per day.
Catering: Yes. Bar. **Facilities:** Putting green.
Accommodation: Dean Park Hotel.

LOCHGILPHEAD
LOCHGILPHEAD GOLF CLUB

Address: Blarbuie Road, Lochgilphead, Argyll PA31 8LE (01546-604230).
Location: From church in Lochgilphead, take Manse Brae towards Argyll and Bute Hospital. Turn left before hospital grounds.
Secretary: A. Law (01546-886302).
Description: Challenging parkland course in beautiful surroundings. Water hazards on five holes. Some tight fairways. Nine holes, 4,484 yards. Par 64 (SSS 63). Amateur record 58. Pro record 61.
Visitors: Any time, except during competitions.
Green fees: £10 per day. Juniors £5.
Catering: By arrangement for societies. **Facilities:** Putting green, practice ground.
Accommodation: Victoria Hotel, Stag Hotel, Argyll Hotel.
Signature hole: FIFTH (177 yards, par three) – Aptly named 'The Graveyard'. A 177-yard carry to a slightly elevated green with trees on both sides and a sloping fairway.

CARD OF THE COURSE

Hole	Yds	Par
1	366	4
2	370	4
3	114	3
4	257	4
5	177	3
6	392	4
7	139	3
8	264	4
9	163	3
Out	2,242	32
Total	**4,484**	**Par**	**64**

LOCHMABEN
LOCHMABEN GOLF CLUB

Address: Castlehillgate, Lochmaben, Lockerbie DG11 1NT (01387-810552).
Location: Four miles from Lockerbie, off A709.
Secretary: J. Dickie.
Description: Attractive parkland course between two lochs. Excellent scenery. 18 holes, 5,357 yards. Par 67 (SSS 66). Amateur record 62. Pro record 64.
Visitors: Weekdays; weekends by arrangement. **Green fees:** £14 per round weekdays, £16 per day. £16 per round weekends, £22 per day.
Catering: Yes. Bar. **Facilities:** Putting green, practice ground.
Accommodation: Balcastle Hotel, Kings Arms Hotel.
Signature hole: EIGHTH (120 yards, par three) – Over water.

CARD OF THE COURSE

Hole	Yds	Par	Hole	Yds	Par
1	314	4	10	143	3
2	188	3	11	425	4
3	190	3	12	522	5
4	311	4	13	445	4
5	359	4	14	343	4
6	404	4	15	141	3
7	291	4	16	426	4
8	120	3	17	328	4
9	295	4	18	132	3
Out	2,452	33	In	2,905	34
Total	**5,357**		**Par**	**67**	

LOCHWINNOCH
LOCHWINNOCH GOLF CLUB

Address: Burnfoot Road, Lochwinnoch PA12 4AN (01505-842153).
Location: West of town, off A760.
Professional: Gerry Reilly.

Description: Hilly parkland course with testing holes overlooking bird sanctuary. 18 holes, 6,243 yards. Par 71 (SSS 70).
Visitors: Not weekends and bank holidays unless accompanied by member. Restricted on competition days.
Green fees: £15 per round weekdays, £20 per day.
Catering: Bar. **Facilities:** Pro shop.
Accommodation: Bowfield Hotel and Country Club.

LOCKERBIE
HODDOM CASTLE GOLF CLUB
Address: Hoddom, Lockerbie, Dumfriesshire DG11 1AS (01576-300251).
Location: From A74(M), take Junction 19 (Ecclefechan). Follow signs to Hoddom Castle Caravan Park.
Description: Parkland holiday course bounded on one side by the River Annan. Short but testing. Nine holes, 4,548 yards. Par 68 (SSS 66).
Visitors: Any time. **Green fees:** £7–£8.
Catering: Restricted.
Accommodation: Ravenshill Hotel, Golf Hotel.
Signature hole: FIFTH – Dogleg left with River Annan running the full length of the hole on the right. Green is guarded by mature hardwoods.

LOCKERBIE GOLF CLUB
Address: Corrie Road, Lockerbie DG11 2ND (01576-202462; 01576-203363).
Location: East of town, off B7068.
Description: Parkland course with fine views. Only pond hole in Dumfriesshire. 18 holes, 5,614 yards. Par 68 (SSS 67). Course record 64.
Visitors: Restricted Sundays. Contact in advance. **Green fees:** £18 per day weekdays, £22 per day Saturdays, £18 per round Sundays.
Catering: Bar. **Facilities:** Trolley hire, putting green, practice ground.
Accommodation: Dryfesdale Hotel.

LONGNIDDRY
LONGNIDDRY GOLF CLUB
Address: Links Road, Longniddry, East Lothian EH32 0NL.
Location: From south and north, access from A1. Take slip road, signposted Cockenzie (A198) to Longniddry. Golf course access via Links Road.
Secretary: Neil Robertson (01875-852141).
Professional: John Gray (01875-852228).
Description: Mixture of parkland and links. No par fives. Out of bounds to left of 11 holes. Very scenic, overlooking the Firth of Forth to Fife. 18 holes, 6,219 yards. Par 68 (SSS 70). Amateur record 63 (R. Russell, J. Noon). Pro record 63 (C. Hardin).
Visitors: Monday to Thursday 9.30 a.m. to 4 p.m. Limited number of start times on Fridays. Three tee times allocated at 11.30 a.m. on Saturdays and 2.30 p.m. on Sundays.
Green fees: £27 per round weekdays, £38 per day. £35 per round weekends.

Catering: Full service. Snacks and meals as requested.
Facilities: Trolley hire, putting green, pro shop, practice ground.
Accommodation: Kilspindie House Hotel.
Signature hole: FIFTH (314 yards, par four) – Dogleg left to elevated double green. Trees on left, gorse and trees on right. Must hit upper tier of green

CARD OF THE COURSE

Hole	Yds	Par	Hole	Yds	Par
1	398	4	10	364	4
2	416	4	11	333	4
3	461	4	12	281	4
4	199	3	13	174	3
5	314	4	14	403	4
6	168	3	15	425	4
7	430	4	16	145	3
8	367	4	17	434	4
9	374	4	18	433	4
Out	3,127	34	In	3,092	34
Total	**6,219**		**Par**	**68**	

LONGSIDE
LONGSIDE GOLF CLUB
Address: West End Main Street, Longside, Peterhead AB4 (01779-821558).
Location: Six miles west of Peterhead on A950.
Description: Short, flat inland course with small greens. Nine holes, 3,992 yards. SSS 60.
Visitors: Not on Wednesday evenings or on Sundays before 10.30 a.m.
Green fees: £10 per round weekdays, £12 Saturdays, £16 Sundays.
Catering: Yes.

LOSSIEMOUTH
MORAY GOLF CLUB
Address: Lossiemouth IV31 6QS (01343-812018).
Location: North side of town.
Professional: Alistair Thomson.
Description: Two fine Scottish championship links courses, situated on the Moray Firth. Mild weather.
Old Moray: 18 holes, 6,643 yards. Par 71 (SSS 73).
New Moray: 18 holes, 6,005 yards. Par 69 (SSS 69).
Visitors: Contact in advance. **Green fees:** *Old Moray*: £22 per round weekdays, £32 per day. £33 per round weekends, £43 per day. *New Moray*: £17 per round weekdays, £22 per day. £22 per round weekends, £27 per day.
Facilities: Putting green, practice ground.
Accommodation: Stotfield Hotel.

LUNDIN LINKS
LUNDIN GOLF CLUB

Address: Golf Road, Lundin Links, Fife KY8 6BA (01333-320202).
Location: A915 Kirkcaldy to St Andrews road. From Kirkcaldy, through Leven into Lundin Links. Turn right in dip, left, right and left.
Secretary: David Thomson. **Professional:** David Webster (01333-320051).
Description: Principally links with four holes more akin to parkland. Every hole has the potential to ruin a card, even what may seem an innocuous short par four. Several holes have narrow burns crossing fairways. The old railway line provides an out-of-bounds area which runs through the course. Much praised for the quality of the greens which provide subtle borrows to test golfers of all levels. 18 holes, 6,394 yards. Par 71 (SSS 71). Amateur record 64. Pro record 63.
Visitors: Yes. Monday to Thursday 9 a.m. to 3.30 p.m.; Friday 9 a.m. to 3 p.m.; Saturday after 2.30 p.m. (Societies limited to 32.)
Green fees: £25 per round weekdays, £35 per day. £35 per round Saturdays.
Catering: Very welcome. Full facilities Tuesday to Saturday. Monday: hot soup, cold rolls. **Facilities:** Trolley hire, 18-hole putting green, pro shop, practice ground, practice net.
Accommodation: The Old Manor House Hotel, Lundin Links Hotel, Crusoe Hotel, Upper Largo Hotel.
Signature hole: FOURTEENTH (175 yards, par three) – Called 'Perfection', you'll understand why when you survey the shot in front of you. From an elevated tee, there is a magnificent view of the entire course and an outlook over the Firth of Forth. The green is virtually all carry with some impenetrable gorse bushes right on line with the flag. Green is surrounded by five bunkers. (See diagram opposite.)

CARD OF THE COURSE

Hole	Yds	Par	Hole	Yds	Par
1	424	4	10	353	4
2	346	4	11	466	4
3	335	4	12	150	3
4	452	4	13	512	5
5	140	3	14	175	3
6	330	4	15	418	4
7	273	4	16	314	4
8	364	4	17	345	4
9	555	5	18	442	4
Out	3,219	36	In	3,175	35
Total	**6,394**		**Par**	**71**	

LUNDIN LADIES GOLF CLUB

Address: Woodielea Road, Lundin Links, Fife KY8 6AJ (01333-320832).
Location: Follow A915 to St Andrews, turn left at Royal Bank of Scotland in Lundin Links.
Secretary: Mrs Elizabeth Davidson.

Description: Parkland course with coastal views. Nine holes, 4,730 yards. Par 68 (SSS 67).
Visitors: Yes. Restricted play on Wednesdays during season.
Green fees: £8 per day weekdays, £9.50 per day weekends.
Catering: No. **Facilities:** Trolley hire, putting green.
Accommodation: Old Manor Hotel, Lundin Links Hotel, Crusoe Hotel.
Signature hole: SECOND (262 yards, par four) – This fairway is home to famous ancient Roman standing stones.

CARD OF THE COURSE

Hole	Yds	Par	
1	327	4	
2	262	4	
3	355	4	
4	287	4	
5	309	4	
6	145	3	
7	234	4	
8	260	4	
9	186	3	
Out	2,365	34	
Total	**4,730**	**Par**	**68**

LUSS

LOCH LOMOND GOLF CLUB

The very title is evocative and exciting. It conjures up thoughts of spectacular Scottish scenery and the romance of one of the best-known old love songs recorded by, among many others, jazz great Benny Goodman at New York's Carnegie Hall. That Scottish–American link forged many years ago has been continued by the acquisition of the club three years ago by Arizona developer Lyle Anderson. Despite his Scottish-sounding name, however, the new owner does not have even a hint of tartan in his veins. Nor did the creator of the superlative four-course complex at Desert Mountain in Scottsdale have any intention of expanding his bulging portfolio (he also has huge interests in Hawaii and New Mexico) to include a Scottish golf club. Until Loch Lomond's imaginative and sensitive designer Tom Weiskopf bent his ear, that is.

In the early 1990s, Weiskopf and then partner Jay Morrish were recruited by London developer David Brench to create two courses on the bonnie, bonnie banks on a gorgeous piece of property leased from Sir Ivar Colquhoun of Luss, with the clan's ancestral home Rossdhu House as an imposing clubhouse.

'They will, of course, be the High Road and the Low Road,' Weiskopf proudly proclaimed before recessionary forces clamped down on Brench and many others like a bear trap. For a long time banks maintained the first course, the High Road, and Weiskopf feared for the future of his wonderful creation, the first Scottish course to be designed by an American. Eventually he and a close friend, renowned Scottish golf photographer Brian Morgan, prevailed upon a somewhat reluctant Lyle Anderson to at least look at the club. Within one hour of setting foot on the property he was so captivated that he decided there and then to buy it.

165

The result is one of the world of golf's most exclusive members-only golf clubs with a globally acclaimed course – and none other than Jack Nicklaus already signed up to start work on the Low Road, probably in 1997. Songs of praise for Weiskopf's work have been sung by such notables as 1996 Masters champion Nick Faldo, 1996 Open champion Tom Lehman and Europe's undisputed No. 1 Colin Montgomerie, a club member along with World No. 1 Greg Norman. Indeed, after his first look at the course on the eve of last year's hugely successful Loch Lomond World Invitational, Faldo exclaimed, 'This is the finest golf course in Europe and in fantastic condition. It simply cannot be faulted. This is the standard all other European courses have to strive to attain.'

From the championship tees it is a severe examination for the very best of players, but from forward tees – and Weiskopf has offered a varied selection – the course is eminently playable for the less skilled. There is a huge variety of trees, some many hundreds of years old, wildlife abounds and there is an overwhelming sense of serenity. Owner Lyle Anderson never tires of referring to 'the spirit of Loch Lomond', and there is definitely an indefinable 'something' in the air.

Each and every hole has its own charm and its own challenge. No two are alike, although the ninth and the 14th – the latter where Weiskopf almost lost his life in the quicksands of a peat bog during construction – are both driveable par fours under favourable conditions, while the sixth, at 625 yards all along the lochside, is the longest hole in Scottish golf.

Weiskopf is reluctant to select a so-called signature hole, but he is inordinately and justifiably proud of two of his creations. The 455-yard 10th hole, Arn Burn, is played downhill away from the loch, and as the tee shot arcs into the sky the ball can seem suspended against the mountain backdrop of the hillsides of Glen Fruin, and one can sense the ghosts of Rob Roy MacGregor and his marauding band. A burn cuts across the fairway, and a loch teeming with all kinds of aquatic activity guards the left of the green. It is, quite simply, a gem from both the visual and the physical aspects.

Tom's other favourite is the short 205-yard 17th, The Bay. He describes it as a 'classic par three', and in time it, and the other 17 holes, are destined to become as world famous as the song sung so enchantingly by such jazz legends as Maxine Sullivan and Martha Tilton.

Membership is exclusive and enquiries should be directed to 01436-860223. In the meantime, do everything legally possible to elicit an invitation to play with a member or a member of the excellent staff. The staff includes former Walker Cup player and captain Charlie Green who, at 64, beat his age by one towards the end of 1996. No wonder he has been scratch or better for 40 years – and gets to play Loch Lomond every day. It is a very special place.

Alister Nicol

Address: Rossdhu House, Luss G83 8NT (01436-860223).
Location: Take Luss turn-off on A82.
Professional: Colin Campbell.
Description: 18 holes, 7,060 yards. Par 71 (medal par 72, SSS 74).
Visitors: May only play as guests of members.
Catering: Full service. Bar. **Facilities:** Putting green, pro shop, practice ground.
Signature hole: TENTH (455 yards, par four) – Weiskopf says, 'Hitting the fairway is a must. The pond on the left does not really threaten the second shot, as

it is much further from the big receptive green, which will accept long shots, than it looks.' (See diagram opposite.)

CARD OF THE COURSE

Hole	Yds	Par	Hole	Yds	Par
1	425	4	10	455	4
2	455	4	11	235	3
3	505	5	12	415	4
4	385	4	13	560	5
5	190	3	14	345	4
6	625	5	15	415	4
7	440	4	16	480	4
8	155	3	17	205	3
9	340	4	18	430	4
Out	3,520	36	In	3,540	35
Total	**7,060**		**Par**	**71**	

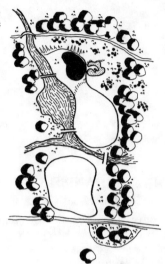

LYBSTER
LYBSTER GOLF CLUB
Address: Main Street, Lybster KW3 6AE (01593-721201).
Location: East of village.
Description: Short heathland course. Easy walking. Nine holes, 3,792 yards. Par 62 (SSS 62).
Visitors: Any time. **Green fees:** £6 per day.
Accommodation: Portland Arms Hotel.

MACDUFF
ROYAL TARLAIR GOLF CLUB
Address: Buchan Street, Macduff AB44 1TA (01261-832897).
Location: From Deveron Bridge at Banff take the Shore Road to Fraserburgh. As you leave Macduff, course is on left.
Secretary: Mrs Mary Law.
Description: Seaside cliff-top links course. 18 holes, 5,866 yards. Par 71 (SSS 68). Course record 64.
Visitors: Very welcome. No problem weekdays. Advance booking for weekends.
Green fees: £10 per round weekdays, £15 per day. £15 per round weekends, £20 per day. £50 for 7 days.
Catering: Full catering all summer.
Facilities: Trolley/buggy hire, putting green, shop.
Accommodation: The Highland Haven Hotel.
Signature hole: THIRTEENTH (152 yards, par three) – Testing tee shot over a gully.

CARD OF THE COURSE

Hole	Yds	Par	Hole	Yds	Par
1	292	4	10	353	4

2	365	4	11	345	4
3	125	3	12	331	4
4	477	5	13	152	3
5	289	4	14	276	4
6	410	4	15	363	4
7	176	3	16	477	5
8	483	5	17	221	3
9	351	4	18	380	4
Out	2,968	36	In	2,898	35
Total	**5,866**		**Par**	**71**	

MACHRIHANISH
MACHRIHANISH GOLF CLUB

Address: Machrihanish, Campbeltown, Argyll PA28 6PT (01586-810213).

Location: Situated 160 miles from Glasgow on Kintyre peninsula. A82 to Tarbet on Loch Lomond, then A83 via Inveraray and Lochgilphead. 25 minutes by air from Glasgow Airport.

Secretary: Anna Anderson. **Professional:** Ken Campbell (01586-810277).

Description: Has a world-wide reputation as a first-class natural links course. Described in 1878 by Old Tom Morris as 'specifically designed by the Almighty for playing golf', little has changed to disturb the natural scenic beauty and inspiring challenge. Outward nine follow the hills and hollows along the sand dunes bordering the Atlantic. Each hole requires accurate tee shots and carefully chosen irons to reach the expertly maintained greens. Inward stretch is no less demanding. Two par fives and three tricky par threes have to be negotiated until, within sight of the clubhouse, the Machrihanish burn has to be driven while avoiding the out of bounds which borders the final two holes. 18 holes, 6,228 yards. Par 70 (SSS 71).

Visitors: Yes. Contact professional to reserve tee times.

Green fees: £21 per round Sunday to Friday, £30 per day. £36 per day Saturday.

Catering: By arrangement with club steward.

Facilities: Trolley/buggy hire, putting green, pro shop, practice ground.

Accommodation: Balegreggan Country House, Ardshiel Hotel, Argyll Arms Hotel, Ardell House, White Hart Hotel, Putechan Lodge, Seafield Hotel.

Signature hole: FIRST (423 yards, par four) – Has been voted the finest in the world. You open with a challenging and spectacular drive across Machrihanish Bay.

CARD OF THE COURSE

Hole	Yds	Par	Hole	Yds	Par
1	423	4	10	497	5
2	395	4	11	197	3
3	376	4	12	505	5
4	123	3	13	370	4
5	385	4	14	442	4
6	315	4	15	167	3
7	432	4	16	233	3
8	337	4	17	362	4
9	354	4	18	315	4

| Out | 3,140 | 35 | In | 3,088 | 35 |
| Total | **6,228** | | **Par** | **70** | |

MARKINCH
BALBIRNIE PARK GOLF CLUB

Address: Balbirnie Park, Markinch KY7 6NR (01592-752006).
Location: Two miles east of Glenrothes.
Description: Scenic parkland course with several interesting holes. 18 holes, 6,214 yards. Par 71 (SSS 70). Course record 65.
Visitors: Contact in advance. Numbers restricted at weekends. Visitors must play from yellow tees. **Green fees:** £20 per round weekdays, £28 per day. £28 per round weekends, £36 per day.
Catering: Full service. Bar. **Facilities:** Trolley hire, putting green, pro shop.
Accommodation: Balbirnie House Hotel.

MAUCHLINE
BALLOCHMYLE GOLF CLUB

Address: Catrine Road, Mauchline KA5 6LE (01290-550469).
Location: One mile south-east on B705.
Description: Wooded parkland course. Burns out of bounds, and small undulating greens guarded by bunkers. 18 holes, 5,952 yards. Par 70 (SSS 69). Course record 65.
Visitors: Not Mondays from October to March, except with member.
Green fees: £18 per round weekdays, £25 per day. £30 per day weekends.
Catering: Yes, by prior arrangement. Bar.
Facilities: Trolley hire, putting green, pro shop, practice ground.
Accommodation: The Royal Hotel.

MAYBOLE
MAYBOLE GOLF CLUB

Address: Memorial Park, Maybole KA19 7DX (01292-282842).
Location: 10 miles south of Ayr on Girvan road.
Professional: Philip Cheyney.
Description: Parkland course situated on hill. Nine holes, 5,270 yards. Par 66 (SSS 66). Course record 64.
Visitors: Any time. **Green fees:** £7 per round, £11 per day.
Accommodation: Ladyburn Hotel.

MELROSE
MELROSE GOLF CLUB

Address: Dingleton TD6 9HS (01896-822855; 01896-822391).
Location: South side of town on B6359.
Description: Set at foot of Eildon Hills. Undulating tree-lined fairways with splendid views. Nine holes, 5,579 yards. Par 70 (SSS 68). Course record 61.

Visitors: Yes, but competitions have priority on all Saturdays and many Sundays (April to October). Ladies have priority on Tuesdays. Juniors have priority on Wednesday mornings in holidays. **Green fees:** £15 per round/day.
Catering: Yes, by prior arrangement. Bar. **Facilities:** Practice ground.
Accommodation: Burt's Hotel.

MILNATHORT
MILNATHORT GOLF CLUB LTD

Address: South Street, Milnathort KY13 7XA (01577-864069).
Location: One mile north of Kinross. M90 junction 6 (north) or junction 7 (south).
Secretary: K. Dziennik.
Description: Undulating parkland course. Lush fairways and excellent greens. Nine holes, 5,993 yards. Par 71 (SSS 69). Course record 65.
Visitors: Yes, apart from Saturdays. **Green fees:** £10 per round weekdays, £15 per day. £14 per round weekends, £18 per day.
Catering: Bar. **Facilities:** Putting green, practice ground, driving range.
Accommodation: Thistle Hotel, Jolly Beggars Hotel, Royal Hotel.
Signature Hole: SEVENTH (451 yards, par four) – Trying to get home in two causes all sorts of problems. Bunkers and trees make for a difficult second shot.

CARD OF THE COURSE

Hole	Yds	Par	
1	403	4	
2	328	4	
3	286	4	
4	141	3	
5	380	4	
6	495	5	
7	451	4	
8	205	3	
9	277	4	
Out	2,966	35	
Total	**5,993**	**Par**	**71**

MINTO
MINTO GOLF CLUB

Address: Minto, Hawick TD9 8SH (01450-870220).
Location: Five miles north-east of Hawick. Leave A698 at Denholm.
Secretary: I. Todd.
Description: Wooded parkland. Not a long course but quite testing. Fine views. 18 holes, 5,453 yards. Par 68 (SSS 67). Amateur record 63.
Visitors: Very welcome. Phone for tee times. **Green fees:** £15–£25. Discounts for parties. Tourist Board Freedom of Fairways scheme.
Catering: Full, except Thursdays.
Facilities: Trolley/buggy hire, putting green, practice ground.
Accommodation: Kirklands Hotel.

Signature hole: TWELFTH (267 yards, par four) – Short, steep uphill. Called 'Everest'. Drive through trees. Approach to shelf green.

CARD OF THE COURSE

Hole	Yds	Par	Hole	Yds	Par
1	396	4	10	252	4
2	309	4	11	369	4
3	421	4	12	267	4
4	236	3	13	311	4
5	248	4	14	409	4
6	226	3	15	355	4
7	188	3	16	297	4
8	347	4	17	122	3
9	325	4	18	375	4
Out	2,696	33	In	2,757	35
Total	**5,453**		**Par**	**68**	

MOFFAT
THE MOFFAT GOLF CLUB

Address: Coatshill, Moffat DG10 9SB (01683-220020).
Location: Leave A74 at Beattock. A701 to Moffat for one mile.
Secretary: T. Rankin.
Description: Scenic moorland course. Overlooks the town. 18 holes, 5,263 yards. Par 69 (SSS 67). Amateur record 60.
Visitors: Any time, except Wednesdays from noon onwards.
Green fees: £18 per round weekdays, £20 per day. £27.50 per day weekends.
Catering: Meals Monday to Friday 11 a.m. to 2.30 p.m. (Wednesdays 6 p.m. to 9 p.m.) Weekends 11 a.m. to 8 p.m.
Facilities: Trolley/buggy hire, putting green, shop.
Accommodation: Moffat House Hotel.
Signature hole: NINTH (125 yards, par three) – Not the best but certainly the best-known hole on the course. Hitting over a rock face to an elevated green will remain in your memory for a long time.

CARD OF THE COURSE

Hole	Yds	Par	Hole	Yds	Par
1	203	3	10	342	4
2	331	4	11	381	4
3	346	4	12	251	4
4	292	4	13	141	3
5	291	4	14	505	5
6	267	4	15	364	4
7	334	4	16	144	3
8	390	4	17	285	4
9	125	3	18	271	4
Out	2,579	34	In	2,684	35
Total	**5,263**		**Par**	**69**	

MONREITH

ST MEDAN GOLF CLUB

Address: Monreith, Port William, Newton Stewart DG8 8NJ (01988-700358).
Location: One mile south-east off A747.
Secretary: E. Richards.
Description: Links course. Fairly fast greens. Magnificent views of the Solway and Isle of Man. Nine holes, 4,454 yards. Par 64 (SSS 62). Course record 61.
Visitors: All year round. Societies April to September.
Green fees: £12 per round, £15 per day.
Catering: Full. **Facilities:** Putting green.
Accommodation: Corsemalzie House Hotel.

CARD OF THE COURSE

Hole	Yds	Par	
1	220	3	
2	270	4	
3	205	3	
4	274	4	
5	276	4	
6	340	4	
7	273	4	
8	233	3	
9	186	3	
Out	2,227	32	
Total	**4,454**	**Par**	**64**

MONTROSE

MONTROSE LINKS TRUST

Address: Traill Drive, Montrose DD10 8SW (01674-672932).
Location: From south follow A90, turn off at Brechin and take A935 to Montrose.
Secretary: Mrs M. Stewart.
Professional: Kevin Stables (01674-672634).
Description: Links on common land, shared by three clubs. Medal Course is the fifth-oldest in the world. Typical of Scottish seaside links with narrow undulating fairways, it stretches along the dunes from the first to the seventh holes and then turns landward. Broomfield Course is flatter and easier.
Medal Course: 18 holes, 6,470 yards. Par 71 (SSS 72). Course record 64.
Broomfield Course: 18 holes, 4,815 yards. Par 66 (SSS 63).
Visitors: Not on Medal Course on Saturdays and not before 10 a.m. on Sundays. Must have

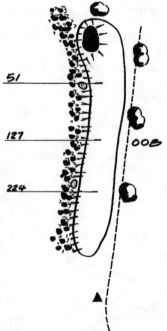

51

127

224

OOB

handicap certificate and contact in advance. No restrictions on Broomfield Course.

Green fees: *Medal Course*: £20 per round weekdays, £30 per day. £28 per round weekends, £42 per day. *Broomfield Course*: £10 per round weekdays, £14 weekends.

Catering: Full service. Bar.

Facilities: Trolley hire, putting green, pro shop, practice ground.

Accommodation: Park Hotel, Links Hotel.

Signature hole: SEVENTEENTH (418 yards, par four) – A truly testing hole on the Medal Course with out of bounds all down the right, trouble on the left and an elevated green. (See diagram on previous page.)

CARD OF THE MEDAL COURSE

Hole	Yds	Par	Hole	Yds	Par
1	391	4	10	379	4
2	391	4	11	444	4
3	154	3	12	150	3
4	365	4	13	320	4
5	292	4	14	414	4
6	489	5	15	541	5
7	368	4	16	235	3
8	329	4	17	418	4
9	444	4	18	346	4
Out	3,223	36	In	3,247	35
Total	**6,470**		**Par**	**71**	

MOTHERWELL

COLVILLE PARK GOLF CLUB

Address: Jerviston Estate, Merry Street, Motherwell ML1 3AP (01698-265779).

Location: One and a half miles north-east from Motherwell Cross and railway station.

Description: Parkland course. First nine mature, tree-lined. Back nine more open. Relatively flat. 18 holes, 6,265 yards. Par 71 (SSS 70). Amateur record 66. Pro record 65.

Visitors: Weekdays. Parties must book through secretary. **Green fees:** £20 per day.

Catering: Full catering available.

Facilities: Putting green, pro shop, practice ground.

Accommodation: Moorings Hotel.

Signature hole: SIXTH (315 yards, par four) – Mature, tree-lined. Picturesque approach to raised green.

CARD OF THE COURSE

Hole	Yds	Par	Hole	Yds	Par
1	204	3	10	180	3
2	421	4	11	400	4
3	429	4	12	486	5
4	162	3	13	492	5
5	264	4	14	386	4
6	315	4	15	260	4

7	416	4	16	444	4
8	533	5	17	190	3
9	388	4	18	295	4
Out	3,132	35	In	3,133	36
Total	**6,265**		**Par**	**71**	

MUCKHART
MUCKHART GOLF CLUB LTD

Address: Muckhart, by Dollar FK14 7JN (01259-781423).
Location: Off A91 south-west of village.
Secretary: A. Robertson. **Professional:** Keith Salmoni.
Description: Heathland, parkland course with first nine holes ascending. Second nine open and undulating with magnificent scenic views of Ochil Hills and Lothians. 18 holes, 6,034 yards. Par 71 (SSS 70). Amateur record 66.
Visitors: Yes. Weekdays after 9.30 a.m. Weekends reserved for visitors between 10 a.m. and 12 noon, and between 2.30 p.m. and 4.30 p.m. **Green fees:** £15 per round weekdays, £22 per day. £22 per round weekends, £30 per day.
Catering: Yes.
Facilities: Trolley/buggy hire, putting green, pro shop, practice ground.
Accommodation: Castle Campbell Hotel.
Signature hole: EIGHTEENTH (535 yards, par five) – Heather in front of the tee with rough to the left and water to the right. The approach to the green is over a burn. A generous fairway but straight driving required.

CARD OF THE COURSE

Hole	Yds	Par	Hole	Yds	Par
1	269	4	10	109	3
2	300	4	11	374	4
3	291	4	12	429	4
4	170	3	13	326	4
5	361	4	14	424	4
6	196	3	15	279	4
7	525	5	16	449	4
8	484	5	17	309	4
9	204	3	18	535	5
Out	2,800	35	In	3,234	36
Total	**6,034**		**Par**	**71**	

MUIR OF ORD
MUIR OF ORD GOLF CLUB

Address: The Great North Road, Muir of Ord IV6 6SX (01463-870825).
Location: South of village on A862.
Professional: Graham Vivers.
Description: Established 1875. Heathland course with tight fairways and easy walking. 18 holes, 5,202 yards. Par 67 (SSS 66). Course record 61.
Visitors: Not before 11 a.m. weekends without prior agreement and not during club

competitions. **Green fees:** £12.50 per round weekdays, £14.50 per day. £16.50 per round weekends, £18.50 per day.
Catering: Yes, by prior arrangement. Bar.
Facilities: Trolley hire, putting green, pro shop, practice ground.
Accommodation: Priory Hotel.

MULL (Isle of)
CRAIGNURE GOLF CLUB

Address: Scallastle, Isle of Mull, Argyll PA65 6PB.
Location: One mile from Oban to Craignure ferry terminal.
Secretary: D. Howitt, The Pierhead, Craignure PA65 6AY (01680-812487; 01680-300402).
Description: Links course first laid out in 1895. Nine holes, 5,072 yards. Par 70 (SSS 65). Amateur record 68.
Visitors: Most times except when Sunday competitions are played.
Green fees: £10 per round, £12 per day.
Catering: No catering. Clubhouse open to visitors.
Accommodation: Isle of Mull Hotel.
Signature hole: SEVENTH (soon to be extended to 475 yards, par five) – Out of bounds on left, wicked river to play over. Beach to the right – a very long lateral water hazard. Not for the faint-hearted.

CARD OF THE COURSE

Hole	Yds	Par
1	255	4
2	270	4
3	255	4
4	328	4
5	120	3
6	392	4
7	448	5
8	217	3
9	251	4
Out	2,536	35
Total	**5,072**	**Par** 70

TOBERMORY GOLF CLUB

Address: Tobermory, Isle of Mull, Argyll PA75 6PS (01688-302020).
Location: Above the town of Tobermory.
Secretary: J. Weir.
Description: A cliff-top course with small but good greens. Magnificent views from all parts of the course. Nine holes, 4,890 yards. Par 64 (SSS 64). Amateur record 65 (G. Davidson).
Visitors: Yes, most days. **Green fees:** £12 per day.
Catering: No. **Facilities:** Practice ground.
Accommodation: Fairways Lodge, on the course. Western Isles Hotel.
Signature hole: SEVENTH (142 yards, par three) – Difficult hole with out of

bounds close on the right. Rocks behind and a steep slope in front of the two-tiered green.

CARD OF THE COURSE

Hole	Yds	Par	
1	356	4	
2	359	4	
3	230	3	
4	208	3	
5	274	4	
6	398	4	
7	142	3	
8	358	4	
9	120	3	
Out	2,445	32	
Total	**4,890**	**Par**	**64**

MUSSELBURGH
THE MUSSELBURGH GOLF CLUB
Address: Monktonhall, Musselburgh EH21 6SA (0131-665-2005).
Location: One mile south on B6415.
Professional: Fraser Mann.
Description: Testing parkland course with natural hazards, including a burn. 18 holes, 6,614 yards. Par 71 (SSS 73). Course record 65.
Visitors: Contact in advance. **Green fees:** £17 per round weekdays, £25 per day. £21 per round weekends, £30 per day.
Catering: Full service. Bar.
Facilities: Trolley/buggy hire, putting green, pro shop, practice ground.
Accommodation: Donmaree Hotel.

MUSSELBURGH OLD COURSE GOLF CLUB
Address: Musselburgh Links, Millhill EH21 7RP (0131-665-6981; Starter: 0131-665-5438).
Location: One mile east of town, off A1.
Description: Possibly the first proper golf course. The game was played here as long ago as 1672. Some records claim Mary, Queen of Scots played the course. Within Musselburgh Racecourse. Nine holes, 4,742 yards. Par 66 (SSS 66). Course record 67.
Visitors: Not at weekends. **Green fees:** £9.60 per round.
Catering: Bar.
Accommodation: Donmaree Hotel.

MUTHILL
MUTHILL GOLF CLUB
Address: Peat Road, Muthill, Perthshire PH5 2DA (01764-681523).
Location: Two miles from Crieff on outskirts of village.

Description: Parkland course of reasonably level terrain. Tight fairways and small greens. Nine holes, 4,700 yards. Par 66 (SSS 63). Amateur record 61. Pro record 67.
Visitors: Yes, except Wednesday and Thursday evenings.
Green fees: £12 per day weekdays, £15 per day weekends.
Catering: Yes. **Facilities:** Trolley hire.
Accommodation: Drummond Arms.
Signature hole: NINTH (205 yards, par three) – Small, very difficult green to land on with tempting out of bounds on right.

CARD OF THE COURSE

Hole	Yds	Par	
1	224	4	
2	186	3	
3	268	4	
4	274	4	
5	144	3	
6	395	4	
7	322	4	
8	332	4	
9	205	3	
Out	2,350	33	
Total	**4,700**	**Par**	**66**

NAIRN

NAIRN DUNBAR GOLF CLUB

Address: Lochloy Road, Nairn IV12 5AE (01667-452741).
Location: Off A96.
Secretary: Mrs S. MacLennan. **Professional:** Brian Mason.
Description: Championship links with gorse- and whin-lined fairways. Medium greens. 18 holes, 6,712 yards. Par 72 (SSS 73).
Visitors: Yes. Weekdays preferred. **Green fees:** £23 per round weekdays, £28 per day. £28 per round weekends, £35 per day.
Catering: Yes. **Facilities:** Trolley hire, putting green, pro shop, practice ground.
Accommodation: Links Hotel, Claymore Hotel, Golf View Hotel.
Signature hole: THIRTEENTH (529 yards, par five) – Stroke Index 6, but 'Long Peter' is one of the most testing on the course.

CARD OF THE COURSE

Hole	Yds	Par	Hole	Yds	Par
1	418	4	10	414	4
2	333	4	11	126	3
3	189	3	12	381	4
4	448	4	13	529	5
5	453	4	14	346	4
6	419	4	15	161	3
7	395	4	16	503	5
8	155	3	17	442	4
9	501	5	18	499	5

Out	3,311	35	In	3,401	37
Total	**6,712**		**Par**	**72**	

THE NAIRN GOLF CLUB

Address: Seabank Road, Nairn IV12 4HB. (01667-453208).
Location: 15 miles east of Inverness. From Inverness, turn left at church with tower along Seabank Road. From Aberdeen, on A96, turn right at church with tower.
Secretary: James Somerville. **Professional:** Robin Fyfe.
Description: Traditional Scottish links. A championship course, which was the venue for the Amateur Championship in 1994 and will be hosting the 37th Walker Cup in 1999. Fast greens. Founded in 1887 and designed by Old Tom Morris, James Braid and A. Simpson. 18 holes, 6,745 yards. Par 72 (SSS 74). Amateur record 66 (S. Tomisson). Pro record 65 (D. Small).
Visitors: Yes.
Green fees: £40 weekdays, £50 weekends.
Catering: Full facilities all year round. Restricted in winter.
Facilities: Trolley hire, putting green, pro shop, practice ground, driving range.
Accommodation: The Golf View, the Newton Hotel.
Signature hole: FOURTEENTH (221 yards, par three) – Out of bounds on left. 191 yards to the front of the two-tiered green, which is guarded by bunkers right and left. Picturesque hole. (See diagram opposite.)

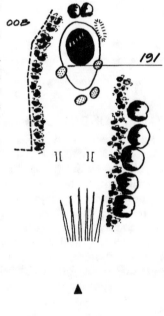

CARD OF THE COURSE

Hole	Yds	Par	Hole	Yds	Par
1	400	4	10	540	5
2	499	5	11	163	3
3	400	4	12	445	4
4	146	3	13	435	4
5	390	4	14	221	3
6	185	3	15	309	4
7	552	5	16	424	4
8	359	4	17	364	4
9	358	4	18	555	5
Out	3,289	36	In	3,456	36
Total	**6,745**		**Par**	**72**	

NETHY BRIDGE
ABERNETHY GOLF CLUB

Address: Nethy Bridge PH25 3EB (01479-821305).
Location: B970 Nethy Bridge to Grantown-on-Spey.
Description: Interesting moorland course. Nine holes, 5,040 yards. Par 66 (SSS 66). Amateur record 61 (I. Murray).

Visitors: Any time, except during club competitions.
Green fees: £10 per day weekdays, £12 per day weekends.
Catering: Yes, April to October. **Facilities:** Trolley/buggy hire, putting green.
Accommodation: Mountview Hotel, Nethy Hotel, Heatherbrae Hotel.

NEWBURGH-ON-YTHAN
NEWBURGH-ON-YTHAN GOLF CLUB

Address: Newburgh Links, Newburgh-on-Ythan AB41 0FD (01358-789058; 01358-789436).
Location: East of village on A975.
Description: Seaside course founded in 1888. Adjacent to bird sanctuary. 18 holes, 6,162 yards. Par 72 (SSS 69).
Visitors: Contact in advance.
Green fees: £13 per day weekdays, £15 weekends.
Catering: Snacks. **Facilities:** Practice ground.
Accommodation: Udny Arms Hotel.

NEWCASTLETON
NEWCASTLETON

Address: Newcastleton Golf Club, Holm Hill, Newcastleton TD9 0QD (01387-375257).
Location: From Carlisle, M6 to A7. Turn off Canonbie/Newcastleton.
Secretary: F. Ewart.
Description: Hilly course with several very steep holes. Nine holes, 5,748 yards. Par 70 (SSS 68).
Visitors: Any time, except on competition weekends.
Green fees: £7 weekdays, £8 weekends.
Catering: If required. **Facilities:** Putting green.
Accommodation: Local hotels.
Signature hole: NINTH (521 yards, par five) – Dogleg right.

CARD OF THE COURSE

Hole	Yds	Par	
1	396	4	
2	153	3	
3	386	4	
4	312	4	
5	163	3	
6	322	4	
7	299	4	
8	322	4	
9	521	5	
Out	2,874	35	
Total	**5,748**	**Par**	**70**

NEW CUMNOCK
NEW CUMNOCK GOLF CLUB
Address: Lochill, New Cumnock, Ayrshire KA18 4PN (01290-338848).
Location: North-west of New Cumnock on A76.
Secretary: Dickson Scott.
Description: Parkland, overlooking loch. Nine holes, 5,176 yards. Par 68 (SSS 68).
Course record 68.
Visitors: Any time, except Sundays before 4 p.m. **Green fees:** £7 per day.
Catering: Lochside House Hotel on the course.
Accommodation: Lochside House Hotel, Crown Hotel.
Signature hole: THE ROAD HOLE – Starts at the highest point of the course, driving down over a small burn with the road on the right. Second shot uphill into the corner of the course to a small green.

NEW GALLOWAY
NEW GALLOWAY GOLF CLUB
Address: New Galloway, Kirkcudbrightshire DG7 3RN (01644-430455).
Location: South side of town on A762.
Secretary: Alan Brown.
Description: Mixed woodland and moorland course with excellent tees and first-class greens. Some steep inclines. The first and second fairways lead up to magnificent views over Loch Ken. Nine holes, 5,006 yards. Par 68 (SSS 67). Course record 63.
Visitors: Very welcome. **Green fees:** £10 per day. Juniors £5.
Catering: Bar open 12 noon to 2 p.m. **Facilities:** Putting green, practice ground.
Accommodation: Douglas Arms.

CARD OF THE COURSE

Hole	Yds	Par	
1	302	4	
2	252	4	
3	358	4	
4	133	3	
5	377	4	
6	256	4	
7	121	3	
8	367	4	
9	337	4	
Out	2,503	34	
Total	**5,006**	**Par**	**68**

NEWTONMORE
NEWTONMORE GOLF CLUB
Address: Golf Course Road, Newtonmore PH20 1AT (01540-673328; 01540-673878).
Location: East of town, off A9.

Professional: Robert Henderson.
Description: Flat parkland course beside the River Spey. Beautiful views and easy walking. 18 holes, 6,029 yards. Par 70 (SSS 68). Course record 68.
Visitors: Contact in advance. **Green fees:** £10 per round weekdays, £15 per day. £14 per round weekends, £20 per day.
Catering: Full service. Bar.
Facilities: Trolley/buggy hire, putting green, pro shop, practice ground.
Accommodation: The Scot House Hotel.

NEWTON STEWART

NEWTON STEWART GOLF CLUB

Address: Kirroughtree Avenue, Newton Stewart D68 6PF (01671-402172).
Location: A75 Carlisle to Stranraer. Course on outskirts of town.
Secretary: J. Tait.
Description: Parkland course which is a very good test for all standards of golfer. Relatively flat but has a hill with wonderful views. 18 holes, 5,970 yards. Par 69 (SSS 70). Amateur record 68.
Visitors: Any time. **Green fees:** £17 per round weekdays, £20 per round weekends.
Catering: Full catering.
Facilities: Trolley/buggy hire, putting green, practice ground.
Accommodation: Discounts available through majority of local hotels.
Signature hole: NINTH (337 yards, par four) – Pond, stream and wall give player a choice of tee shots. The easier the option taken, the more difficult the second shot.

CARD OF THE COURSE

Hole	Yds	Par	Hole	Yds	Par
1	346	4	10	152	3
2	443	4	11	520	5
3	177	3	12	197	3
4	371	4	13	523	5
5	426	4	14	405	4
6	175	3	15	328	4
7	353	4	16	345	4
8	383	4	17	164	3
9	337	4	18	325	4
Out	3,011	34	In	2,959	35
Total	**5,970**		**Par**	**69**	

WIGTOWNSHIRE COUNTY GOLF CLUB

Address: Mains of Park, Glenluce, Newton Stewart DG8 0NN (01581-300420).
Location: Eight miles east of Stranraer on A75.
Secretary: Robert McKnight.
Description: A links course, situated on the shores of the scenic Luce Bay with the Isle of Man visible on a clear day. Subtly sloping greens and changing sea breezes provide a test for both the high and the low handicappers. 18 holes, 5,847 yards. Par 70 (SSS 68). Course record 67.
Visitors: Any time.

Green fees: £17 per round weekdays, £21 per day. £19 per round weekends, £23 per day.
Catering: All year. Bar.
Facilities: Trolley/buggy hire, putting green, pro shop, practice ground.
Accommodation: Glenbay Hotel, Kelvin Hotel.
Signature hole: TWELFTH (392 yards, par four) – 'Cunningham's Best', named after designer Gordon Cunningham. Scenic dogleg right with out of bounds to the right.

CARD OF THE COURSE

Hole	Yds	Par	Hole	Yds	Par
1	332	4	10	332	4
2	350	4	11	294	4
3	402	4	12	392	4
4	301	4	13	152	3
5	162	3	14	341	4
6	491	5	15	376	4
7	363	4	16	325	4
8	300	4	17	106	3
9	341	4	18	397	4
Out	3,042	36	In	2,805	34
Total	**5,847**		**Par**	**70**	

NORTH BERWICK
THE GLEN GOLF CLUB

Address: East Links, North Berwick, East Lothian EH39 4LE (01620-895288; 01620-892726).
Location: Half a mile east of town centre.
Secretary: David Montgomery.
Description: Seaside links with magnificent panoramic views of the Forth estuary, Bass Rock and the town. 18 holes, 6,043 yards. Par 69 (SSS 69). Amateur record 64.
Visitors: At all times. No restrictions. **Green fees:** £16 per round weekdays, £23 per day. £21 per round weekends, £28 per day.
Catering: Available all day.
Facilities: Trolley/buggy hire, putting green, pro shop, practice ground.
Accommodation: The Marine Hotel, Belhaven Hotel, Fairways Guest House.
Signature hole: THIRTEENTH (144 yards, par three) – Elevated tee to a green below with the seashore on two sides. Tee-shot is semi-blind. Club selection is crucial according to the elements. This can vary from a two-iron to a pitching wedge.

CARD OF THE COURSE

Hole	Yds	Par	Hole	Yds	Par
1	333	4	10	346	4
2	373	4	11	321	4
3	349	4	12	464	4
4	184	3	13	144	3
5	369	4	14	370	4

6	476	5	15	397	4
7	381	4	16	191	3
8	357	4	17	416	4
9	207	3	18	365	4
Out	3,029	35	In	3,014	34
Total	**6,043**		**Par**	**69**	

THE NORTH BERWICK GOLF CLUB

Address: Beach Road, North Berwick EH39 4BB (01620-892135).
Location: From Edinburgh, A1 to Meadowmill turn-off then A198. From the south, A1 to A198 at Biel Gates.
Secretary: W. Gray. **Professional:** David Huish.
Description: Championship links course. The many interesting hazards include the beach, light rough, walls intersecting fairways and streams crossing three of the fairways. Most interesting holes are the world famous 'Redan' and the 376-yard par-four 14th 'Perfection'. 18 holes, 6,420 yards. Par 71 (SSS 71). Amateur record 66 (Gordon Sherry). Pro record 64 (Nick Job).
Visitors: Yes, from 10 a.m. **Green fees:** £30 per round weekdays, £45 per day. £45 per round weekends, £60 per day.
Catering: Yes.
Facilities: Trolley/buggy hire, putting green, pro shop, practice ground.
Accommodation: Marine Hotel, Nether Abbey, Golf Hotel.
Signature hole: FIFTEENTH (192 yards, par three) – 'Redan' is played across a hummocky valley to an angled plateau green guarded by a formidable bunker in front and 20 feet below the flag. To the right are three bunkers. (See diagram opposite.)

OUT OF BOUNDS

CARD OF THE COURSE

Hole	Yds	Par	Hole	Yds	Par
1	328	4	10	176	3
2	431	4	11	550	5
3	464	4	12	389	4
4	175	3	13	365	4
5	373	4	14	376	4
6	162	3	15	192	3
7	354	4	16	381	4
8	495	5	17	425	4
9	510	5	18	274	4
Out	3,292	36	In	3,128	35
Total	**6,420**		**Par**	**71**	

OBAN
GLENCRUITTEN GOLF CLUB

Address: Glencruitten Road, Oban PA34 5PU (01631-62868).
Location: One mile north-east of town centre, off A816.

Secretary: A. Brown.

Description: Picturesque, hilly parkland course with many elevated tees and greens. Beautiful isolated situation. 18 holes, 4,500 yards. Par 61 (SSS 63). Course record 55.

Visitors: Yes, except Thursday afternoons, Saturdays and Sundays, which are competition days. Small groups can play at weekends by arrangement.

Green fees: £15 per round .

Catering: Full service. Bar. **Facilities:** Trolley hire, pro shop, practice ground.

Accommodation: Kilchrenan Hotel, Barriemore Hotel.

Signature hole: FIRST – Daunting par four. Second shot is blind, over a hill, to a saucer-shaped green.

OLDMELDRUM

OLDMELDRUM GOLF CLUB

Address: Kirk Brae, Oldmeldrum, Aberdeenshire AB51 0DJ (01651-872648).

Location: 17 miles north of Aberdeen on A947.

Secretary: Douglas Petrie.

Professional: John Caven.

Description: Undulating parkland course with tree-lined fairways and water features. On the 14th fairway can be seen the 'Groaner Stone' which dates back to the days of Robert the Bruce. 18 holes, 5,988 yards. Par 70 (SSS 69). Amateur record 66.

Visitors: Yes, except during club competitions.

Green fees: £12 per day weekdays, £18 per day weekends.

Catering: Yes, licensed.

Facilities: Trolley hire, putting green, pro shop, practice ground.

Accommodation: Meldrum Arms Hotel.

Signature hole: ELEVENTH (196 yards, par three) – Over two ponds to a small green flanked on three sides by bunkers. (See diagram opposite.)

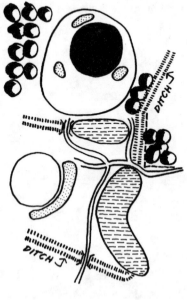

CARD OF THE COURSE

Hole	Yds	Par	Hole	Yds	Par
1	260	4	10	466	4
2	482	5	11	196	3
3	192	3	12	440	4
4	417	4	13	425	4
5	274	4	14	295	4
6	476	5	15	301	4
7	148	3	16	301	4
8	410	4	17	163	3
9	423	4	18	319	4
Out	3,082	36	In	2,906	34
Total	**5,988**		**Par**	**70**	

ORKNEY ISLES
ORKNEY GOLF CLUB
Address: Grainbank, Kirkwall, Orkney KW15 1RD (01856-872457).
Location: At western boundary of Kirkwall.
Secretary: L. Howard.
Description: Inland parkland course. 18 holes, 5,411 yards. Par 70 (SSS 67). Course record 65.
Visitors: Any time. **Green fees:** £10 per day.
Catering: Lunch times during summer.
Facilities: Trolley hire, putting green, practice ground.
Accommodation: Ayre Hotel.

STROMNESS GOLF CLUB
Address: Ness, Stromness, Orkney KW16 3DW (01856-850772).
Location: South of town on A965.
Secretary: F. Groundwater (01856-850622).
Description: Seaside parkland course. Easy walking but testing. Views of Scapa Flow. 18 holes, 4,762 yards. Par 65 (SSS 63). Amateur record 61. Pro record 66.
Visitors: Any time. **Green fees:** £12 per day.
Catering: No.
Accommodation: Ayre Hotel.
Signature hole: TENTH (163 yards, par three) – Played over war-time gun emplacements. Out of bounds behind green.

CARD OF THE COURSE

Hole	Yds	Par	Hole	Yds	Par
1	335	4	10	163	3
2	186	3	11	142	3
3	219	3	12	279	4
4	403	4	13	266	4
5	355	4	14	376	4
6	186	3	15	199	3
7	402	4	16	251	4
8	105	3	17	333	4
9	263	4	18	299	4
Out	2,454	32	In	2,308	33
Total	**4,762**		**Par**	**65**	

WESTRAY GOLF CLUB
Address: Westray, Orkney KW17 2DH (01857-677373).
Location: One mile north-west of Pierowall off B9066.
Treasurer: Billy Tulloch.
Description: Interesting seaside links course. Easy walking but watch out for the rabbit holes. Nine holes, 4,810 yards. Par 66.
Visitors: Any time. **Green fees:** £3 per day, £15 per week.
Catering: No.
Accommodation: Cleaton House Hotel.

PAISLEY
BARSHAW GOLF CLUB

Address: Barshaw Park, Glasgow Road, Paisley, Renfrewshire PA1 3TJ (0141-889-2908).
Location: Three-quarters of a mile from Paisley town centre, heading for Glasgow.
Secretary: W. Collins (0141-884-2533). **Professional:** John Scott.
Description: Municipal parkland course with a variety of flat and hilly holes. No bunkers. 18 holes, 5,704 yards. Par 68 (SSS 67). Course record 63.
Visitors: Any time.
Green fees: £6.50 per round. £3.50 for senior citizens, unemployed and juniors.
Catering: None. **Facilities:** Putting green.
Accommodation: Watermill Hotel, Brabloch Hotel.

THE PAISLEY GOLF CLUB

Address: Braehead, Paisley PA2 8TZ (0141-884-3903; 0141-884-4114).
Location: South of town, off B774.
Professional: Grant Gilmour.
Description: Windy moorland course. Good views. 18 holes, 6,466 yards. Par 71 (SSS 72). Course record 66.
Visitors: Contact in advance. Not at weekends or public holidays. Societies weekdays only. **Green fees:** £20 per round, £28 per day.
Catering: Full service. Bar.
Facilities: Trolley hire, putting green, pro shop, practice ground.
Accommodation: Glynhill Hotel and Leisure Club.

RALSTON CLUB

Address: Strathmore Avenue, Paisley PA1 3DT (0141-882-1503).
Location: Two miles east, off A737.
Description: Parkland course. 18 holes, 6,071 yards. Par 71 (SSS 69).
Visitors: Must be accompanied by member.
Green fees: £19 per round weekdays, £27 per day.
Catering: Bar. **Facilities:** Pro shop.
Accommodation: Swallow Hotel.

PANMURE
PANMURE GOLF CLUB

Address: Burnside Road, Barry, by Carnoustie DD7 7RT (01241-855120; Pro shop: 01241-852460).
Location: Nine miles east of Dundee. One mile west of Carnoustie.
Description: Traditional tight links course, established in 1845 and designed by St Andrews architect, requiring accuracy. 18 holes, 6,317 yards. SSS 71. Amateur record 66.
Visitors: Any time, except after 4 p.m. Not Saturdays.
Green fees: £28 per round, £42 per day.
Catering: Yes. **Facilities:** Pro shop, practice ground.
Accommodation: Panmure Hotel.

PATNA
DOON VALLEY GOLF CLUB

Address: Hillside, Patna, Ayrshire KA6 7JT (01292-531607).
Location: 10 miles south of Ayr on A713.
Secretary: Hugh Johnstone MBE.
Description: Undulating hillside parkland course. Has tight out of bounds and a number of water hazards. Little shelter on this course. Nine holes, 5,654 yards. Par 70 (SSS 69).
Visitors: Welcome weekdays. Weekends by arrangement.
Green fees: £10 per round, £15 per day.
Catering: Full catering at Parsons Lodge Hotel nearby.
Accommodation: Parsons Lodge Hotel.

CARD OF THE COURSE

Hole	Yds	Par	
1	344	4	
2	290	4	
3	368	4	
4	398	4	
5	149	3	
6	314	4	
7	496	5	
8	160	3	
9	308	4	
Out	2,827	35	
Total	**5,654**	**Par**	**70**

PEEBLES
PEEBLES GOLF CLUB

Address: Kirkland Street, Peebles EH45 8EU (01721-720197).
Location: North-west corner of town, only five minutes' walk from High Street.
Secretary: Hugh Gilmore.
Description: Undulating parkland with panoramic views. 18 holes, 6,160 yards. Par 70 (SSS 70). Course record 63.
Visitors: Yes. **Green fees:** £18 per round weekdays, £25 per day. £24 per round weekends, £35 per day.
Catering: Full service available. **Facilities:** Trolley/buggy hire, putting green, pro shop (opening mid 1997), practice ground.
Accommodation: Peebles Hydro Hotel.

CARD OF THE COURSE

Hole	Yds	Par	Hole	Yds	Par
1	196	3	10	365	4
2	440	4	11	326	4
3	359	4	12	173	3
4	295	4	13	319	4
5	342	4	14	377	4

6	401	4	15	431	4
7	135	3	16	193	3
8	359	4	17	411	4
9	497	5	18	541	5
Out	3,024	35	In	3,136	35
Total	**6,160**		**Par**	**70**	

PENICUIK
GLENCORSE GOLF CLUB

Address: Milton Bridge, Penicuik, Midlothian EH26 0RD (01968-677189).
Location: On A701, nine miles south of Edinburgh on the Peebles road.
Secretary: W. Oliver. **Professional:** C. Jones (01968-676481).
Description: Inland parkland course with trees. Burn affects 10 holes. Eight par threes – only one under 200 yards. 18 holes, 5,217 yards. Par 64 (SSS 66). Amateur record 60 (N. Shillinglaw). Pro record 60 (C. Brooks).
Visitors: Any time, depending on club competitions. Societies Monday to Thursday and Sunday afternoons. **Green fees:** £18.50 per round. £24.50 per day and holidays and weekends. Packages available on request.
Catering: All day. **Facilities:** Trolley hire, putting green, pro shop, practice ground, driving range (half a mile from course).
Accommodation: Roslin Glen Hotel.
Signature hole: FIFTH (237 yards, par three) – Over a burn. One of the most difficult in the country.

CARD OF THE COURSE

Hole	Yds	Par	Hole	Yds	Par
1	225	3	10	335	4
2	355	4	11	211	3
3	208	3	12	211	3
4	451	4	13	434	4
5	237	3	14	329	4
6	273	4	15	236	3
7	308	4	16	375	4
8	164	3	17	215	3
9	331	4	18	319	4
Out	2,552	32	In	2,665	32
Total	**5,217**		**Par**	**64**	

PERTH
CRAIGIE HILL GOLF CLUB

Address: Cherrybank, Perth PH2 0NE (01738-620829; 01738-622644).
Location: One mile south-west of city centre, off A952.
Professional: Steven Harrier.
Description: Slightly hilly parkland course. Views over Perth. 18 holes, 5,386 yards. Par 66 (SSS 67). Course record 60.
Visitors: Restricted on Saturdays. Telephone three days in advance.

Green fees: £15 per round, £20 per day. £25 Sundays.
Catering: Full service. Bar.
Facilities: Trolley hire, putting green, pro shop, practice ground.
Accommodation: The Royal George.

KING JAMES VI GOLF CLUB

Address: Moncreiffe Island, Perth PH2 8NR (01738-445132).
Location: South-east of city.
Professional: Tom Coles (01738-632460).
Description: Perth's oldest course, established in 1858. Parkland course situated on island in the middle of River Tay. Easy walking. 18 holes, 6,038 yards. Par 70 (SSS 69). Course record 62.
Visitors: Restricted on competition days. Contact pro for bookings.
Green fees: £15 per round weekdays, £22 per day. £18 per round weekends, £28 per day.
Catering: Full service. Bar. **Facilities:** Trolley/buggy hire, putting green, pro shop, practice ground.
Accommodation: Queens Hotel.

MURRAYSHALL COUNTRY HOUSE HOTEL AND GOLF COURSE

Address: Murrayshall, Scone PH2 7PH (01738-552784).
Location: East of village, off A94.
Professional: George Finlayson.
Description: Parkland, tree-lined fairways. 18 holes, 6,446 yards. Par 73 (SSS 71).
Visitors: No restrictions. **Green fees:** £22.50 per round weekdays, £35 per day. £27.50 per round weekends, £45 per day. Discounts for residents.
Catering: Full service. Bar. **Facilities:** Trolley/buggy hire, putting green, pro shop, practice ground, driving range.
Accommodation: Murrayshall Country House Hotel.

NORTH INCH GOLF CLUB

Address: off Hay Street, Perth PH1 5PH (01738-636481).
Location: North of Perth centre.
Description: Flat, open parkland course by River Tay. 18 holes, 5,178 yards. Par 65. Course record 60.
Visitors: Contact in advance. **Green fees:** £6 per round weekdays, £7.50 weekends.
Catering: Yes. Bar. **Facilities:** Trolley hire, putting green.
Accommodation: The Royal George.

PETERCULTER
PETERCULTER GOLF CLUB

Address: Oldtown, Burnside Road, Peterculter, Aberdeen AB14 0LN (01224-735245; 01224-734994).
Location: A90 from Aberdeen. Eight miles west of city on main Deeside Road.
Secretary: Keith Anderson. **Professional:** Dean Vannet.
Description: Tight inland course. Undulating. On the banks of the River Dee. Very scenic with spectacular views up the Dee Valley. 18 holes, 5,947 yards. Par 68 (SSS 68). Course record 68.

Visitors: Any time. No outings at weekends. **Green fees:** £11 per round weekdays, £16 per day. £15 per round weekends, £21 per day. £6 member's guest.
Catering: Full bar and catering facilities, apart from Mondays.
Facilities: Trolley/buggy hire, putting green, pro shop, practice ground.
Accommodation: Gordon Arms Hotel, Maryculter House.

PETERHEAD
PETERHEAD GOLF CLUB
Address: Craigewan Links, Peterhead AB42 6LT (01779-472149).
Location: North of town, off A952.
Description: Natural links course bounded by the sea and the River Ugie.
Old Course: 18 holes, 6,173 yards. Par 70 (SSS 71). Course record 64.
New Course: Nine holes, 4,456 yards.
Visitors: Contact in advance. Competition day Saturdays. Societies not weekends.
Green fees: *Old Course*: £16 per round weekdays, £22 per day. £20 per round weekdays, £27 per day. *New Course*: £9 per round/day.
Catering: Yes. Bar. **Facilities:** Practice ground.
Accommodation: Waterside Inn.

PITLOCHRY
PITLOCHRY GOLF COURSE LTD
Address: Golf Course Road, Pitlochry PH16 5QY (01796-472792).
Location: North end of village off A924.
Secretary: D. Mackenzie JP. **Professional:** George Hampton.
Description: Hilly parkland course with lush turf. 18 holes, 5,811 yards. Par 69 (SSS 69).
Visitors: Yes. **Green fees:** £20 per day weekdays, £25 weekends.
Catering: Yes. **Facilities:** Trolley/buggy hire, putting green, pro shop, practice ground.
Accommodation: Pine Trees Hotel.

PORT GLASGOW
PORT GLASGOW GOLF CLUB
Address: Devol Road, Port Glasgow PA14 5XE.
Location: One mile south of town.
Description: Moorland course on hilltop overlooking the Clyde with views to the Cowal Hills. 18 holes, 5,712 yards. Par 68 (SSS 68).
Visitors: Not on Saturdays. **Green fees:** On application.
Catering: Bar. **Facilities:** Putting green, pro shop.
Accommodation: Gleddoch House Hotel.

PORTMAHOMACK
TARBET GOLF CLUB
Address: Portmahomack, Ross-shire IV20 1YQ (01862-871236).

190

Location: East side of village.
Secretary: Roy Pettit, 1 East Tarrel Cottages, Portmahomack.
Description: Links course overlooking the Dornoch Firth and Moray Firth. Magnificent backdrop of mountains. Nine holes, 5,082 yards. Par 67 (SSS 65). Amateur record 67.
Visitors: Any time, except Saturday mornings.
Green fees: £7 weekdays, £9 weekends.
Catering: No, but locals pubs and restaurant. **Facilities:** Practice ground.
Accommodation: Caledonian Hotel, Castle Hotel.
Signature hole: EIGHTH (302 yards, par four) – Approach to an elevated green is protected by undulating land for some 100 yards before the green.

CARD OF THE COURSE

Hole	Yds	Par	Hole	Yds	Par
1	290	4	10	290	4
2	324	4	11	324	4
3	414	4	12	385	4
4	265	4	13	180	3
5	177	3	14	177	3
6	355	4	15	355	4
7	166	3	16	130	3
8	302	4	17	302	4
9	323	4	18	323	4
Out	2,616	34	In	2,466	33
Total	**5,082**		**Par**	**67**	

PORTPATRICK

PORTPATRICK (DUNSKEY) GOLF CLUB

Address: Golf Course Road, Portpatrick, Wigtownshire DG9 8TB (01776-810273 or answer phone 01776-810811).
Location: From north, A77 to Stranraer and to Portpatrick. From east, A75 to Stranraer and to Portpatrick.
Secretary: J. Horberry. **Professional:** K. Hughes.
Description: *Dunskey*: Links set on cliffs above Portpatrick. 18 holes, 5,882 yards. Par 70 (SSS 68). Course record 63.
Dinvin: Nine holes, 1,504 yards. Par 27 (SSS 27). Course record 23.
Visitors: Yes, all year round. Book in advance. **Green fees:** *Dunskey*: £17 per round weekdays, £25 per day. £20 per round weekends, £30 per day. *Dinvin*: £6 per round, £12 per day.
Catering: All day. Breakfast through to dinner.
Facilities: Trolley hire, putting green, golf shop, practice ground.
Accommodation: Fernhill Hotel, Portpatrick Hotel, Downshire Arms Hotel, Crown Hotel.
Signature hole: SEVENTH (165 yards, par three) – Though fairly short, is uphill to a raised green. Plays one club more than the yardage. Deep gully 30 yards in front of green which falls away downhill to the left. Putting green has more slopes than one imagines.

CARD OF THE COURSE

Hole	Yds	Par	Hole	Yds	Par
1	393	4	10	329	4
2	375	4	11	163	3
3	544	5	12	390	4
4	160	3	13	293	4
5	405	4	14	293	4
6	382	4	15	101	3
7	165	3	16	393	4
8	349	4	17	301	4
9	311	4	18	535	5
Out	3,084	35	In	2,798	35
Total	**5,882**		**Par**	**70**	

PRESTONPANS

ROYAL MUSSELBURGH GOLF CLUB

Address: Prestongrange House, Prestonpans EH32 9RP (01875-810276).
Location: West of town, off A59.
Professional: John Henderson.
Description: Opened in 1926 and designed by James Braid. Tree-lined parkland course overlooking Firth of Forth. 18 holes, 6,237 yards. Par 70 (SSS 70). Course record 64.
Visitors: Contact pro in advance. Restricted Friday afternoons and weekends.
Green fees: £20 per round weekdays, £35 per day. £35 per round weekends.
Catering: Full service. Bar.
Facilities: Trolley hire, putting green, pro shop, practice ground.
Accommodation: Kilspindie House Hotel.

PRESTWICK

THE PRESTWICK GOLF CLUB

If you are as interested in the history of golf as the playing of the game, then Prestwick, the birthplace of the Open Championship on the west coast of Scotland, demands a visit. Here you will be walking in the footsteps of legends. Although when the Open was first played in 1860 it was over a 12-hole course of 3,799 yards with a par in the mid-50s, the distinctive flavour of the Prestwick Old Course remains and seven of the original greens are in the same place.

Whether playing or just lunching at the vast table which stretches the length of the room with history all around you, take time to visit the stone cairn, close to the putting green, which is on the site of the original first tee. Imagine all those years ago Young Tom Morris, perhaps the first superstar of golf, facing the monster of the then first which stretched to 578 yards, and ponder how, using hickory shaft and a gutty ball, he managed to hole out in three on what is now the 16th green.

Around the time America was preparing for the Civil War, the members of Prestwick, which had been founded nine years earlier, decided to hold an annual Open competition to find a successor to the great Allan Robertson. Nowadays the Open Championship is a multi-million pound event with the winner becoming a millionaire overnight and receiving world-wide acclaim. At the birth, the prize was an elegant red morocco leather belt, with anyone winning three times in succession getting to keep it.

The first Open had only eight entrants, with Willie Park, from the east coast, carrying off the prize after rounds of 55, 59 and 60. Old Tom Morris was the professional at Prestwick and runner-up in the first championship. He later won the Open four times between 1861 and 1867, but it was his son, Young Tom, who made the belt his own, winning three in a row from 1868 to 1870. He was only 17 when he won his first title, carding a record score of 157 and recording the first official hole in one. The following year he broke 50 for the 12 holes and in achieving the hat-trick scored a 47.

With the influence of St Andrews and Muirfield growing, along with the need to be able to entertain large crowds, Prestwick staged its last Open in 1925. It is still a championship course, though, having hosted the Amateur Championship in 1987.

Although the course expanded to 18 holes in 1883, you will still be playing in the divots of Old and Young Tom, facing the same Pow Burn, which comes into play at several holes, humps and hillocks, deep bunkers, steep sandhills, and heather and gorse that they had to contend with. From the back tees, Prestwick is not the longest of courses at 6,544 yards, with a par of 71, but it is challenging.

Today's first hole is nowhere near as intimidating as that in Tom's day. However, although now a mere 346 yards, it is certainly not easy, with out of bounds and Prestwick Station and the railway line on the right. There is a ruined church and graveyard beside the green. The vast Cardinal Bunker awaits on the third, and the fifth, called the 'Himalayas', is a testing 206-yard par three. You have to play a blind tee shot over the burn and a vast sand dune to a heavily bunkered green.

The 10th, a 454-yard hole, takes you towards the sea and there are magnificent views of Ailsa Craig and the Isle of Arran. The 460-yard 13th is played along a gully to a narrow, slanting green. The 391-yard 17th, the 'Alps', is the last major test before getting back to the haven of the clubhouse, involving a blind second shot over the 'Alps' to a green guarded by a huge bunker. It is not as mountainous as it sounds, but when you step off the 18th just ponder awhile how they did it all those years ago.

Address: 2 Links Road, Prestwick, Strathclyde KA9 1QG (01292-477404).
Location: In town centre off A79.
Secretary: I.T. Bunch. **Professional:** Frank Rennie.
Description: 18 holes, 6,544 yards. Par 71 (SSS 73).
Visitors: Restricted. Not weekends or Thursday afternoons. Book well in advance.
Green fees: £50 per round, £75 per day.
Catering: Full. **Facilities:** Trolley hire, putting green, pro shop, practice ground.
Accommodation: Parkstone Hotel.
Signature hole: THIRD (482 yards, par five) – With the Pow Burn running all down the right and the famous and huge Cardinal Bunker stretching the entire width of the fairway at the point of the dogleg, this is an outstanding hole. Once two good hits were needed to clear the bunker, but this is the age of the big hitters.

CARD OF THE COURSE

Hole	Yds	Par	Hole	Yds	Par
1	346	4	10	454	4
2	167	3	11	195	3

3	482	5	12	513	5
4	382	4	13	460	4
5	206	3	14	362	4
6	362	4	15	347	4
7	430	4	16	288	4
8	431	4	17	391	4
9	444	4	18	284	4
Out	3,250	35	In	3,294	36
Total	**6,544**		**Par**	**71**	

PRESTWICK ST CUTHBERT GOLF CLUB

Address: East Road, Prestwick KA9 2SX (01292-477101).
Location: Half a mile east of town, off A77.
Description: Flat and partially wooded parkland course. Natural hazards. Easy walking. 18 holes, 6,470 yards. Par 71 (SSS 71). Course record 64.
Visitors: Contact in advance. Not weekends or bank holidays. Societies weekdays.
Green fees: £20 per round, £27 per day.
Catering: Full service. Bar. **Facilities:** Trolley hire, putting green, practice ground.
Accommodation: St Nicholas Hotel.

PRESTWICK ST NICHOLAS GOLF CLUB

Address: Grangemuir Road, Prestwick KA9 1SN (01292-477608).
Location: From Prestwick town centre along Main Street heading for Ayr. Right at traffic lights into Grangemuir Road.
Secretary: G. Thomson.
Description: Links course with tight fairways. Easy walking. 18 holes, 5,952 yards. Par 69 (SSS 69). Amateur record 65 (Gavin Lawrie). Pro record 63 (Tony Johnstone).
Visitors: Yes. Weekdays and Sunday afternoons.
Green fees: £25 per round weekdays, £40 per day. £30 per round Sundays.
Catering: Full facilities. **Facilities:** Trolley hire, putting green, golf shop.
Accommodation: Parkstone Hotel.
Signature hole: SECOND (172 yards, par three) – From elevated tee. Challenging and picturesque. (See diagram opposite.)

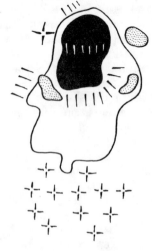

CARD OF THE COURSE

Hole	Yds	Par	Hole	Yds	Par
1	342	4	10	165	3
2	172	3	11	498	5
3	281	4	12	139	3
4	420	4	13	456	4
5	406	4	14	412	4
6	326	4	15	276	4
7	454	4	16	379	4
8	360	4	17	301	4
9	338	4	18	227	3
Out	3,099	35	In	2,853	34
Total	**5,952**		**Par**	**69**	

PUMPHERSTON
PUMPHERSTON GOLF CLUB
Address: Drumshoreland Road, Pumpherston EH53 0LH (01506-432869)
Location: Two miles east, between A71 and A89.
Secretary: A. Docharty.
Description: Undulating parkland course with trees, bunkers and a large pond providing the hazards. Nine holes, 5,434 yards. Par 66 (SSS 67). Amateur record 64 (P. Drake 1996).
Visitors: No casual visitors. Societies Monday to Thursday.
Green fees: £4 with ticket, £11 without.
Catering: Snack meals. **Facilities:** Putting green, practice ground.
Signature hole: SIXTH (251 yards, par four) – Green built in the pond leaving only a seven-yard-wide entrance. Three bunkers short of pond. Out of bounds from tee to green on the left and a lateral water hazard on the right.

CARD OF THE COURSE

Hole	Yds	Par	
1	410	4	
2	440	4	
3	184	3	
4	340	4	
5	185	3	
6	251	4	
7	165	3	
8	302	4	
9	440	4	
Out	2,717	33	
Total	**5,434**	**Par**	**66**

RATHO
RATHO PARK GOLF CLUB
Address: Ratho EH28 8NX (0131-333-2566; 0131-333-1752).
Location: Eight miles west of Edinburgh on A71. Adjacent to Edinburgh Airport.
Professional: Alan Pate.
Description: Flat parkland course. 18 holes, 5,900 yards. Par 69 (SSS 68). Course record 62.
Visitors: Contact in advance. **Green fees:** On application.
Catering: Bar. **Facilities:** Trolley hire, putting green, pro shop, practice ground.
Accommodation: Forte Posthouse.

REAY
REAY GOLF CLUB
Address: The Club House, Reay, Caithness KW14 7RE (01847-811288).
Location: 11 miles west of Thurso on A836.
Secretary: Miss P. Peebles.
Description: Beautiful seaside course. The most northerly 18-hole links on the

British mainland. Alongside Sandside Bay, it has excellent greens and contoured fairways providing enjoyable golf for high and low handicap players alike. 18 holes, 5,884 yards. Par 69 (SSS 69). Course record 64.

Visitors: Any time. Societies by prior arrangement.
Green fees: £15 per round or day.
Catering: Limited. During summer months only.
Facilities: Putting green, practice ground.
Accommodation: Forss Hotel, Melvich Hotel.
Signature hole: FOURTH (584 yards, par five) – Requires a solid tee shot and fairway wood to set up an approach to a sheltered green protected by a burn.

CARD OF THE COURSE

Hole	Yds	Par	Hole	Yds	Par
1	238	3	10	360	4
2	431	4	11	414	4
3	370	4	12	349	4
4	584	5	13	309	4
5	145	3	14	479	5
6	492	5	15	138	3
7	198	3	16	309	4
8	400	4	17	334	4
9	174	3	18	160	3
Out	3,032	34	In	2,852	35
Total	**5,884**		**Par**	**69**	

RENFREW

RENFREW GOLF CLUB

Address: Blythswood Estate, Inchinnan Road, Renfrew PA4 9EG (0141-886-6692).
Location: M8 Junction 26 then A8 to Renfrew. Turn in at Stakis Glasgow Airport Hotel.
Secretary: Ian Murchison. **Professional:** Stuart Kerr.
Description: Wooded parkland course with featured rivers. 18 holes, 6,818 yards. Par 72 (SSS 73).
Visitors: Yes. Introduction by member. Societies by arrangement.
Green fees: £25 per round, £35 per day.
Catering: Yes. **Facilities:** Trolley hire, putting green, pro shop, practice ground.
Accommodation: Glynhill Hotel, Dean Park Hotel, Stakis Glasgow Airport Hotel.

CARD OF THE COURSE

Hole	Yds	Par	Hole	Yds	Par
1	356	4	10	178	3
2	485	5	11	500	5
3	215	3	12	315	4
4	455	4	13	389	4
5	434	4	14	207	3
6	420	4	15	557	5
7	175	3	16	421	4
8	419	4	17	395	4

9	549	5	18	348	4
Out	3,508	36	In	3,310	36
Total	**6,818**		**Par**	**72**	

ROSEHEARTY
ROSEHEARTY GOLF CLUB

Address: Castle Street, Rosehearty AB43 4JP (01346-571250).
Location: Three miles north-west of Fraserburgh.
Description: Links course. Nine holes, 3,368 yards.
Visitors: Any time. **Green fees:** £8 per day weekdays, £10 weekends.

ROTHES
ROTHES GOLF CLUB

Address: Blackhall, Rothes, Moray AB38 7AN (01340-831443).
Location: Nine miles south of Elgin on A941. Turn off at Glen Spey Distillery entrance.
Secretary: J. Tilley.
Description: Constructed six years ago from derelict farmland. Magnificent views over the River Spey and Rothes Castle from its elevated position between woodland and a distillery. Challenging for all abilities. Nine holes, 4,972 yards. Par 68 (SSS 65).
Visitors: Yes, weekdays. Weekends by arrangement.
Green fees: £8 per day weekdays, £10 weekends.
Catering: By arrangement for parties only.
Accommodation: Seafield Arms Hotel, Ben Aigen Hotel, East Bank Hotel, Rothes Glen Hotel.
Signature hole: SIXTH (145 yards, par three) – Although one of the shortest holes, is very close to a steep drop into the valley. The green is narrow, and accuracy rather than power is required.

CARD OF THE COURSE

Hole	Yds	Par	
1	345	4	
2	306	4	
3	372	4	
4	116	3	
5	404	4	
6	145	3	
7	290	4	
8	252	4	
9	256	4	
Out	2,486	34	
Total	**4,972**	**Par**	**68**

ST ANDREWS

One of the recurring charms of golf is that even the humble duffer can stand on the hallowed ground where great deeds have been performed by past heroes, and

197

savour the challenge they experienced. It is a bond between champion and devotee few other sports can offer.

There are moments when that awareness can be quite overwhelming, and nowhere is the presence of past ghosts and great occasions more apparent than on the first tee of the Old Course at St Andrews – because the game of golf, both in form and doctrine, was created upon this somewhat forbidding stretch of shore on the east coast of Scotland. The Old Course stands on the edge of a medieval town which was once the hub of the country's religious, academic and commercial affairs. The game itself has been played at St Andrews for at least five centuries. It is therefore unquestionably the home of golf. But, quite apart from being both shrine and spiritual Mecca for millions of golfers worldwide, the Old Course has also extended an active influence on the game and the manner in which it is played.

By definition, a round of golf is conducted over 18 holes because in 1764 the players at St Andrews decided upon that number. And such was the influence of this 'auld grey toon' that in 1897 the Royal and Ancient Golf Club, one of several to play regularly over this public land, was given the responsibility of framing and maintaining the rules of the sport throughout most of the world.

The Old Course exerts an even stronger hold because it has also defined the spirit of the game and its philosophies by establishing the fundamental doctrine that golf was never meant to be fair and consequently will always be a test of a player's character as well as personal skill. In a sense, these enduring principles were determined by the bleak nature of the terrain from which the sea had receded and over which the ball was played. The uneven landscape which lacked definition, the hidden tracts of sand that formed penal hazards and the constantly changing coastal weather conditions all contributed to an exhaustive test of physical and mental stamina that remains an intrinsic challenge.

In truth, the Old Course, which runs out and back along a peninsula, has to be played from memory, cruel experience and preferably with the wise counsel of a local caddie whose instructions must be observed to the letter without question. The playing strategy is simple enough and demands a kind of stepping-stone approach in which various safe and pre-determined areas of the terrain are found *en route* to the massive undulating greens. Sometimes, the judicious line of attack ignores the intended flagstick in the distance because of the perils that lie in between. There is also a constant need for saint-like patience because temper and skill are tested to the limit, especially when a perfectly struck shot finds an uneven lie or is ambushed by a cavernous pot bunker.

The old campaigners at St Andrews observe one golden rule: 'Never tease the bunkers.' In other words, these hazards must be given the widest possible berth because the ground around them invariably slopes in their direction, effectively making them much larger penalties than they appear. The other essential tenet is to find an immediate way out of a sand trap even if that means playing out backwards, as Australian Peter Thomson did when winning the Open Championship in 1955.

What makes the Old Course such a complete test is that it combines the two basic elements of golf-course architecture in that it is both strategic and punitive. By definition the strategic concept demands positional play for the best results and provides proportionate rewards, while the punitive style imposes massive sanctions for the slightest deviation from the prescribed route.

To stand on the first tee and aim an opening shot at that huge expanse of land which also includes the adjacent 18th fairway is to experience the strategic concept.

The sharp line to the left will be safe enough, but it then imposes a very long and difficult approach over the Swilcan Burn which menaces the front edge of the green. Thereafter, the Old Course remains both punitive and strategic in that the safe tee shot is played to the left and sometimes as far as the adjacent fairways to avoid the constant trouble on the right, but this tactic can make the approach more difficult, particularly to the seven huge greens that are shared by outward and inward holes. (Aim for the white flags on the outward nine and reds on the homeward stretch.)

The overriding rule of play at the Old Course is that no matter how savage the setback or disaster, there is no good reason to surrender all hope. That said, the inward run presents a succession of challenges that can undermine the prospects of a reasonable score and tee shots must always be placed precisely to avoid escalating drama. From the 14th tee, the church spire in the distant town is the safe line on which to aim in order to pass to the right of the hazardous Beardies and find that level known as the Elysian Fields, from where the second shot is directed left of Hell Bunker for a third stroke to the green. Pure stepping-stone stuff and essentially a double dogleg in open countryside.

The mark of a great hole is the manner in which it makes players worry long before they reach it. Such is the awe in which the 17th – the Road Hole – is held. It is the most famous golf hole in the world. Some claim it is the best. The drive has to find a fairway over sheds and a wall to set up an approach to the green that is protected by the infamous Road Bunker at the front edge, while the road itself at the rear punishes any stroke that is too powerful. It contains the definitive elements of strategic and punitive golf and for lesser mortals is best played as a five to avoid heartbreak. Once completed, the ritual of the final tee shot remains, and it should be aimed towards the Royal and Ancient clubhouse clock to avoid the right-hand out of bounds road – as well as the house and shops – which runs all the way to the green.

No matter who you are, some local citizen will lean over the fence to watch how you tackle the Valley of Sin, that hollow in front of the green that has wrecked so many scores. The pitch and run can be risky if not played with confidence. The high wedge is safer, although it may leave a downhill putt. But even if you miss, the journey is complete and you share an experience with all the great heroes of the past who strode the same fairways. At the home of golf, too. But try not to think about it on the first tee.

Michael McDonnell

Daily Mail Golf Correspondent and member of the Royal and Ancient Golf Club

Address: St Andrews Links Trust, St Andrews, Fife KY16 9SF (01334-466666).
Location: A91 from Cupar. Once in town, take third turning on left into Golf Place and follow for 500 yards.
Secretary: D.N.H. James.
Visitors: All year.
Catering: Full service in Links Clubhouse. Bar. **Facilities:** Trolley hire, putting green, pro shop, practice ground, driving range.
Accommodation: St Andrews Tourist Board (01334-472021)

Old Course
Description: Traditional links course – the oldest in the world. Its layout is unique

and challenging. The sense of history is almost overwhelming. 18 holes, 6,933 yards (championship), 6,566 yards (medal). Par 72 (SSS 72). Course record 62.

Green fees: High season (April 1 to October 31) £70. Low season £50.

Signature hole: SEVENTEENTH (461 yards, par four) – 'The Road Hole', the most famous hole in golf. Blind drive over hotel grounds. Very long second to extremely narrow green with road hard against back edge and a fearsome bunker front left.

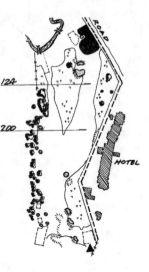

Old Course 17th

CARD OF THE COURSE

Hole	Yds	Par	Hole	Yds	Par
1	370	4	10	342	4
2	411	4	11	172	3
3	371	4	12	316	4
4	463	4	13	425	4
5	564	5	14	567	5
6	416	4	15	413	4
7	372	4	16	382	4
8	178	3	17	461	4
9	356	4	18	354	4
Out	3,501	36	In	3,432	36
Total	**6,933**		**Par**	**72**	

New Course

Description: Traditional links course, laid out by Old Tom Morris and opened in 1894. A tough test. 18 holes, 6,604 yards. Par 71 (SSS 72).

Green fees: High season £30. Low season £24.

Signature hole: EIGHTEENTH (408 yards, par four) – The line is slightly left but tempered by the rough edge bunker at driving range. Green is protected on the right by a single bunker and on the left by a pair backed up by gorse. If left, you should have a clear line to the pin. No trouble at the back, so play long for safety.

Jubilee Course

Description: Traditional links course. First laid out in 1897 and upgraded to championship standard in 1989. A severe test. 18 holes, 6,805 yards. Par 72 (SSS 73).

Green fees: High season £25. Low season £20.

Signature hole: TWELFTH (538 yards, par five) – Shortest route hugs the edge of the left-hand dogleg. The placing of the second wood is critical. Too wide and you may need two or three more clubs to the green. Too tight and the mound to the left of the green

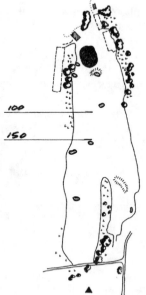

New Course 18th

and the bunker come into play. The green is 40 yards deep, so pin placement should be carefully assessed.

Eden Course
Description: Traditional links course laid out by H.S. Colt and opened in 1914. A good test and home of one of Scotland's oldest amateur tournaments, the Eden Trophy. 18 holes, 6,112 yards. Par 70 (SSS 70).
Green fees: High season £20. Low season £16.
Signature hole: SEVENTEENTH (432 yards, par four) – Running along the curve of the old railway, this is more of a banana than a dogleg. Out of bounds on the right. The line of the drive is on the most distant visible bunker. The green is reasonably deep but the gap between the bunker on the left of the green and the out of bounds is tight.

Strathtyrum Course
Description: Traditional links course but with parkland features and few bunkers providing an enjoyable round. 18 holes, 5,904 yards. Par 69 (SSS 64).
Green fees: High season £15. Low season £13.

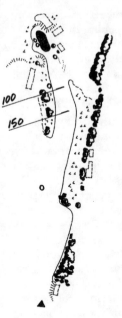

Jubilee Course 12th

Balgove
Description: Primarily for children, beginners and those who can manage only nine holes. Nine holes, 1,530 yards. Par 30
Green fees: High season £7. Low season £5.

THE BRITISH GOLF MUSEUM
When was the first written reference to golf? Why did King James II ban the game? Why did every well-dressed lady golfer once wear the 'Miss Higgins Elastic Hoop'? What is the difference between a cleek and a mashie?

All these questions and more can be answered by a visit to The British Golf Museum in St Andrews, which traces the 500-year history of the game. Themed galleries and interactive displays explore subjects such as the development of golfing equipment and costume, the history of major championships and biographies of famous players.

Audio-visual displays and touch-activated screens bring the game to life. In the 48-seat theatre you can watch a variety of historical golfing films, including instructional clips featuring Bobby Jones and a guided tour of the Old Course with Old Tom Morris. There is also a permanent exhibition of the work of golfing artist Harold Riley and a souvenir shop.
Location: Opposite the Royal and Ancient Golf Club at

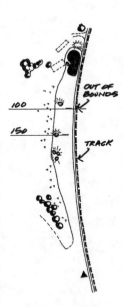

Eden Course 17th

201

Bruce Embankment, St Andrews, Fife KY16 9AB (01334-478880).
Opening times: Mid April to Mid October: 10 a.m. to 5.30 p.m., 7 days a week. Winter: 11 a.m. to 3 p.m., Closed Tuesdays and Wednesdays.
Admission charges: Adults £3.75; senior citizens and students £2.75; children (15 and under) £1.50; family £9.50.

THE DUKE'S COURSE

Address: Craigtoun, St Andrews KY16 8NS (01334-479947).
Location: Five minutes from Old Course Hotel.
Administration Manager: Heidi Orr. **Professional:** John Kelly.
Description: Classic inland parkland course, which is a contrast to the Old Course and its neighbouring links courses that lie along the beach. The fairways are characterised by many small undulations and groups of small bunkers, often pot bunkers built into mounds. Designed by former Open champion Peter Thomson. Opened in 1995. Well worth a visit. 18 holes, 7,171 yards (championship), 6,649 yards (medal). Par 72.
Visitors: Any time. **Green fees:** £50 per round, £65 per day. If residents of the Old Course Hotel, £35 per round, £50 per day. Society packages from £60 per day (minimum party of 12).
Catering: Full service from 7.30 a.m. to 10 p.m. Bar.
Facilities: Trolley/buggy hire, putting green, pro shop, practice ground, chipping and bunker practice area.
Accommodation: Old Course Hotel Golf Resort and Spa.

CARD OF THE COURSE

Hole	Yds	Par	Hole	Yds	Par
1	479	5	10	403	4
2	421	4	11	478	5
3	140	3	12	192	3
4	404	4	13	366	4
5	343	4	14	435	4
6	510	5	15	501	5
7	431	4	16	410	4
8	185	3	17	177	3
9	393	4	18	381	4
Out	3,306	36	In	3,343	36
Total	**6,649**		**Par**	**72**	

ST BOSWELLS

ST BOSWELLS GOLF CLUB

Address: Braeheads, St Boswells, Roxburghshire TD6 0DE (01835-823527; 01835-823858).
Location: Centre of the Borders off A68.
Secretary: J. Phillips.
Description: Course is situated close to village of St Boswells along the south bank of the River Tweed, which is renowned for its salmon fishing. On the opposite side of the river is Dryburgh Abbey, founded in 1150 and the burial place of Sir Walter

Scott. Original course laid out by William Park. Unlike other Borders courses, the terrain is flat and presents few difficulties other than the River Tweed, which is defined as a lateral water hazard. Nine holes, 5,250 yards. Par 66 (SSS 66).
Visitors: Weekdays 9 a.m. to 4 p.m.
Green fees: £12 per round weekdays, £15 per day, £15 weekends.
Catering: By arrangement only.
Accommodation: Buccleuch Arms Hotel.

CARD OF THE COURSE

Hole	Yds	Par	
1	148	3	
2	161	3	
3	316	4	
4	198	3	
5	425	4	
6	321	4	
7	430	4	
8	370	4	
9	256	4	
Out	2,625	33	
Total	**5,250**	**Par**	**66**

ST FILLANS
ST FILLANS GOLF CLUB

Address: South Loch Earn Road, St Fillans, Perthshire PH6 2NJ (01679-685312).
Location: Off A85 at east end of village.
Secretary: K. Foster.
Description: Inland flat parkland course suitable for all standards of golfer, including the elderly. Beautiful mountain scenery. Nine holes, 5,796 yards. Par 68 (SSS 67). Amateur record 73.
Visitors: Individuals any time. Parties by arrangement.
Green fees: £12 per day weekdays, £15 per day weekends and bank holidays.
Catering: Snacks and light meals, April to October. **Facilities:** Trolley hire.
Accommodation: Four Seasons Hotel, Achray House Hotel, Drummond Arms Hotel.

CARD OF THE COURSE

Hole	Yds	Par	
1	337	4	
2	462	4	
3	272	4	
4	420	4	
5	272	4	
6	224	3	
7	453	4	
8	171	3	
9	287	4	
Out	2,898	34	
Total	**5,796**	**Par**	**68**

SALINE
SALINE GOLF CLUB

Address: Kinneddar Hill, Saline, Fife KY12 9NF (01383-852591).
Location: Junction 4 off M90. Seven miles on B914 Dollar road.
Secretary: R. Hutchison.
Description: Hillside parkland course with excellent turf. Panoramic views. Nine holes, 5,302 yards. Par 68, (SSS 66). Amateur record 63.
Visitors: Unrestricted, except on Saturdays and certain Sundays.
Green fees: £9 weekdays, £11 per day Sundays.
Catering: Full service. Bar.
Facilities: Putting green, practice ground, practice nets.
Accommodation: King Malcolm Thistle Hotel.
Signature hole: EIGHTH (160 yards, par three) – Downhill. Must pitch on green. Very difficult if any cross-wind, but best chance of hole in one.

CARD OF THE COURSE

Hole	Yds	Par	
1	279	4	
2	314	4	
3	166	3	
4	289	4	
5	372	4	
6	378	4	
7	329	4	
8	160	3	
9	364	4	
Out	2,651	34	
Total	**5,302**	**Par**	**68**

SANQUHAR
SANQUHAR GOLF CLUB

Address: Blackaddie Road, Sanquhar DG4 6JZ (01659-50577).
Location: 30 miles south of Ayr, off A76.
Secretary: Mrs J. Murray.
Description: Inland course. Undulating but easy walking. Fine views. Nine holes, 5,594 yards. Par 70 (SSS 68). Course record 63.
Visitors: Any time. **Green fees:** £10 per day, £12 weekends.
Catering: Yes, by prior arrangement. Bar.
Facilities: Putting green, practice ground.
Accommodation: Blackaddie House Hotel.
Signature hole: SECOND (444 yards, par four) – Out of bounds right side, down length of hole.

CARD OF THE COURSE

Hole	Yds	Par
1	259	4
2	444	4
3	384	4

4	314	4
5	294	4
6	149	3
7	332	4
8	156	3
9	465	5
Out	2,797	35
Total	**5,594**	**Par**	**70**

SELKIRK
SELKIRK GOLF CLUB
Address: Selkirk Hill, Selkirk TD7 4NW (01750-20621).
Location: Half a mile south of Selkirk on A7.
Secretary: Alistair Wilson.
Description: Set on the side of Selkirk Hill, undulating with heather- and gorse-lined fairways. Offers a full range of shots. Exceptionally scenic. Nine holes, 5,620 yards. Par 68 (SSS 67). Amateur record 60.
Visitors: Yes. **Green fees:** £12 per round, £15 per day.
Catering: Book in advance. **Facilities:** Trolley/buggy hire, putting green.
Accommodation: County Hotel, Woodburn House Hotel, Heatherlie House Hotel.
Signature hole: EIGHTH (518 yards, par five) – Drive into narrow fairway flanked by heather slopes. Second shot sets up approach to green, hidden behind grassy mounds. Dogleg to right.

CARD OF THE COURSE

Hole	Yds	Par	
1	383	4	
2	265	4	
3	401	4	
4	379	4	
5	384	4	
6	119	3	
7	210	3	
8	518	5	
9	151	3	
Out	2,810	34	
Total	**5,620**	**Par**	**68**

SHETLAND ISLES
SHETLAND GOLF CLUB
Address: PO Box 18, Shetland Isles ZE1 0YW (01595-84369).
Location: Four miles north of Lerwick on A970.
Description: Undulating moorland course. Wide fairways but hard walking. Burn runs full length of course and provides a natural hazard. 18 holes, 5,800 yards. Par 68 (SSS 68). Course record 68.
Visitors: Contact in advance. **Green fees:** £10 per day.

Catering: Bar. **Facilities:** Putting green.
Accommodation: Lerwick Hotel.

WHALSAY GOLF CLUB

Address: Skaw Taing, Island of Whalsay ZE2 9AA (01806-566705).
Location: Half an hour's drive north from Lerwick, then half an hour on ferry.
Secretary: Charles Hutchison (01806-566450).
Description: Most northerly golf course in Britain. Moorland course, exposed with spectacular cliff-top scenery. Fairways defined by marker posts. 18 holes, 6,009 yards. Par 70 (SSS 68). Course record 65.
Visitors: Welcome any time. **Green fees:** £10 per day.
Catering: By arrangement. New clubhouse built in 1996. **Facilities:** Putting green.
Accommodation: Bed and breakfast only on island.
Signature hole: EIGHTEENTH (386 yards, par four) – Dogleg left around (or over) East Loch of Skaw.

CARD OF THE COURSE

Hole	Yds	Par	Hole	Yds	Par
1	401	4	10	381	4
2	399	4	11	398	4
3	150	3	12	529	5
4	311	4	13	202	3
5	140	3	14	342	4
6	337	4	15	346	4
7	165	3	16	510	5
8	482	5	17	175	3
9	355	4	18	386	4
Out	2,740	34	In	3,269	36
Total	**6,009**		**Par**	**70**	

SHOTTS

SHOTTS GOLF CLUB

Address: Blairhead, Shotts ML7 5BJ (01501-820431; 01501-826628).
Location: Leave M8 at junction for B7057.
Description: Undulating moorland course, designed by James Braid. 18 holes, 6,205 yards. Par 70 (SSS 70). Course record 63.
Visitors: Not weekends. **Green fees:** £17 per day.
Catering: Full service. Bar.
Facilities: Trolley/buggy hire, putting green, pro shop, practice ground.
Accommodation: The Hilcroft Hotel.

SKYE (Isle of)

ISLE OF SKYE GOLF CLUB

Address: Sconser, Isle of Skye IV48 8TD (01478-650351).
Location: On main road from Skye Bridge to Portree.
Secretary: M. Macdonald.

Description: Seaside parkland course. Magnificent views. Nine holes, 4,677 yards. Par 66 (SSS 64). Amateur record 62.
Visitors: Any time. Avoid 10 a.m. to 11 a.m. on Saturdays.
Green fees: £10 per day.
Catering: 200 yards from course. **Facilities:** Trolley hire.
Accommodation: Two hotels adjacent.

CARD OF THE COURSE

Hole	Yds	Par	Hole	Yds	Par
1	288	4	10	307	4
2	447	4	11	417	4
3	153	3	12	129	3
4	280	4	13	280	4
5	162	3	14	122	3
6	349	4	15	349	4
7	146	3	16	142	3
8	294	4	17	276	4
9	268	4	18	268	4
Out	2,387	33	In	2,290	33
Total	**4,677**		**Par**	**66**	

SKEABOST GOLF CLUB

Address: Skeabost House Hotel, Isle of Skye IV51 9NP (01470-532202).
Location: Six miles out of Portree on Dunvegan road.
Description: Wooded, taxing seaside course. Tight fairways and greens. Nine holes, 3,056 yards. Par 62 (SSS 60). Course record 58.
Visitors: Contact in advance. **Green fees:** £6 per day.
Catering: Full service. Bar.
Facilities: Trolley hire, putting green, pro shop, practice ground.
Accommodation: Skeabost House Hotel.

SKELMORLIE

SKELMORLIE GOLF CLUB

Address: Skelmorlie, Ayrshire PA17 5ES (01475-520152).
Location: Off A78, through Skelmorlie village.
Secretary: Mrs A. Fahey.
Description: Hilly moorland course. Designed by James Braid in 1891. First five holes are played twice. 13 holes, 5,056 yards. Par 64 (SSS 65).
Visitors: Weekdays and some Sundays. **Green fees:** £13 per round weekdays, £17.50 per day. £14 per round weekends, £20 per day (Saturdays after 4 p.m.).
Catering: Weekend and visiting parties.
Accommodation: Manor Park Hotel.

CARD OF THE COURSE

Hole	Yds	Par	Hole	Yds	Par
1	345	4	10	252	4
2	462	4	11	272	4
3	108	3	12	197	3

4	366	4	13	210	3
5	228	3	14	345	4
6	323	4	15	462	4
7	430	4	16	108	3
8	191	3	17	366	4
9	163	3	18	228	3
Out	2,616	32	In	2,440	32
Total	**5,056**		**Par**	**64**	

SOUTH QUEENSFERRY
DUNDAS PARKS GOLF CLUB
Address: Dundas Castle Estate, South Queensferry EH30 9SP.
Location: One mile south on A8000.
Secretary: Mrs Joan Pennie (0131-331-3179).
Description: Moderately undulating parkland course. Nine holes, 6,024 yards. Par 70 (SSS 69). Course record 66.
Visitors: Contact in advance. **Green fees:** £8 per round.
Facilities: Putting green, practice ground, bunker and driving bay.
Accommodation: Forth Bridges Hotel.

SOUTH UIST (Isle of)
ASKERNISH GOLF CLUB
Address: Loch Boisdale, South Uist PA81 5SY (01878-700541).
Location: Five miles north-west of Loch Boisdale.
Description: On shores of Atlantic Ocean. Nine holes, 5,042 yards. Par 68 (SSS 67). Course record 64.
Visitors: Any time. **Green fees:** £3.50 per round, £5 per day.
Catering: Bar.

SOUTHEND
DUNAVERTY GOLF CLUB
Address: Campbeltown, Argyll PA28 6RW (01586-830677).
Location: 10 miles south of Campbeltown on B842.
Description: Undulating seaside links course. 18 holes, 4,799 yards. Par 66 (SSS 63). Course record 59.
Visitors: Limited Saturdays. Contact in advance.
Green fees: £12 per round, £18 per day, £45 per week.
Catering: By prior arrangement. **Facilities:** Putting green, practice ground.
Accommodation: Seafield Hotel.

SOUTHERNESS
SOUTHERNESS GOLF CLUB
Address: Southerness, Dumfries DG2 8AZ (01387-880677).

Location: A710 from Dumfries, marked Solway coast. Follow Southerness sign after 15 miles.

Secretary: W. Ramage.

Description: Championship links course. Designed by MacKenzie Ross and opened in 1947. Set beneath the Galloway Hills along the Solway Firth coastline. Crisp, sandy turf and rolling fairways and greens, but stray off the fairways and there is heather and gorse in abundance. 18 holes, 6,566 yards. Par 69 (SSS 73). Amateur record 65. Pro record 71.

Visitors: Weekdays 10 a.m. to 12 noon, 2 p.m. to 5 p.m. Thursdays 11 a.m. to 1 p.m., 2.30 p.m. to 5 p.m. Weekends and bank holidays 10 a.m. to 11.30 am., 2.30 p.m. to 4.30 p.m. **Green fees:** £25 per day weekdays. £35 per day weekends, including bank holidays.

Catering: Full catering and bar service.

Facilities: Trolley hire, putting green, practice ground.

Accommodation: Paul Jones Hotel, Cavens House Hotel, Clonyard Hotel, Cairndale Hotel, Barons Craig Hotel.

Signature hole: TWELFTH (421 yards, par four) – Dogleg right towards the sea and into the prevailing wind. Accurate drive needed. Approach to an almost blind green up on a shelf amidst humps and bunkers.

CARD OF THE COURSE

Hole	Yds	Par	Hole	Yds	Par
1	393	4	10	168	3
2	450	4	11	390	4
3	408	4	12	421	4
4	169	3	13	467	4
5	496	5	14	458	4
6	405	4	15	217	3
7	215	3	16	433	4
8	371	4	17	175	3
9	435	4	18	495	5
Out	3,342	35	In	3,224	34
Total	**6,566**		**Par**	**69**	

SPEY BAY

SPEY BAY GOLF CLUB

Address: Spey Bay, Fochabers IV32 7PJ (01343-820424).

Location: Four and a half miles north of Fochabers on B9104.

Professional: Hamish McDonald.

Description: Undulating links course. 18 holes, 6,092 yards. Par 70 (SSS 69). Course record 66.

Visitors: Contact in advance. **Green fees:** £10 per round weekdays, £15 per day. £13 per round weekends, £18 per day.

Catering: Full service. Bar.

Facilities: Trolley hire, putting green, practice ground, driving range.

Accommodation: Mill House Hotel.

STEVENSTON
ARDEER GOLF CLUB

Address: Greenhead, Stevenston KA20 4JX (01294-464542).
Location: Half a mile off A78, Ayr to Greenock road.
Secretary: P. Watson (01294-465316).
Professional: G. Thomson (01294-601327).
Description: Fairly hilly parkland course with fast greens. 18 holes, 6,409 yards. Par 72 (SSS 71). Course record 64.
Visitors: Yes, except Saturdays and competition days.
Green fees: £12 per round weekdays, £22 per day. £20 per round weekends, £30 per day.
Catering: Full service. **Facilities:** Putting green, pro shop, practice ground.
Accommodation: Hospitality Inn, Bay Hotel.
Signature hole: NINTH (339 yards, par four) – Trees on right, bunker on left. Burn meanders on right and crosses in front of two-tiered green. (See diagram below.)

CARD OF THE COURSE

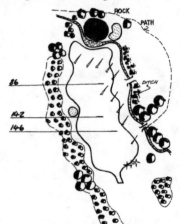

Hole	Yds	Par	Hole	Yds	Par
1	190	3	10	373	4
2	328	4	11	425	4
3	304	4	12	480	5
4	378	4	13	420	4
5	561	5	14	252	4
6	363	4	15	417	4
7	501	5	16	355	4
8	161	3	17	395	4
9	339	4	18	167	3
Out	3,125	36	In	3,284	36
Total	**6,409**		**Par**	**72**	

AUCHENHARVIE GOLF CLUB

Address: Moor Park Road West, Stevenston KA20 3HU (01294-603103).
Location: 12 miles north of Ayr.
Professional: Bob Rogers.
Description: Although a seaside course, is not a links. Long and flat municipal course with narrow greens and water on third and 12th holes. Nine holes, 5,048 yards. Par 65 (SSS 65).
Visitors: Six-day advance booking system.
Green fees: £3.30 per nine holes weekdays, £5.50 weekends.
Catering: Full service. Bar.
Facilities: Trolley hire, putting green, pro shop, practice ground, driving range.
Accommodation: The Montgreenan Mansion House Hotel.

STIRLING
STIRLING GOLF CLUB

Address: Queens Road, Stirling FK8 3AA (01786-464098).
Location: 10 minutes' walk from town centre on the ring road below Stirling Castle.

Secretary: W. McArthur. **Professional:** Ian Collins.
Description: Rolling parkland course with magnificent views of Stirling Castle and the Grampian mountains. 18 holes, 6,450 yards. Par 72 (SSS 71). Course record 65.
Visitors: Weekdays. **Green fees:** £20 per round, £30 per day.
Catering: Yes.
Facilities: Trolley/buggy hire, putting green, pro shop, practice ground.
Accommodation: Terraces Hotel.

STONEHAVEN
STONEHAVEN GOLF CLUB

Address: Cowie, Stonehaven AB39 3RH (01569-762124).
Location: North of Stonehaven.
Secretary: W. Donald.
Description: Parkland set on cliffs overlooking Stonehaven Bay. Three gullies. 18 holes, 5,103 yards. Par 66 (SSS 65). Amateur record 61 (R. Forbes, F. McCarron).
Visitors: Yes, except Saturdays.
Green fees: £15 weekdays, £20 weekends.
Catering: Full catering facilities.
Facilities: Trolley/buggy hire, putting green, practice ground.
Accommodation: Heugh Hotel, Commodore Hotel, St Leonard Hotel.
Signature hole: FIFTEENTH (161 yards, par three) – All carry over a gully 75 feet deep. Very challenging. Club selection can vary due to wind conditions. Green well bunkered with gorse on left. (See diagram opposite.)

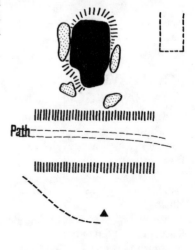

CARD OF THE COURSE

Hole	Yds	Par	Hole	Yds	Par
1	305	4	10	329	4
2	203	3	11	272	4
3	331	4	12	416	4
4	364	4	13	252	4
5	376	4	14	169	3
6	190	3	15	161	3
7	170	3	16	482	5
8	159	3	17	315	4
9	398	4	18	211	3
Out	2,496	32	In	2,607	34
Total	**5,103**		**Par**	**66**	

STRANRAER
STRANRAER GOLF CLUB

Address: Creachmore, Leswalt, Stranraer DG9 0LF (01776-870245).
Location: Two miles north of Stranraer on the Kirkcolm road.
Description: Parkland course on the shores of Loch Ryan. Designed by James Braid, it is a blend of links and parkland. 18 holes, 6,308 yards. Par 70 (SSS 72).

Amateur record 66 (C. Findlay 1969).
Visitors: Weekdays 9.15 a.m. to 12.30 p.m., 1.30 p.m. to 5 p.m. Weekends 9.30 a.m. to 11.45 a.m., 1.45 p.m. to 5 p.m.
Green fees: £18 weekdays, £24 weekends.
Catering: Full service.
Facilities: Trolley/buggy hire, putting green, practice ground.
Accommodation: North West Castle Hotel, Mount Stewart Hotel, Windyridge Bed and Breakfast.
Signature hole: FIFTH (397 yards, par four) – From elevated tee, the curved fairway skirts the shore of Loch Ryan. Strategically placed bunkers for tee shot. (See diagram opposite.)

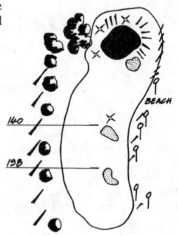

CARD OF THE COURSE

Hole	Yds	Par	Hole	Yds	Par
1	319	4	10	346	4
2	338	4	11	377	4
3	420	4	12	185	3
4	324	4	13	335	4
5	397	4	14	513	5
6	160	3	15	165	3
7	381	4	16	470	4
8	315	4	17	462	4
9	458	4	18	343	4
Out	3,112	35	In	3,196	35
Total	**6,308**		**Par**	**70**	

STRATHAVEN
STRATHAVEN GOLF CLUB

Address: Glasgow Road, Strathaven ML10 6NL (01357-520421).
Location: North-east side of town on A726.
Secretary: A. Wallace. **Professional:** Matt McCrorie (01357-521812).
Description: Gently undulating, tree-lined, championship parkland course. 700 feet above sea level. Good challenge without being too strenuous. 18 holes, 6,224 yards. Par 71 (SSS 71). Amateur record 65 (Robert Scott). Pro record 63 (David Huish).
Visitors: Yes. **Green fees:** £20 per round, £30 per day.
Catering: All day. **Facilities:** Trolley hire, putting green, pro shop, practice ground.
Accommodation: Strathaven Hotel, Springvale Hotel.

CARD OF THE COURSE

Hole	Yds	Par	Hole	Yds	Par
1	365	4	10	487	5
2	204	3	11	410	4
3	482	5	12	338	4
4	159	3	13	323	4
5	335	4	14	298	4
6	348	4	15	148	3

7	384	4	16	446	4
8	507	5	17	356	4
9	226	3	18	408	4
Out	3,010	35	In	3,214	36
Total	**6,224**		**Par**	**71**	

STRATHPEFFER
STRATHPEFFER SPA GOLF CLUB

Address: Strathpeffer Spa IV14 9AS (01997-421219).
Location: Quarter of a mile north of village, off A834.
Description: Testing upland course with many natural hazards, including burns. No sand bunkers. Hard walking. 18 holes, 4,792 yards. Par 65 (SSS 64). Course record 60.
Visitors: Contact in advance.
Green fees: £12 per round, £16 per day, £50 per week (Monday to Friday).
Catering: Bar. **Facilities:** Trolley hire, pro shop, practice ground.
Accommodation: Brunstane Lodge Hotel.

STRATHTAY
STRATHTAY GOLF CLUB

Address: Strathtay PH15 (01350-727797).
Location: Eastern end of road to Weem, off A827.
Secretary: T. Lind, Lorne Cottage, Dalguise, Dunkeld PH8 0JX.
Description: Wooded parkland course. First three holes and ninth hole are flat. The remainder are hilly, particularly the fifth and seventh. Scenic views from the sixth and eighth tees. Nine holes, 4,086 yards. Par 62 (SSS 63).
Visitors: Any time. **Green fees:** £10 per day. Juniors £5.
Catering: At Grandtully Hotel, half a mile away. **Facilities:** Practice ground.
Accommodation: Grandtully Hotel.
Signature hole: FIFTH (256 yards, par four) – Green is hidden below a steep hill. If hill is not cleared by your drive, the ball is likely to roll back down to the foot of the hill. Few succeed in getting over the top with their drive.

CARD OF THE COURSE

Hole	Yds	Par
1	286	4
2	218	3
3	212	3
4	155	3
5	256	4
6	370	4
7	144	3
8	288	4
9	114	3
Out	2,043	31
Total	**4,086**	**Par**	**62**

213

TAIN

TAIN GOLF CLUB

Address: Chapel Road, Tain, Ross-shire IV19 1PA (01862-892314).
Location: 35 miles north of Inverness. Half a mile from town centre on B9174.
Secretary: Mrs K. Ross.
Description: Part inland, part links course with fast greens. River Tain winds through course at three holes. Designed by Tom Morris. 18 holes, 6,271 yards. Par 70 (SSS 69). Amateur record 62.
Visitors: Whenever tee is available. Pre-booking required. **Green fees:** £20 per round weekdays, £26 for two rounds. £26 per round weekends, £30 for two rounds.
Catering: Yes.
Facilities: Trolley/buggy hire, putting green, pro shop, practice ground.
Accommodation: Morangie House Hotel, Carnegie Lodge Hotel, Royal Hotel, Mansfield Hotel.
Signature hole: ELEVENTH (380 yards, par four) – Green is hidden behind two huge sand hills. Pin position must be checked on indicator board on the tee.

CARD OF THE COURSE

Hole	Yds	Par	Hole	Yds	Par
1	369	4	10	390	4
2	361	4	11	380	4
3	435	4	12	378	4
4	499	5	13	501	5
5	181	3	14	438	4
6	309	4	15	346	4
7	377	4	16	147	3
8	189	3	17	215	3
9	355	4	18	371	4
Out	3,105	35	In	3,166	35
Total	**6,271**		**Par**	**70**	

TARBERT

TARBERT GOLF CLUB

Address: Kilberry Road, Tarbert PA29 6XX (01880-820536).
Location: One mile west on B8024.
Description: Hilly, wooded heathland course. Streams cross four fairways. Nine holes, 4,460 yards. Par 66 (SSS 63). Course record 62.
Visitors: Not Saturday afternoons.
Green fees: £10 per round, £15 per day. £5 for nine holes.
Accommodation: Stonefield Castle Hotel.

TARLAND

TARLAND GOLF CLUB

Address: Tarland Golf Club, Aberdeen Road, Tarland, Aboyne AB34 4TB (013398-81413).
Location: North of Aboyne. Off B9119.

Secretary: Raymond Reid.
Description: Parkland course, easy walking. Very difficult. Always maintained in the best condition. Nine holes, 5,875 yards. Par 67 (SSS 68). Course record 66.
Visitors: Yes, but check availability at weekends.
Green fees: £11 weekdays, £13 per day weekends.
Catering: Available most days. **Facilities:** Trolley hire, practice ground.
Accommodation: Commercial Hotel, Aberdeen Arms Hotel.
Signature hole: FIFTH (236 yards, par three) – Narrow driving with out of bounds all the way up the right. A pond and trees on the left.

CARD OF THE COURSE

Hole	Yds	Par	Hole	Yds	Par
1	309	4	10	311	4
2	350	4	11	350	4
3	171	3	12	221	3
4	373	4	13	379	4
5	236	3	14	208	3
6	450	4	15	415	4
7	172	3	16	211	3
8	437	4	17	486	5
9	398	4	18	398	4
Out	2,896	33	In	2,979	34
Total	**5,875**		**Par**	**67**	

TAYNUILT
TAYNUILT GOLF CLUB

Address: Laroch, Taynuilt, Argyll PA35 1JE.
Location: 12 miles east of Oban on A85.
Secretary: Murray Sim (01866-822429).
Description: Undulating parkland course. Good views. Nine holes, 4,018 yards. SSS 62.
Visitors: Any time. **Green fees:** £10 per round.

TAYPORT
SCOTSCRAIG GOLF CLUB

Address: Golf Road, Tayport, Fife DD6 9DZ (01382-552515).
Location: 10 miles north of St Andrews, off B945.
Secretary: K. Gourlay. **Professional:** S. Campbell.
Description: Established in 1817. Part links, part parkland with excellent greens. Sheltered. Open qualifying course. 18 holes, 6,550 yards. Par 71 (SSS 72).
Visitors: Yes, by prior booking. **Green fees:** £27 per round weekdays, £36 per day. £32 per round weekends, £44 per day.
Catering: Yes. **Facilities:** Trolley hire, putting green, pro shop, practice ground.
Accommodation: The Queen's Hotel.
Signature hole: FOURTH (366 yards, par four) – Included in Henry Longhurst's *Best 18 Holes of Golf*.

215

CARD OF THE COURSE

Hole	Yds	Par	Hole	Yds	Par
1	402	4	10	404	4
2	374	4	11	459	4
3	214	3	12	389	4
4	366	4	13	165	3
5	402	4	14	523	5
6	150	3	15	175	3
7	401	4	16	479	5
8	387	4	17	380	4
9	484	5	18	396	4
Out	3,180	35	In	3,370	36
Total	**6,550**		**Par**	**71**	

THORNHILL

THORNHILL GOLF CLUB

Address: Blacknest, Thornhill, Dumfriesshire DG3 5DW (01848-330546).
Location: On A76 Dumfries to Kilmarnock road. One mile from the village cross.
Secretary: J. Crichton.
Description: Founded in 1893. Delightful mixture of heathland and parkland set in the midst of the scenic southern uplands. 18 holes, 6,085 yards. Par 71 (SSS 70). Course record 63.
Visitors: Any time, except open competition days.
Green fees: £18 per day, £22 weekends and bank holidays.
Catering: Full service available.
Facilities: Trolley/buggy hire, putting green, practice ground.
Accommodation: Gillbank Hotel, Trigony House Hotel, George Hotel.
Signature hole: FOURTH (426 yards, par four) – Stroke Index 1. Dogleg right with burn on right. Intimidating drive. Difficult second shot to two-tiered green which has a collective bank on right, falling sharply left. (See diagram opposite.)

CARD OF THE COURSE

Hole	Yds	Par	Hole	Yds	Par
1	158	3	10	396	4
2	477	5	11	342	4
3	359	4	12	363	4
4	426	4	13	429	4
5	267	4	14	156	3
6	421	4	15	497	5
7	317	4	16	191	3
8	160	3	17	266	4
9	332	4	18	528	5
Out	2,917	35	In	3,168	36
Total	**6,085**		**Par**	**71**	

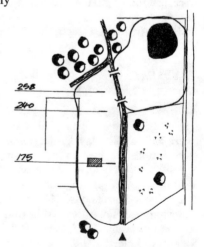

THORNTON
THORNTON GOLF CLUB

Address: Station Road, Thornton KY1 4DW (01592-771111; Starter: 01592-771173).

Location: One mile east of town, off A92. **Secretary:** B. Main.

Description: Wooded, undulating parkland course. Challenging last five holes. Bounded by River Ore on two sides. 18 holes, 6,177 yards. Par 70 (SSS 69). Course record 64.

Visitors: Very welcome. Restricted at weekends before 10 a.m. and between 12 noon and 2 p.m.; also Tuesdays between 1 p.m. and 2 p.m., Wednesdays after 4 p.m. and Thursdays between 9 a.m. and 10 a.m. Contact in advance. **Green fees:** £14 per round weekdays, £20 per day. £20 per round weekends, £30 per day.

Catering: Full service. Bar. **Facilities:** Trolley hire, putting green, practice ground.

Accommodation: Crown Hotel, Royal Hotel, Rescobie Hotel.

CARD OF THE COURSE

Hole	Yds	Par	Hole	Yds	Par
1	343	4	10	399	4
2	364	4	11	139	3
3	209	3	12	422	4
4	395	4	13	528	5
5	431	4	14	190	3
6	476	5	15	361	4
7	395	4	16	253	4
8	405	4	17	286	4
9	188	3	18	393	4
Out	3,206	35	In	2,971	35
Total	**6,177**		**Par**	**70**	

THURSO
THURSO GOLF CLUB

Address: Newlands of Geise, by Thurso, Caithness KW14 7XF (01847-63807).

Location: Two miles west of Thurso on B874 to Reay.

Secretary: R. Black.

Description: Windy parkland course with magnificent views of Pentland Firth to the Orkney Isles. 18 holes, 5,828 yards. Par 69 (SSS 69). Course record 63.

Visitors: No restrictions.

Green fees: £11 per day, £25 per week, £45 per month. Juniors half price.

Catering: All day (July to September).

Facilities: Putting green, pro shop, practice ground, driving range.

Accommodation: Pentland Hotel, John O'Groats Hotel, Ormlie Hotel, MacKays Hotel.

Signature hole: THIRTEENTH (274 yards, par four) – Demands a straight drive over a burn with heather to left and unplayable rough on the right. Driveable with wind behind.

CARD OF THE COURSE

Hole	Yds	Par	Hole	Yds	Par
1	406	4	10	410	4
2	373	4	11	365	4
3	186	3	12	219	3
4	514	5	13	274	4
5	189	3	14	158	3
6	353	4	15	354	4
7	492	5	16	429	4
8	270	4	17	372	4
9	158	3	18	306	4
Out	2,941	35	In	2,887	34
Total	**5,828**		**Par**	**69**	

TIGHNABRUAICH
KYLES OF BUTE GOLF CLUB

Address: Tighnabruaich PA21 2EE.
Location: 400 yards from Kames crossroads on B8000.
Secretary: Dr J. Thomson (01700-811603).
Description: Hilly moorland course with striking views of the Kyles of Bute and Arran. Heather rough and much wildlife. Nine holes, 4,748 yards. Par 66 (SSS 64). Course record 62.
Visitors: All times, except Sunday mornings. **Green fees:** £6 per round/day.
Catering: Soft drinks, confectionery when staff present. **Facilities:** Trolley hire.
Accommodation: Royal Hotel, Kames Hotel, Kilfinan Hotel.
Signature hole: FIRST (110 yards, par three) – Heather-covered rocks in front of sloping green with burn behind. Out of bounds to right and heavy rough on left.

CARD OF THE COURSE

Hole	Yds	Par
1	110	3
2	343	4
3	260	4
4	329	4
5	245	3
6	402	4
7	254	4
8	243	4
9	188	3
Out	2,374	33
Total	**4,748**	**Par**	**66**

TILLICOULTRY
TILLICOULTRY GOLF CLUB

Address: Alva Road, Tillicoultry FK13 6BL (01259-750124).

Location: Nine miles east of Stirling on A91.
Description: Undulating inland parkland course at foot of Ochil Hills. Hard walking. Nine holes, 5,365 yards. Par 68 (SSS 66). Course record 61.
Visitors: Contact in advance.
Green fees: £10 per round before 4 p.m., £12 afterwards. £15 weekends.
Catering: Full service. Bar.
Accommodation: Harviestoun Country Inn.

TORPHINS
TORPHINS GOLF CLUB

Address: Bog Road, Torphins, Aberdeenshire AB31 4JU (013398-82115).
Location: West of village off A980.
Secretary: S. MacGregor (013398-82402).
Description: Inland parkland with good views of the Highlands. Nine holes, 4,684 yards. Par 64 (SSS 64). Course record 63.
Visitors: Weekdays and weekends on non-competition days.
Green fees: £10 weekdays, £12 weekends.
Catering: Weekends. **Facilities:** Putting green.
Accommodation: Learney Arms Hotel.

CARD OF THE COURSE

Hole	Yds	Par	
1	207	3	
2	253	4	
3	291	4	
4	243	3	
5	120	3	
6	366	4	
7	310	4	
8	193	3	
9	359	4	
Out	2,342	32	
Total	**4,684**	**Par**	**64**

TORRANCE
BALMORE GOLF CLUB LTD

Address: Golf Course Road, Balmore G64 4AW (01360-620240).
Location: Two miles north of Glasgow, off A807.
Description: Parkland course. Fine views. 18 holes, 5,530 yards. Par 66 (SSS 67). Course record 63.
Visitors: Contact in advance. Must be accompanied by member.
Green fees: £25 per round weekdays, £35 per day.
Catering: Yes. **Facilities:** Putting green, practice ground.
Accommodation: Black Bull Thistle Hotel.

TROON
KILMARNOCK (BARASSIE) GOLF CLUB

Address: 29 Hillhouse Road, Troon KA10 6SY (01292-313920).
Location: East of village on B746.
Professional: W. Lockie.
Description: Established in 1887. Qualifying course for the Open. Flat seaside course with much heather. Great turf and greens. More challenging than it looks. 18 holes, 6,473 yards. Par 71 (SSS 72). Course record 63.
Visitors: With member only Wednesdays and weekends. May not play Friday mornings. Contact in advance. **Green fees:** £30 per round, £40 per day.
Catering: Full service. Bar.
Facilities: Trolley hire, putting green, pro shop, practice ground.
Accommodation: Marine Highland Hotel.

ROYAL TROON GOLF CLUB

'Dramatic' would perhaps be the best way to describe Royal Troon, host of the 1997 Open Championship. When the wind blows on the Old Course, strange things can happen on this classic undulating links, which is full of bumps and hollows and rated amongst the world's best. Founded in 1878 by 24 local enthusiasts, the course then consisted of only five holes but rapidly grew in stature and hosted the Open Championship five times between 1923 and 1989 – and every time there was high drama.

In 1989, Mark Calcavecchia executed a Houdini act to win the championship. First he holed out from deep rough on the 12th in the final round and then birdied the 425-yard par-four 18th to take the competition into extra time. Then at the 18th, the final hole in the four-hole play-off with Greg Norman and Wayne Grady, he hit an exquisite five-iron again from deep rough and needed only a single putt to win. Earlier Norman, who had a final round 64, made a mark of his own, birdieing the first six holes.

Those golfing greats Arnold Palmer and Jack Nicklaus also go down in the history of the course, Palmer for winning the 1962 Open by six shots at the same time as Nicklaus, of all people, was taking a 10 at the 11th. Gene Sarazen holed in one at the Postage Stamp, the world's most famous par-three, in 1973, and nine years later Bobby Clampett, a runaway leader after two rounds, carded a confidence-shaking eight at the sixth, and slumped to a 78 and 77 to finish out of the running.

Royal Troon boasts both the longest and the shortest holes of any Open Championship. When you think of Troon invariably you think of the Postage Stamp, the 126-yard eighth which can take anything from a three-iron to a wedge depending on the wind. To the delight of the spectators and a large television audience, Sarazen, then 71, holed his punched five-iron in 1973. Then, as if to prove that this gem of a hole held no psychological terrors for him, the inventor of the sand-wedge holed his second shot from a cavernous bunker in the next round.

Not everyone has happy memories of the par-three. In the same tournament, Palmer scored a seven there and in 1950 Herman Tissies, a German amateur, took 15 blows to get down. When you prepare for your shot from a high tee with a troublesome gully between you and the green, it is hard to put all the problems facing you to the back of your mind. On the left is a hugh sandhill and the green is surrounded by five bunkers. Hitting into the crater bunker on the right approach could mean you going from bunker to bunker as Herr Tissies did. With a green 25 feet across at its widest point, it is a daunting target.

The sixth is the longest in British championship golf at 577 yards, and it is a dangerous hole. With a slight dogleg to the right, the drive has to pitch on the upper half of the fairway, which is tilted right to left. There are three bunkers positioned to catch the less-than-accurate drive. The second shot should be aimed slightly left to avoid a bunker on the right, ready for a pitch into a long, narrow green with sand dunes on three sides. Miss the target and expect to have to do some exploring in the rough.

But this magnificent course is not just about those holes. The 438-yard 10th is not the longest but must rate the trickiest par-four on the course. There is not a bunker on this hole but, from a low tee, you have to be long and straight to clear a range of sandhills. Get it wrong and you are in impenetrable rough. The plateau green falls sharply to the right. A bogey here is a result.

The 11th has been cut to 463 yards for the Open, but in the prevailing winds it plays every inch and is reckoned to be the toughest hole on the course. Hit your drive left and you are in thick gorse; go right and you are out of bounds on the railway line, which runs the whole length of the hole and gets so close to the little green that the guard could almost punch your ticket without leaving his cab. Just to complicate matters the fairways tighten almost to the narrowness of a Victorian lady's waist. Anything can happen here – and it usually does.

That gives you the flavour of Troon's testing finish, of which the 15th (457 yards, par-four) is most difficult. The drive is slightly blind to a plateau fairway with three bunkers in a landing area of about 30 yards, and the approach is to a well-guarded, sunken green. Troon can be a terror, and that is why you can expect a tale of the unexpected from any Open Championship contender there.

Address: Craigend Road, Troon, South Ayrshire KA10 6EP (01292-311555).
Location: Three miles from A77 (Glasgow to Ayr road). Follow signs for Prestwick Airport.
Secretary: J.D. Montgomerie.
Professional: Brian Anderson (01292-313281).
Description: *Old Course*: 18 holes, 7,079 yards. Par 71 (SSS 73). Course record 64 (Greg Norman). *Portland Course*: Resembles moorland course but has the challenges of a links. 18 holes, 6,274 yards. Par 71 (SSS 71).
Visitors: May not play Wednesdays, Fridays and weekends. Must write in advance, have introductory letter and handicap certificate of under 20. Ladies and under-18s may play only on the Portland.
Green fees: £100 per day (includes a round on both courses and lunch). £65 Portland only.
Catering: Full service. Bar.
Facilities: Trolley hire, putting green, pro shop, practice ground.
Accommodation: Lochgreen House Hotel, Marine Highland Hotel, Highgrove House Hotel, Piersland House Hotel.

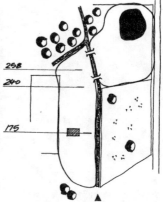

Signature hole: EIGHTH (126 yards, par three) – You can say no more. (See diagram on previous page.)

CARD OF THE OLD COURSE

Hole	Yds	Par	Hole	Yds	Par
1	364	4	10	438	4
2	391	4	11	463	4
3	379	4	12	431	4
4	557	5	13	465	4
5	210	3	14	179	3
6	577	5	15	457	4
7	402	4	16	542	5
8	126	3	17	223	3
9	423	4	18	452	4
Out	3,340	36	In	3,650	35
Total	**7,079**		**Par**	**71**	

TROON MUNICIPAL GOLF COURSES

Address: Harling Drive, Troon KA10 6NE (01292-312464).
Location: In centre of Troon beside railway station.
Professional: Gordon McKinlay.
Description: Three links courses, two championship.
Lochgreen Course: 18 holes, 6,785 yards. Par 74 (SSS 73).
Darley Course: 18 holes, 6,360 yards. Par 71 (SSS 72).
Fullarton: 18 holes, 4,870 yards. Par 64 (SSS 63).
Visitors: Any time. **Green fees:** *Lochgreen*: £17 per round, £24 per day. *Darley*: £13 per round, £24 per day. *Fullarton*: £11 per round, £18 per day.
Catering: Bar. **Facilities:** Trolley hire, putting green, pro shop, practice ground.
Accommodation: Crailea Hotel.

LOCHGREEN CARD OF THE COURSE

Hole	Yds	Par	Hole	Yds	Par
1	473	4	10	188	3
2	476	5	11	413	4
3	487	5	12	408	4
4	293	4	13	318	4
5	429	4	14	306	4
6	197	3	15	203	3
7	496	5	16	491	5
8	323	4	17	360	4
9	429	4	18	495	5
Out	3,603	38	In	3,182	36
Total	**6,785**		**Par**	**74**	

TURNBERRY
TURNBERRY HOTEL GOLF COURSES

The locals have a saying that if you can see Ailsa Craig, the 1,208-foot-high granite rock off the Ayrshire coast, it is about to rain; if you can't, it is raining. They do a disservice to an area of Scotland that is home to a glorious course which is amongst the best. Often when the rest of Britain is shivering in a freezing winter, the sun is shining on Turnberry and the temperature is mild. Play Turnberry's Ailsa Course on one of those days with a light breeze from the sea, and there is nowhere you would rather be; play it in the rain and high winds and your step quickens towards the beckoning lights of the hotel – which is as magnificent as its two courses.

The hotel provides spectacular views of a breathtaking coastline and out to the Isle of Arran, the Mull of Kintyre and, on a clear day, all the way to Ireland. With the Ailsa and its friendlier sister, the Arran, dominating Turnberry's 800 acres, a non-golfer could keep track of their partner's progress with a powerful pair of binoculars.

As an Open Championship course Turnberry is a newcomer, first staging golf's most prestigious prize in 1977 – and what a championship it turned out to be. It ended up a head to head between Jack Nicklaus and Tom Watson, the two greatest players of the day. It was tagged 'the duel in the sun', and many still believe it to be the greatest ever finale to the championship. Nicklaus was two up after 12 holes and covered the final six in one under par. On the 18th tee, Watson led by a stroke and hit his drive down the middle. Nicklaus drove right and to the edge of trouble. Watson struck his seven-iron approach to within a yard of the hole, while Nicklaus was 15 yards away and holed a tricky putt to stay in it. But Watson holed out for his second Open title.

If the weather had been benign on that occasion, it showed its true colours nine years later when Greg Norman shot a record second-round 63 to win by five strokes. Some say that that was the finest round in championship golf.

In 1994 Nick Price won after a final nine of 31. But it was the eagle-three putt on the 71st green that clinched it for him. From 50 feet, he struck the ball firmly. It took a break to the right, slowed up and then dropped almost with relief into the cup. Price couldn't contain himself, leaping into the air and waving his putter above his head. 'I couldn't believe the putt went in,' he said. 'When it did, I just about jumped out of my skin.'

Turnberry is a youngster compared to most of the other great courses of Scotland. The first 13 holes were laid out by Willie Fernie in 1903 and three years later it was the first hotel and golf complex in the world, with the wealthy travelling down by train from Glasgow to visit. During the Second World War it was used as an airfield, and many dunes were levelled and bunkers filled in. Part of the old runway remains and can be found if you play a particularly wayward shot. It looked like the end of Turnberry as a golf course, but thanks to the restoration work of Mackenzie Ross it reopened in 1951.

The first three holes are parallel, relatively flat and not the toughest of starts to an Open, although the 462-yard third is directly into the wind, but the club golfer would be happy to come away with three par-fours even from the shorter medal tees. With the short fourth, you now have a run of eight holes along the rugged coastline. It is 165 yards and not the hardest of holes, but be careful not to go left or you could end up on the beach. There is another par three at the sixth and this is something else. It needs a hefty clout from the championship tee of 231 yards, or even the medal tee some 10 yards shorter, to get up on top of a raised green. There are three bunkers to the left with jungle farther left and a deep, deep bunker just in front for the drive that doesn't quite have the legs. Stray right and you will find yourself at the bottom of a slope. Even if you make the green it can be three-putt territory, depending on pin placement.

The seventh, a classic 529-yard par-five from the championship tees and possibly an even harder 475-yard par-four from the medal markers, is regarded as the hardest hole on the course. Your tee shot has to carry a burn and be right to give yourself a decent second shot. The ninth is Turnberry's lighthouse hole, one of the most photographed signature holes in the world. Even if you are not playing it, it is worth a stroll out to look at it. The rocks are 390 million years old and at that time there were several active volcanoes along this stretch of Ayrshire coast. From the green you can see the remains of Robert the Bruce's castle.

The 10th demands a solid strike and, if down the left of this 452-yard hole, it could set you up for a birdie-three. From the 174-yard 11th, you head inland. The 13th has a tricky raised green which is slower than any of the rest. The 15th, a 209-yard par-three, can be a destructive hole. Any error is heavily punished. With a ravine to the front, bunkers to the left and a huge drop to the right, you have got to hit the small green.

The 16th is called the Wee Burn, but it is not so wee. Not that long, 380 yards from the medal tees, it presents an intriguing approach shot. You often need a club more than you think to get over, because there is a danger of the ball rolling back into it.

If you have had a tough day on the links, you might be inclined to try your hand at the nine-hole pitch-and-putt course on the front lawns of the hotel. Be warned, it is tougher than you think – but then again that's Turnberry.

Address: Turnberry, Ayrshire KA26 9LT (01655-331000).
Location: 15 miles south-west of Ayr on A77.
Golf Manager: Ewen Bowman.
Professional: Brian Gunson.
Description: Two championship links courses.
Ailsa: 18 holes, 6,976 yards (6440 yards medal tees). Par 70 (69 medal) (SSS 72). Course record 63 (Greg Norman, Mark Hayes).
Arran: 18 holes, 6,014 yards. Par 68 (SSS 69). Course record 66 (P. Parkin).
Visitors: Yes, providing they are residents of Turnberry Hotel.
Green fees: *Ailsa*: £70, *Arran*: £40.
Catering: Full service. Bar.
Facilities: Trolley hire (not permitted on Ailsa course), putting green, pro shop, practice ground.
Accommodation: Turnberry Hotel.
Signature hole: Ailsa Course: NINTH (454 yards, par four) – The championship tee is perched out on a promontory of cliff with a sheer drop of 50 feet. Not for someone suffering with vertigo. The medal tee is some 40 yards further on but still a

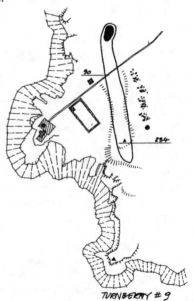

TURNBERRY #9

224

spectacular tee shot. It takes a 200-yard drive from the championship tee just to reach the fairway and a white stone marker shows you where to aim for. If you are on this line, playing from the medal tees, you will have a shot of about 180 yards to a large green unbothered by bunkers. (See diagram on previous page.)

CARD OF THE AILSA COURSE

Hole	Yds	Par	Hole	Yds	Par
1	350	4	10	452	4
2	430	4	11	174	3
3	462	4	12	446	4
4	165	3	13	412	4
5	442	4	14	449	4
6	231	3	15	209	3
7	529	5	16	409	4
8	431	4	17	497	5
9	454	4	18	434	4
Out	3,494	35	In	3,482	35
Total	**6,976**		**Par**	**70**	

TURRIFF
TURRIFF GOLF CLUB

Address: Rosehall AB53 7HB (01888-562982).
Location: One mile west off B9024.
Professional: Robin Smith (01888-563025).
Description: Parkland course alongside River Deveron. 18 holes, 6,145 yards. Par 69 (SSS 68). Course record 63.
Visitors: Not before 10 a.m. at weekends. Contact in advance.
Green fees: £15 per round weekdays, £20 per day. £20 per round weekends, £25 per day.
Catering: Bar. **Facilities:** Trolley hire, putting green, pro shop, practice ground.
Accommodation: Banff Springs Hotel, The County Hotel.

UDDINGSTON
CALDERBRAES GOLF CLUB

Address: 57 Roundknowe Road, Uddingston, Lanarkshire G71 7TS (01698-813425).
Location: Beginning of M74, east of Glasgow next to Glasgow Zoo.
Secretary: Seamus McGuigan.
Description: Inland, hilly, very tight woodland course. Extremely difficult. Nine holes, 5,186 yards. Par 66 (SSS 67). Course record 65.
Visitors: Weekdays only. **Green fees:** £12 per day.
Catering: Yes. Bar. **Facilities:** Putting green, practice ground.
Accommodation: Black Bear Travel Lodge.
Signature hole: FOURTH (434 yards, par four) – Demanding and long second shot to a green very high up with out of bounds to left and right, only five yards from green.

UPHALL

UPHALL GOLF CLUB

Address: Houston Mains, Uphall EH52 6JT (01506-856404).
Location: Junction 3 off M8. 10 miles from Edinburgh, 30 miles from Glasgow.
Club Captain: T. Flannigan. **Professional:** Gordon Law (01506-855553).
Description: Parkland course. As it is relatively short it is ideal for golf societies. Picturesque with some great character-building holes. 18 holes, 5,600 yards. Par 69 (SSS 67). Course record 62.
Visitors: Yes.
Green fees: £14 per round weekdays, £19 per day. £18 per round weekends, £26 per day. Winter weekend day ticket £13. Winter weekday per round £10.
Catering: A la carte, bar meals, suppers, golf outings and functions catered for.
Facilities: Trolley/buggy hire, putting green, pro shop, practice ground.
Accommodation: Houstoun House Hotel.

UPLAWMOOR

CALDWELL GOLF CLUB

Address: Uplawmoor G78 4AU (01505-850329).
Location: Five miles south-east of Barrhead on A736, Glasgow to Irvine road.
Secretary: H. Harper (01505-850366).
Professional: Stephen Forbes (01505-850616).
Description: Undulating parkland course. 18 holes, 6,294 yards. Par 71 (SSS 70). Amateur record 66. Pro record 63.
Visitors: Yes, but not at weekends or on local public holidays. Phone professional to book. **Green fees:** £20 per round, £28 per day.
Catering: Yes. Not Thursdays.
Facilities: Trolley hire, putting green, pro shop, practice ground.
Accommodation: Uplawmoor Hotel, Dalmenny House Hotel.
Signature hole: THIRD (160 yards, par three) – Aptly named 'Risk an' Hope'. Out of bounds on right for the length of the hole. Long, narrow green.

CARD OF THE COURSE

Hole	Yds	Par	Hole	Yds	Par
1	395	4	10	311	4
2	422	4	11	391	4
3	160	3	12	345	4
4	304	4	13	360	4
5	516	5	14	280	4
6	382	4	15	131	3
7	422	4	16	395	4
8	331	4	17	547	5
9	196	3	18	406	4
Out	3,128	35	In	3,166	36
Total	**6,294**		**Par**	**71**	

WEST CALDER

HARBURN GOLF CLUB

Address: Harburn Village EH55 8RS (01506-871131).
Location: On B7008.
Professional: Tom Stangoe.
Description: Moorland course laid out on a slope 600 feet above sea level. 18 holes, 5,921 yards. Par 69 (SSS 69). Course record 62.
Visitors: Contact in advance. Limited at weekends.
Green fees: £16 per round weekdays, £21 for two rounds. £19/£26 Fridays. £21/£32 weekends and bank holidays.
Catering: Yes. Bar.
Facilities: Trolley/buggy hire, putting green, pro shop, practice ground.
Accommodation: The Hilcroft Hotel.

WEST KILBRIDE

WEST KILBRIDE GOLF CLUB

Address: 33–35 Fullerton Drive, Seamill KA23 9NQ (01294-823911).
Location: On A78, Greenock to Ayr road.
Professional: Gregor Howie.
Description: Seaside links course on Firth of Clyde. 18 holes, 5,974 yards. Par 70 (SSS 70). Course record 63.
Visitors: Not at weekends. Contact in advance.
Green fees: £21 per round, £35 per day.
Catering: Yes. Bar.
Facilities: Trolley hire, putting green, pro shop, practice ground, driving range.
Accommodation: Elderslie Hotel.

WEST LINTON

WEST LINTON GOLF CLUB

Address: Medwyn Road, West Linton, Peeblesshire EH46 7HN (01968-660256).
Location: 18 miles south-west of Edinburgh on A702.
Secretary: G. Scott. **Professional:** Ian Wright.
Description: Scenic moorland course with views of the Pentland Hills and Moorfoot Hills. A real challenge of golf. 18 holes, 6,132 yards. Par 69 (SSS 70). Amateur record 63 (S. Walker). Pro record 71 (Bernard Gallacher).
Visitors: Weekdays, except on medal days. Weekends, non-medal days after 1 p.m.
Green fees: £18 per round weekdays, £27 per day. £28 per round weekends.
Catering: Yes.
Facilities: Trolley/buggy hire, putting green, pro shop, practice ground.
Accommodation: Gordon Arms Hotel.
Signature hole: EIGHTEENTH (230 yards, par three) – Tee shot over gully. Out of bounds on right.

CARD OF THE COURSE

Hole	Yds	Par	Hole	Yds	Par
1	307	4	10	348	4

2	143	3	11	469	4
3	353	4	12	203	3
4	525	5	13	295	4
5	470	4	14	376	4
6	360	4	15	503	5
7	330	4	16	415	4
8	447	4	17	196	3
9	162	3	18	230	3
Out	3,097	35	In	3,035	34
Total	**6,132**		**Par**	**69**	

WHITBURN
POLKEMMET COUNTRY PARK

Address: Whitburn EH47 0AD (01501-743905).
Location: Two miles west, off B7066.
Description: Public parkland course surrounded by mature woodland. River Almond bisects the course. Nine holes, 6,496 yards. Par 74 (SSS 74).
Visitors: Any time. **Green fees:** £2.85 for nine holes, £3.60 on Sundays.
Catering: Bar. **Facilities:** Trolley hire, practice ground, driving range.
Accommodation: The Hilcroft Hotel.

WICK
WICK GOLF CLUB

Address: Reiss, Wick KW1 4RW (01955-602726).
Location: North of Wick, off A9.
Description: Challenging seaside links course. 18 holes, 5,976 yards. Par 69 (SSS 69). Course record 63.
Visitors: Any time. **Green fees:** £15 per round.
Catering: Bar.
Accommodation: Mackay's Hotel.

WIGTOWN
WIGTOWN AND BLADNOCH GOLF CLUB

Address: Lightlands Terrace, Wigtown, Newton Stewart DG8 9EF (01988-403354).
Location: A714 from Newton Stewart. Follow Whithorn/Port William signs and turn left at crossroads with B733.
Secretary: J. Alexander.
Description: Parkland course, part hilly, with several quite tricky holes. Nine holes, 5,462 yards . Par 68 (SSS 67). Course record 62.
Visitors: Welcome weekdays without prior booking. Check at weekends. Societies by prior arrangement.
Green fees: £10 per round, £15 per day. Senior citizens and juniors half price.
Catering: Available from 11.30 a.m. to 2.30 p.m., April to September. Other times by arrangement. **Facilities:** Putting green.

Accommodation: Creebridge House Hotel.
Signature hole: THIRD (195 yards, par three) – Only pin visible from tee. Out of bounds on left. Fairway slopes from left to right with rough and trees on right. Sloping green.

CARD OF THE COURSE

Hole	Yds	Par	
1	306	4	
2	370	4	
3	195	3	
4	275	4	
5	149	3	
6	362	4	
7	356	4	
8	342	4	
9	376	4	
Out	2,731	34	
Total	**5,462**	**Par**	**68**

WINCHBURGH
NIDDRY CASTLE GOLF CLUB

Address: Castle Road, Winchburgh EH52 6RQ (01506-891097).
Location: Nine miles west of Edinburgh between Kirkliston and Linlithgow.
Description: Wooded parkland course. Tight with small greens. Nine holes, 5,514 yards. Par 70 (SSS 67).
Visitors: Contact at weekends. Restricted during competitions.
Green fees: £12 per round weekdays, £17 weekends.

WISHAW
WISHAW GOLF CLUB

Address: 55 Cleland Road, Wishaw ML2 7PH (01698-372869).
Location: North-west of town, off A721.
Professional: John Campbell.
Description: Tree-lined parkland course. Bunkers on 17 greens. 18 holes, 6,073 yards. Par 69 (SSS 69). Course record 64.
Visitors: Not Saturdays.
Green fees: £12 per round weekdays, £20 per day. Sundays £25 per round/day.
Catering: Full service. Bar.
Facilities: Trolley/buggy hire, putting green, pro shop, practice ground.
Accommodation: Popinjay Hotel.

INDEX

KEY.

1. ST ANDREWS
2. CARNOUSTIE
3. ROYAL DORNOCH
4. MUIRFIELD
5. TURNBERRY
6. TROON
7. PRESTWICK
8. LOCH LOMOND
9. GLENEAGLES
10. MACHRAHANISH
11. DURNESS
12. SOUTHERNESS

SHETLAND

LERWICK

ORKNEY

KIRKWALL

11

THURSO

WICK

LEWIS

ULLAPOOL

3

HARRIS

FRASERBURGH

PETERHEAD

INVERNESS

SKYE

AVIEMORE

ABERDEEN

STONEHAVEN

FORT WILLIAM

MULL

OBAN

PERTH

DUNDEE

9

2

ST ANDREWS

1

8

STIRLING

GLASGOW

4

BUTE

EDINBURGH

CUMBRAE

GIGHA

6

7

10

ARRAN

AYR

CAMPBELTOWN

5

DUMFRIES

12